I am not asking anyone to accept Christianity
if his best reasoning tells him
that the weight of the evidence is against it.

—C. S. Lewis

C. S. LEWIS
AND THE
SEARCH FOR
RATIONAL
RELIGION

John Beversluis

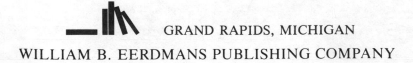

GRAND RAPIDS, MICHIGAN

WILLIAM B. EERDMANS PUBLISHING COMPANY

To Nathaniel
Whose birth was a light to my life.

Copyright © 1985 by John Beversluis

First published 1985 by Wm. B. Eerdmans Publishing Co.
255 Jefferson Ave. S.E., Grand Rapids, Michigan 49503
All rights reserved
Printed in the United States of America

Library of Congress Cataloging in Publication Data

Beversluis, John, 1934-
C.S. Lewis and the search for rational religion.

1. Lewis, C. S. (Clive Staples), 1898-1963.
I. Title.
BX5199.L53B48 1984   230'.092'4   84-26032

ISBN 0-8028-0046-7

CONTENTS

ACKNOWLEDGMENTS

In the course of writing this book I have become indebted to many people in many ways. Most recently, I am lastingly grateful to Harold Ellens for bringing my manuscript to the attention of the William B. Eerdmans Publishing Company and to T. A. Straayer for his felicitous editing and perceptive advice.

I also gratefully acknowledge the Sabbatical Leaves Committee of Butler University for recommending me for a sabbatical during 1981 in order to complete this book, and to the administration for approving it—in particular, President John G. Johnson, Dean David M. Silver, and Paul R. Stewart, at that time Vice President for Academic Affairs. My thanks also go to the current Vice President for Academic Affairs, Thomas J. Hegarty, for his help in arranging for the preparation of the final copy.

For tough criticism and a willingness to discuss C. S. Lewis far beyond the normal limits of human tolerance, I thank Linda Bell, Joanne Edmonds, Grant Luckhardt, and Robert Vorsteg. For encouragement and advice I am grateful to William P. Alston, Alan Donagan, Antony Flew, D. Z. Phillips, W. Norman Pittenger, and Michael Scriven. Nor can I overlook Larry and Jana Bradley, Edmund Byrne, Matthew and Grace Du Pree, Tony Edmonds, Thomas Fox, William Hackett, Norman Morford, Alan Nasser, and Karen Scott—all of whom in one way or another helped keep me afloat. Although their support often elicited little more than dark sayings from me, I want them to know how much it mattered.

My wife, Susan, was involved in this project in more ways than either of us could have ever foreseen. She discussed every aspect of it with me from beginning to end and made extensive criticisms of earlier drafts. Together we learned that writing a book has a way of getting out of hand. As a legitimate interest became a consuming obsession, I began detaching myself by degrees from family concerns in the pious hope that she would "understand."

After all, had not practically every other male author in the history of publishing nervously heaped retroactive praise on his wife for tiptoeing about the premises and keeping the children from disturbing the absorbed recluse? But there is a difference between understanding and domestic martyrdom, and although I often lost sight of it, she seldom did. I thank her for not leaving me alone.

This book was long in the making before I ever wrote a word. Looking back over the years, everyone can identify certain people whose influence shaped them for life in ways that are not only impossible to repay but even hard to acknowledge adequately. In my case, there were three such people: my first and best philosophy teacher, Professor W. Harry Jellema, who died in 1982 at the age of 89; my friend, Paul Dietl, who died in 1972 at the age of 40; and my father, John Beversluis, Sr. They did not know each other and would have differed strongly among themselves as well as with me about the central contentions of this book. But a part of each of them is in it.

All references to Lewis's works in this book are cited parenthetically in the text, using the abbreviations listed below. All quotations are taken from the editions cited.

AGO	*A Grief Observed*. New York: Seabury Press, 1963.
AM	*The Abolition of Man*. New York: Macmillan, 1947.
CR	*Christian Reflections*. Grand Rapids: William B. Eerdmans, 1967.
FL	*The Four Loves*. New York: Harcourt Brace Jovanovich, 1960.
GD	*The Great Divorce*. New York: Macmillan, 1946.
GiD	*God in the Dock*. Grand Rapids: William B. Eerdmans, 1970.
L	*Letters of C. S. Lewis*. London: Geoffrey Bles, 1966.
LM	*Letters to Malcolm*. New York: Harcourt Brace Jovanovich, 1964.
M	*Miracles*. New York: Macmillan, 1947.
M²	*Miracles*. Rev. ed. London: Fontana, 1960.
MC	*Mere Christianity*. New York: Macmillan, 1952.
PP	*The Problem of Pain*. New York: Macmillan, 1943.
PR	*The Pilgrim's Regress*. London: Geoffrey Bles, 1943.

R   *Rehabilitations and Other Essays*. Oxford: Oxford
        University Press, 1939.

RP   *Reflections on the Psalms*. New York: Harcourt
        Brace Jovanovich, 1958.

SbJ   *Surprised by Joy*. New York: Harcourt Brace
        Jovanovich, 1956.

SL   *The Screwtape Letters and Screwtape Proposes a
        Toast*. New York: Macmillan, 1962.

WG   *The Weight of Glory and Other Addresses*. New
        York: Macmillan, 1949.

WLN   *The World's Last Night and Other Essays*. New
        York: Harcourt Brace Jovanovich, 1960.

INTRODUCTION

Clive Staples Lewis died on November 22, 1963. A convert from atheism to Christianity in 1931, he achieved worldwide fame during the last twenty-five years of his life as the author of an impressive number of books on a variety of philosophical and religious topics. *The Case for Christianity, Christian Behaviour, Beyond Personality, The Pilgrim's Regress, The Problem of Pain,* and *Miracles* are apologetic works that set forth a philosophical defense of the Christian faith. *Surprised by Joy*, while neither directly nor chiefly apologetic in intention, is of genuine apologetic significance: it traces Lewis's intellectual development and provides insights into the experiences and arguments that finally led him to believe in Christianity. *A Grief Observed*, on the other hand, finds him overtaken by shattering doubts that forced him to rethink the whole matter of rational religion.

During these years (1938–1963) Lewis wrote many other books bearing directly or indirectly on religious themes—almost forty of them in all—encompassing a wide range of literary forms: expository studies, essays, sermons, allegorical novels, science fiction, fantasy, poetry, and a set of books for children that has become a contemporary classic. Even more remarkable is the fact that he accomplished all this in his spare time and in addition to writing many highly acclaimed scholarly books and articles in his own field. By profession he was neither a philosopher nor a theologian but a tutor of Medieval and Renaissance Literature at Oxford University and later a professor at Cambridge.

However, it is as a Christian apologist that he is best known, and it is on his apologetic writings that I will be focusing. In them we discover the quintessential Lewis: the "mere" Christian[1] who once described himself as "a very ordinary layman of the Church of England, not especially 'high,' nor especially 'low,' nor especially anything else" (*MC*, 6). Lewis always assured us that his views were put forth subject to the correction of "wiser heads,'' but during the course of his own lifetime he became known as "the apostle to the skeptics," "the man who made righteousness readable," and one of the most influential spokesmen for orthodox Christianity in the twentieth century.

The publication of Lewis's apologetic writings during the forties took an unsuspecting reading public by storm. Although his "Broadcast Talks" over the BBC had already attracted considerable attention in England, it was their appearance in book form that first gained for him his enormous reputation and following. There had, of course, been religious best-sellers before, but Lewis's books have little in common with them. Outspokenly impatient with those diluted forms of theological liberalism that he dubbed "Christianity-and-water," Lewis urged his readers to take their Christianity straight or abstain altogether. By posing the issue in these radical terms, he parted company with the reigning theologians of the day who, in his opinion, had whittled away at their Christianity until nothing was left of it. Lewis refused to whittle. Convinced that lines must be drawn beyond which a doctrine ceases to be Christian in any recognizable sense, he offered his readers neither a scientifically chastened version of Christianity nor the usual assortment of uplifting chatter and practical tips. He offered them orthodoxy: sin, repentance, atonement, the new birth, resurrection, miracles—and yes, even the devil and hell. He advocated Christianity not because he thought it would enrich the individual, strengthen the family, and rehabilitate society, but because he thought it true.

The response was unprecedented. Lewis himself reported that by his standards sales were "prodigious." Not only did his books sell, but many readers began corresponding with him, and he eventually found himself spending two or three hours a day just answering mail. Today, more than twenty years after his death, sales are as high as ever. Unlike many popular religious books that create a temporary stir and then pass into the oblivion they so richly deserve, Lewis's works have gone through one printing after another. Thousands, perhaps millions, claim that it was through reading his books that they were converted to Christianity or first persuaded to take it seriously. It is a rare discussion or public debate of Christianity in which his arguments are not conspicuously present. Even the most lavish estimates of his influence are likely to be too conservative.

Those who write about Lewis fall into two categories. First, there are his critics. Lewis never lacked opponents, and one of the earliest charges leveled against him is still worth pondering. During the forties an unfriendly critic attempted to belittle his initial success by attributing it to wartime conditions.[2] Lewis, he grumbled, was simply capitalizing on the uncertainties of the times. Let peace be restored, and the "scare tactics" of this "very unremarkable minor prophet" would be seen for what they were. Seldom has a prediction suffered so complete a reversal.

Far from waning after the war ended, Lewis's influence continued to grow. With it grew the number of critics who considered his reputation to be wildly out of proportion to his achievement.[3] Some complained that he was nothing but a "vulgar" popularizer of Fundamentalist Christianity whose "literalism" and "complete ignorance" of modern biblical studies was "shocking" and "intellectually subversive." Others alleged that he "thoroughly misunderstood" scientific method and that he was "opposed in principle" to science. Still others denounced him as a "slick philosophical charlatan," a "dangerous" and "inept" theologian, a "pious paradox-monger" whose writings were "sheer soapsuds" that substituted "smart superficiality for careful thought" and abounded with "patent absurdities," "half-truths," "misstatements," "evasions," "sleight of hand," and "downright falsehoods."

This is not criticism, of course, but invective. Its unbecoming chip-on-the-shoulder tone and self-indulgent rhetoric generously sprinkled with abusive epithets reveal that the individuals producing it not only disagree with Lewis but are angry with him too. What they have to offer is not an argument but a harangue, not an assessment but a demolition. One begins to suspect that they have reached these negative conclusions a bit too easily—a suspicion confirmed by the fact that all dissenting opinion has been confined to chapters of books dealing with broader subjects, and to articles and reviews.

But if Lewis's critics are too ferocious, his admirers are too benign, erring grievously in the opposite direction. Since his death, they have produced a steady stream of books that, while extraordinarily favorable in their estimate of his achievement, vary greatly in quality. Some are valuable by any standard, including a collection of reminiscences by several of his closest associates published shortly after his death, a generous selection of his letters, two biographies (one dealing just with Lewis, the other treating Lewis, J. R. R. Tolkien, and Charles Williams), his voluminous correspondence with Arthur Greeves, and another collection of informative and admirably balanced reminiscences.[4]

But other more dubious books have also found their way into print. Despite incidental merits, even the best of them are flawed by serious expository weaknesses that have become so common and predictable as to warrant special mention. First, they venerate Lewis to the point of transforming him into a cult figure. Easily the most sensational case is J. B. Phillips's claim that Lewis visited him from beyond the grave on two separate occasions, "ruddier in complexion than ever, grinning all over his face, and . . . positively glowing with health," in order to vouchsafe "a few words" that were "particularly relevant."[5] But many other less jolting examples fill these zealous books. Sections devoted to biography read like hagiography. We seldom encounter a mere fact about Lewis; accounts of his behavior, attitudes, and personal relationships are instead reported in the wide-eyed manner of the impressionable disciple. To describe him as a wonderful friend is a lamentable understatement; we must be assured that no one ever was a better friend. To praise him as brilliant in debate is entirely too lukewarm a compliment; we are told that C. S. Lewis could have matched wits with any man who ever lived. To endorse him as a Christian apologist of the first rank is altogether inadequate; his apocalyptic vision of Christianity must be likened to that of St. John on the Isle of Patmos. After a while, one longs for patches of sunlight to dispel the reverential haze. One tires of enduring these excesses and of having to plow through equally ecstatic testimonials in book after book.

Other works tend to dwell on matters that do not appear to cry out for sustained attention. There exists, for example, one detailed analysis of the tone, pitch, and resonance of Lewis's voice as he delivered the Broadcast Talks, complete with data about his breathing patterns and medical commentary as to the probable cause of his frequent gasping for air. Still other works offer us the opportunity to participate vicariously in Lewis's life. One can peruse a volume of photographs of English landscapes sacramentally entitled *C. S. Lewis: Images of His World*, in which the very natural phenomena upon which he once cast his eye have been lavishly reproduced in full color for anyone wishing to tread imaginatively where he has trod. Nor is this venerating tendency confined to books. The equivalent of C. S. Lewis museums and shrines have been erected in various localities. There are even C. S. Lewis calendars, sweatshirts, aprons, bumper stickers, and tote bags.[6]

The intention underlying all this hero worship and preoccupation with physiological and geographical trivia is to pay tribute to a beloved man. But surely I cannot be the only student of Lewis who has wondered whether much of it is not ill-conceived and self-defeating. On my reading, the man who emerges from Lewis's books would not have been flattered by all this attention. In fact, I cannot help thinking that he would have found it rather embarrassing.

Similar in tone to these transported celebrations of Lewis the man is the increasing crop of almost wholly uncritical studies of Lewis the thinker.[7] Here again, despite considerable effort on the part of his disciples, Lewis has not been well served. On the whole, their expositions of his thought make remarkably unrewarding reading. Inordinately fond of quoting, they can hardly write a page without allowing him "to speak for himself." When they are not simply quoting his words, they are paraphrasing his ideas, often inaccurately and always less interestingly. Their discussions are seldom suggestive or illuminating. They have next to nothing to offer by way of analysis or elucidation. They never probe. Their rare attempts at criticism are timid, addressed to tiny points, and dropped almost the instant they are raised. Wishing (but invariably failing) to do more than repeat what Lewis has already said, they write books that lack direction, thesis, and, in the end, substance. Though brimming over with good intentions, they seldom transcend a sort of doting worshipfulness: "If you thought his last point was good, wait until you hear his next one."

In voicing these opinions, I am not so much scolding other authors as recording my conviction that C. S. Lewis needs to be rescued not only from the evils of excessive hostility but also and equally from the evils of excessive loyalty. His apologetic writings deserve better than cavalier rejection or uncritical acceptance. The question of whether to embrace any particular form of religious belief is important in itself and for its broader intellectual and personal implications. Lewis was committed not only to the truth of Christianity but to debating it with all comers. An open forum of this kind is rare. In what follows, I take up his challenge as I reconstruct and critically examine his case for Christianity.

Chapter One

APOLOGETICS

Lewis's no-nonsense approach to religious belief is nowhere more apparent than in his candid and straightforward admission that "I am not asking anyone to accept Christianity if his best reasoning tells him that the weight of the evidence is against it" (*MC*, 123). Here is a bold reversal of the common view that religious belief is not open to rational discussion. Many Christians are perfectly willing, if not positively eager, to acknowledge that there are no proofs for the existence of God and that it is hard to reconcile their religious beliefs with the observed facts. These damaging concessions do not disturb them in the slightest. They think that belief in God has nothing to do with evidence and that it should be based on faith alone. Which is to say that there are a great many people who *do* ask you to accept Christianity even if your best reasoning tells you that the weight of the evidence is against it.

Lewis rejected this view on the ground that it surrenders the case for rational religion at the very outset. He considered it a serious mistake to define faith as belief in propositions for which there is no evidence, and he maintained that those who advocate "leaps of faith" do a grave disservice to the Christian religion.[1] If the evidence seems unfavorable to believing in God, that is *not* the point at which faith comes in: "A sane man accepts or rejects any statement, not because he wants or does not want to, but because the evidence seems to him good or bad. . . . If he thought the evidence bad but tried to force himself to believe in spite of it, that would be merely stupid" (*MC*, 122). At the initial stage of inquiry, faith is not a virtue but a defect, a refusal to come to terms with the decisive questions of logic and evidence. If it were legitimate to believe in spite of the evidence, anyone could believe anything "by faith."

It follows, according to Lewis, that the question of whether or not to become a Christian is a matter of sorting out and examining the evidence. If the evidence is scanty, faith will not help. If Christianity is not reasonable, it cannot be credible. This is to say that Lewis considered it both important and necessary to reply to what has come to be called the "evidentialist objection"—the contention that it is not only irrational but morally wrong to believe anything without sufficient evidence.[2] The difficulties involved in religious belief, he maintained, should not be skirted but squarely faced and resolved—one way or the other. Because he took Christianity so seriously, Lewis took Christian apologetics equally seriously.

The audience of the apologists is the unbeliever: the atheist, the skeptic, the agnostic—anyone who denies or doubts that there is a God. This fact explains the method they use. In debating with unbelievers, apologists cannot appeal to the Bible, since anyone who denies that there is a God will also deny that the Bible is his word. Instead, they must set forth a philosophical defense of Christianity in the hope of establishing claims independently of faith, on the strength of purely rational considerations. They must try to convince the unbeliever that the claims of Christianity are reasonable, that powerful arguments can be offered in their support, and that it is more rational to believe than to disbelieve in God. As Lewis puts it, apologetics is the attempt to discover how far we can get "on our own steam" (*MC*, 37).

Lewis was confident that these tasks could be accomplished, and his apologetic writings contain the arguments by which he tried to accomplish them. The source of this confidence was his own past experience. An atheist for many years, he gradually came to the realization that as an honest man he could no longer dismiss the claims of the Christian religion. Yet as Christianity itself seemed more and more plausible, the prospect of becoming a Christian grew less and less attractive. Lewis always went out of his way to let people know that he did not *want* to become a Christian and that he became one only because the evidence seemed to allow no other alternative. If there was ever a purely philosophical conversion, it was Lewis's.[3]

His account of that conversion is justly famous, for it is set forth in powerful and unforgettable prose:

> You must picture me alone in that room in Magdalen, night after night, feeling, whenever my mind lifted even for a second from my work, the steady, unrelenting approach of Him whom I so earnestly desired not to meet. That which I greatly feared had at last come upon me. In the Trinity Term of 1929 I gave in, and admitted that God was God, and knelt and prayed: perhaps, that night, the most dejected and reluctant convert in all England. I did not then see what is now the most shining and obvious thing; the Divine humility which will accept a convert even on such terms. The Prodigal Son at least walked home on his own feet. But who can duly adore that Love which will open the high gates to a prodigal who is brought in kicking, struggling, resentful, and darting his eyes in every direction for a chance of escape? (*SbJ*, 228-29)

Lewis knew perfectly well that the average churchgoer would be nonplussed by all this talk about reluctant converts being dragged in by the weight of the evidence. Yet that is exactly what he claimed about his own conversion. His intellectual development convinced him for life that Christianity is more reasonable than its rivals and that rational argument "moves the whole struggle onto [God's] own ground" (*SL*, 8). Seldom has an apologist succeeded so completely in conveying the impression that reason is on the side of faith, and that it is not the believer but the unbeliever for whom rational discussion poses difficulties.

This willingness to confront head-on the decisive questions of logic and evidence is the very quality that attracts so many readers to Lewis. He seems to embody the perfect combination of sound doctrine and rigorous argument: an uncomprisingly orthodox Christian equipped with a logical faculty as devastating and on-target as it is lucid and compelling. What, after all, could be more disarmingly forthright than for someone to say "Look here, if you don't find what I say convincing, then for heaven's sake don't believe it"? Throughout, his appeal is to the clear-headed virtues: straight thinking, facing facts, avoiding nonsense, seeing through fraud, calling a spade a spade—all of it carried off with a mesmerizing blend of effortless brilliance, urbanity, and wit. "Very well, then, atheism is too simple," he will say, as if its refutation were a philosophical bagatelle that the rational man could accomplish after hours. Or again, "All I am doing is to ask people to face the facts—to understand the questions which Christianity claims to answer. And they are very terrifying facts. I wish it was possible to say something more agreeable. But I must say what I think true" (*MC*, 39). The effect is hard to resist. And at those crucial moments when Lewis closes in on his reader and presses the claims of Christianity, it is with such deftness, tact, and apparent reasonableness that disagreeing with him seems like sheer stubbornness, like disputing with a benefactor.

Seldom, too, has an apologist come across to his readers as a person with whom they could so immediately identify. This was a self-consciously adopted technique. At the outset of his career as an apologist, Lewis had observed that Christianity was being presented to the masses either in the emotionally charged form of the revivalist or in the impenetrable jargon of the theologian. Rejecting both approaches, he hit upon a third option—that of the popularizer: "My task was . . . that of a *translator*—one turning Christian doctrine . . . into language that unscholarly people . . . could understand" (*GiD*, 183). He knew his audience. Readers soon discover that instead of being soothingly wooed into accepting yet another innocuous form of "religion," they are being paid the high compliment of an invitation to think hard about important and difficult questions. They quickly sense that the author of these arresting books is not just one more tedious cleric obsessed with "dialogue," but a fiercely independent thinker whose views and personal habits are often controversial enough to raise the eyebrows of other Christians.

Despite his unswerving orthodoxy, Lewis was never entirely comfortable with those many grateful Fundamentalists who almost immediately claimed him as their own. More than once he expressed serious misgivings about the language and stock-in-trade methods of organized evangelism. When a determined member of the Billy Graham Evangelistic Association tried to extract from him the "testimony" that somewhere along the line he had made a personal "decision" for Christ, Lewis doggedly refused to be browbeaten into mouthing the approved formula. Although a firm believer in both the existence and necessity of a nonremedial hell, he objected to terrifying people into embracing Christianity by dwelling on the torments of the damned. When hopefully queried as to whether he had renounced beer and tobacco after his conversion, he replied that he most certainly had not and proceeded to express strong disapproval of "a certain type of bad man [who] cannot give up a thing himself without wanting every one else to give it up" (*MC*, 76).

On more substantive issues, Lewis exhibited the same courage and independence of mind. Ask him whether Jesus was ever mistaken, and he will acknowledge that he was indeed and point you to "the most embarrassing verse in the New Testament." Confide that you have long treasured the four Gospels as great literature, and he will beg to differ on the ground that they are clumsily written and lack all sense of climax. Observe in passing that many of the great world religions anticipated and even duplicated Christianity on certain points, and he will heartily concur and confess that he would have found it hard to believe in Christianity if this were not so. The net result is a freshness, a clarity, and a sense of excitement unparalleled in contemporary apologetic literature. Convinced that Christianity is not contrary to reason, Lewis welcomed debate. He was willing not only to argue for the truth of Christianity but to abide by the conditions of argument. The issues would not be dodged at the last minute by appeals to faith, mystery, or our limited understanding. The case for Christianity stands or falls with the arguments.

But what exactly can reason establish? Although Lewis's views on this question can be pieced together from his more popular apologetic writings, his clearest and most complete discussion occurs in a lesser-known essay entitled "Is Theism Important?" (*GiD*, 172–76).

Since he denies that belief in God should be based on faith, it seems natural to suppose that Lewis thought that reason could establish the existence of God. But this is not quite accurate. If someone claimed that reason could prove the existence of God, Lewis would immediately ask what was meant by the term *God*. This was not so much a request for a definition as an attempt to determine whether the person was using the term philosophically or religiously. In its philosophical sense, *God* has a variety of meanings—the First Cause, the Necessary Being, the Moral Lawgiver, the Designer of the Universe, and so on. In its religious sense, however, *God* means the Creator of the World, the heavenly Father who loved the world and sent his Son to die for the sins of mankind, the Being worshiped by Christians whose nature has been defined and elucidated by the great creeds of Christendom.

Lewis considered these meanings to be radically different and cautioned his readers not to confuse them.

On the basis of this distinction, he held that reason can prove the existence of God only in the philosophical sense, not in the religious sense. It can prove, for example, that a Moral Lawgiver exists, but not that the God of Christianity exists or that the Moral Lawgiver is the God of Christianity.

Corresponding to the philosophical and religious uses of the term *God* are two meanings of the term *faith* that Lewis calls Faith-A and Faith-B. By Faith-A, he meant nothing more than belief understood as intellectual assent. To have faith in this sense is simply to accept the proposition that God exists, that there is in fact such a Being. Those who believe in God in this sense are not Christians but theists. As a form of belief, this kind of faith "hardly differs" from our belief in the uniformity of nature or in the consciousness of other people. There is nothing religious about it. Faith-B, on the other hand, *is* a religious state of mind. Unlike Faith-A, it is not a purely intellectual assent. It is not belief *that* God exists but belief *in* God. As such, it involves the will and manifests itself as trust in the God whose existence has been assented to by Faith-A. So, to say that reason can establish only philosophical conclusions about God is to say that it can produce only Faith-A. With respect to Faith-B it is impotent. Although Faith-A is a "necessary pre-condition" for Faith-B, it does not invariably lead to it.

For these reasons Lewis did not regard attempts to construct philosophical proofs for the existence of God as attempts to establish a religious conclusion. Even if such proofs were successful, the Being whose existence they establish would not be the God of Christianity. A philosophical belief about God remains Faith-A. It is a purely intellectual assent which lacks all that is present in a "living faith." To that extent, Lewis agreed with Pascal's dictum, so often employed by others for mischievous purposes, that the God of the philosophers is not the God of Abraham, Isaac, and Jacob.

The same view is found in Lewis's better-known apologetic writings. In *Mere Christianity*, for example, after arguing that reason can establish the existence of a Power behind the Moral Law, a "Something or Someone" urging us to do what is right and making us uncomfortable when we do wrong, he immediately acknowledges that he is "not yet within a hundred miles of the God of Christian theology" (*MC*, 34). Again, in *Miracles*, after arguing that the validity of human reasoning presupposes the existence of a Mind beyond Nature, he insists that this Mind is not the same thing as the God of Christianity (*M*, 42). Even in *Surprised by Joy*, his spiritual autobiography, he repeatedly emphasizes that to accept theism is not to accept Christianity and informs us that although he became a theist in 1929, it was not until two years later that he became a Christian.

To sum up, philosophical argument can take us just so far. It can produce Faith-A, nothing more. That of course raises the question of just what value there is in Christian apologetics. Lewis's reply is that although no one is likely to be argued into accepting Christianity, philosophical arguments can force people to face certain facts that prepare the way for accepting it. These arguments cannot establish religious conclusions, but they can establish conclusions that are relevant to religious belief and that make Christianity more plausible. Hence, apologists operate on two fronts. First, they try to establish conclusions that have a direct bearing on the claims of Christianity. Although the God of the philosophers is not the God of Abraham, Isaac, and Jacob, "an aridly philosophical God" does not so much repel a personal response as fail to invite it (*GiD*, 174). Second, by replying to objections, apologists remove "inhibitions" and thereby enable the claims of Christianity to get a fair hearing. Those who can accomplish this will have accomplished a great deal. The function of philosophical argument is preliminary but crucial.

Lewis has much more to say about Faith-B, but his further views go far beyond the matter of initial assent and raise difficult questions about continuing to believe in God in the face of apparently contrary evidence. Before we turn to these complications, I want first to consider what Lewis regarded as favorable evidence for the existence of God. In his apologetic writings he gives us three arguments for believing in God: the Argument from Desire, the Moral Argument, and the Argument from Reason. In the next three chapters we will examine these arguments in order to see how far they enable us to get "on our own steam." The fundamental question that Lewis must answer is this: Why believe in God in the first place?

Chapter Two

DESIRE

In his epistle to the Romans, St. Paul declares that God has not left himself without a witness in the world and that the invisible things of the Godhead are clearly discernible in the created universe (Rom. 1:20). The exact meaning of this statement is disputed, but from the earliest days of Christianity apologists have taken it as an endorsement of natural theology—the attempt by reason unaided by faith to prove the existence of God.

Although Lewis considered most of these proofs to be unsuccessful, he did accept a few of them. Of these, one in particular elicited from him a powerful psychological response and came to enjoy a position of special prominence in his writings. Unlike many proofs for God's existence, this one is not an excessively abstract and sterile academic exercise, but rather an experiential argument that speaks directly and intimately to the sensibilities of the religious life by focusing on man's transcendental longings, on our craving for something that no finite object can ever fully satisfy. I call it the Argument from Desire.

This argument did not originate with Christianity. Centuries before the Christian era, Plato had already spoken of certain recurrent stirrings within the human heart, of a deep and unquenchable desire that impels the soul to look beyond the world of the senses to a higher realm where it can find "true pasture."[1] Convinced that man cannot be adequately defined in terms of nature, Plato developed an elaborate argument to show that in all our temporal loves, satisfactions, and goods, we are really desiring some more ultimate good of which these earthly attachments provide only an "inkling."[2] But it was St. Augustine who gave this argument its classic Christian expression. He, too, speaks of a basic restlessness in man, a permanent dissatisfaction with the things of this world, which indicates that we have been created for something more satisfying and ennobling than the impoverished, temporal objects presented to us by our feeble, earthbound imagination. "Thou has created us for Thyself," he declares, "and our hearts are restless until they rest in Thee, oh God."

The more Lewis reflected on this argument, the more convinced he became that its central contention had been confirmed in his own life. Like Plato and St. Augustine, he was mightily impressed by a "bittersweet stab of inconsolable longing" and concluded that the experience of unsatisfied desire provides us with "the truest index" (*WG*, 12) of our real condition: we are cut off from a higher reality for which we unknowingly long. All desire is desire for God. "Joy" is Lewis's name for this experience, and *Surprised by Joy* is his attempt to analyze it and to draw out its philosophical implications.

Although *Surprised by Joy* is commonly regarded as Lewis's autobiography, that is not an accurate description of its contents. Lewis himself stresses that the book is not a general autobiography at all but an account of his conversion, and that he had restricted the content to two categories of material. The first is the conversion story itself: his encounters with Joy, the various ways it manifested itself in his life, the many false paths he took in his attempts to track it down, and his final estimate of its significance. The second is more general. In order to help the reader understand what kind of person he was when his "explicitly spiritual crisis" took place, Lewis provides some additional, carefully selected autobiographical information.

The trouble with these categories is that they are not nearly so straightforward as they look. Lewis goes beyond them in two ways. Clearly he does more than merely describe himself and his early encounters with Joy. The book abounds with tangents and asides: he denounces English boarding schools; he deplores modern educational curricula, which neglect or exclude classical instruction in Greek and Latin; he lays down canons of aesthetic taste; he makes desultory pronouncements about contemporary literature, philosophy, and theology; he criticizes many of the social conventions that had been imposed on him as a child; he bristles about games and other forms of enforced recreation that he says deprive children of their individuality; and he airs many of his well-known pet peeves about modern life. In short, *Surprised by Joy* is a very mixed bag.

A second and more important way in which Lewis trespasses beyond his announced boundaries consists in the fact that the story of his conversion is more than just a factual narrative account. It is clear from the very first page that Lewis thinks that the philosophical and religious implications of Joy apply not only to himself but to everyone who experiences it. Although he does not explicitly argue for the truth of Christianity in this book, the conversion story is buttressed by an implicit argument for the existence of God that he does defend elsewhere. To that extent, *Surprised by Joy*, while not an apologetic work, is nevertheless a work with apologetic implications.[3]

Although the book tends to ramble and suffers from occasional lapses of taste, it is easy to understand its general appeal. Like much of Lewis's work, *Surprised by Joy* contains its share of beautifully written passages. Its diverse and often seemingly disconnected parts are adroitly woven together and brought to bear on the conversion story in a way that seems like pure magic. Clearly this is a book intended not only to persuade but to ravish its reader. For our purposes, however, it is in terms of its implicit argument that *Surprised by Joy* must be assessed.

Lewis had been preoccupied with this argument for a long time. More than twenty years before the publication of *Surprised by Joy*, he set it forth in the allegorical novel *The Pilgrim's Regress*. Little needs to be said about this embarrassing work. Patently lackluster as fiction, it is even less successful as philosophy. Intended as an ambitious critique of modernity, its arguments cannot be taken seriously. Lewis's treatment of opposing positions is maddeningly cavalier. The views that fall before his scourge are so uniformly misrepresented that his "criticism" seldom rises above the level of caricature and ridicule. For example, anthropologists are dismissed as people who travel to "backward villages" in order to collect the "odd stories" that the natives tell (*PR*, 36); the inductive method of science is said to establish its conclusions by guesswork and to be based on the principle that "if you make the same guess often enough it ceases to be a guess and becomes a Scientific Fact" (*PR*, 37); it is said that scientists "pretend" to be objective, but that in fact they assume their conclusions first and "interpret their researches by it" (*PR*, 68); it is claimed that people become atheists because of "wish-fulfillment" (*PR*, 73), and that humanists have no desire to probe issues, for that "would remove the graceful veil of illusion which is so necessary to the *human* point of view" (*PR*, 103).

Lewis's expositors have almost unanimously found it convenient to pass over these astonishing remarks in silence,[4] but in the 1943 preface to the third edition of *The Pilgrim's Regress* Lewis himself owns up to a few of its flaws (e.g., its "needless obscurity" and "uncharitable tone"), even going so far as to confess that in places he had "lost his temper." But no amount of minor misgivings can redeem this gratuitously censorious little book. Surely anyone familiar with the later writings, vintage Lewis, will readily grant that it is a failure, an apprentice work in which Lewis was struggling with ideas that he would one day handle with greater control and sophistication.

Why, then, even mention it? There are two reasons. First, in the 1943 preface Lewis states that this novel sets forth the argument that convinced him of the validity of theism, and that the book should be read as a defense of Christianity as well as of Romanticism and reason. Second, in that same preface he sets forth a version of the Argument from Desire significantly different from that found in *Surprised by Joy*. Since I will be returning to both versions shortly, it will be useful to have the relevant passage before us. Reflecting on what he believed were the many false paths he had taken in pursuit of what he was later to call Joy, Lewis says,

> The sole merit I claim for this book is that it is written by one who has proved [these false paths] all to be wrong. . . . For I have myself been deluded by every one of these false answers in turn, and have contemplated each of them earnestly enough to discover the cheat. To have embraced so many false Florimels is no matter for boasting: it is fools, they say, who learn by experience. But since they do at last learn, let a fool bring his experience into the common stock that wiser men may profit by it. . . .
>
> It appeared to me . . . that if a man diligently followed this desire, pursuing the false objects until their falsity appeared and then resolutely abandoning them, he must come out at last into the clear knowledge that the human soul was made to enjoy some object that is never fully given . . . in our present . . . experience. This Desire was, in the soul . . . the chair in which only one could sit. And if nature makes nothing in vain, the One who can sit in this chair must exist. (*PR*, 8–10)

For the moment, however, I will confine my attention to *Surprised by Joy*.

Lewis begins by telling us that his earliest experiences were "incurably Romantic," that even as a child he had listened for "the horns of elfland." The occasions of his first experiences of Joy had been simple ones: a moss garden his brother once brought into the nursery, Beatrix Potter's *Squirrel Nutkin,* and Longfellow's lines—

> I heard a voice that cried,
> Balder the beautiful
> Is dead, is dead—

The toy garden produced his first awareness of nature, an awareness that was soon to be intensified by the hills visible through his nursery window. Although in fact not very distant, to a child they were inaccessible. They taught him *Sehnsucht,* longing.

A few years later, while standing before a flowering currant bush, there suddenly arose within him "as if from a depth not of years but of centuries" the memory of his brother's garden. He was immediately overwhelmed by a sensation so powerful that words could hardly do it justice. It was a sensation of intense desire. The experience was short-lived, but while it lasted everything that had ever happened to him seemed insignificant by comparison. From then on, whenever Joy struck, whether through nature or poetry or music, he again experienced this "bittersweet stab of inconsolable longing," this "unendurable sense of desire and loss." He was convinced from the very beginning that these experiences were visitations of far-reaching importance, but he was at a loss as to how to explain them. Joy was a desire. But for what?

Noting that all these experiences shared a common character, Lewis proceeds to define Joy as "an unsatisfied desire which is itself more desirable than any other satisfaction" (*SbJ*, 18). As he employs it, *Joy* is a technical term with a precise meaning. It refers to an experience that he sharply distinguishes from aesthetic enjoyment, pleasure, and even happiness. Joy has nothing in common with these beyond the obvious fact that anyone who experiences it will want it again. Nor will anyone who tastes Joy ever exchange it for any other pleasure. Yet it is not the same thing as pleasure. Nor is it a substitute for sex (indeed, sex is often a substitute for Joy). In short, the experience is *sui generis*, unique.

Not only is the experience of Joy fleeting, but even while it lasts, it is a desire for what is absent and never fully possessed. In the experience of Joy, the ordinary distinction between wanting and having breaks down. When we experience Joy, we want to have what we *do* have when we want what we do *not* have.

Is there any escape from this conceptual thicket? I think so. In order to understand Lewis's account of this coveted experience, we must grasp a crucial point: we want to reexperience Joy again and again not in order to gratify our desire but in order to *reawaken* it. The experience depends not only on the absence of its object but on the fact that it is this very absence that makes the experience so wonderful that we want it again and again.

How can we achieve this? One solution immediately suggests itself: in order to reawaken the desire, we must go back to the situations that initially evoked it. We must revisit the landscapes, reread the books, and listen once more to the music that gave rise to the experience of Joy in the first place. And that is exactly what Lewis did. "To 'get it again' became my constant endeavor; while reading every poem, hearing every piece of music, going for every walk, I stood anxious sentinel at my own mind to watch whether the blessed moment was beginning and to endeavor to retain it if it did" (*SbJ*, 169). Oddly, however, this method did not work. No matter how diligently he tried to recapture the experience, he invariably failed.

Lewis finally broke out of this self-defeating predicament by discovering the Corrective: you cannot identify a desire with a sensation or with any other inner state that happens to accompany it. Every desire is a desire *for* something, for some object, and it is only by ignoring your inner state that you can discover what that object is. Divorced from its object, an inner state is of no importance: "If by . . . the use of any drug [the experience] could be produced from within, it would at once be seen to be of no value. For take away the object, and what . . . would be left?—a whirl of images, a fluttering sensation in the diaphragm, a momentary abstraction. And who could want that?" (*SbJ*, 168). The answer is, of course, that C. S. Lewis had wanted it for years. Only after he had discovered the Corrective did he see that his obsessive pursuit of an inner state had been the pursuit of a phantom. Only then did he realize that he had been confusing the object of his desire with the desire itself.

The Corrective first dawned upon him as he pondered a passage from Samuel Alexander's *Space, Time and Deity*. According to Alexander, an important distinction must be drawn between "enjoyment" and "contemplation." When you look at a table, for example, you "enjoy" the act of seeing and you "contemplate" the table. Having accepted this distinction, Lewis found that its consequences were "catastrophic." It immediately convinced him that the enjoyment and the contemplation of our inner states are incompatible. In desiring something, you contemplate the object of your desire. The moment you shift your attention from the object desired to the experience of desire itself and the sensations that happen to accompany it, you begin contemplating yourself. By looking within yourself to discover what is going on, however, you insure that whatever is going on stops. What introspection finds, therefore, is nothing but mental images and physical sensations. The mistake lies in thinking that a desire can be identified with such images and sensations. Lewis immediately realized that his previous efforts to understand Joy by looking within himself had been attempts to do the impossible: to contemplate what was enjoyed. With visible relief, he reveled in the discovery that he would never again have to concern himself with inner states. What he wanted was not an inner state at all.

What was it then? Lewis went about answering this question by the process of elimination. Experience itself was put to the test. Does this world have anything to offer that can satisfy our deepest longings? Lewis thought not. From this he concluded that Joy must be a desire for some infinite Object:

> I had tried everything . . . as it were, asking myself, "Is it this you want?" . . . Last of all I had asked if Joy itself was what I wanted. . . . Joy proclaimed, "You want—I myself am your want of—something other, outside, not you nor any state of you." . . . I thus understood that in deepest solitude there is a road right out of the self, a commerce with something which, by refusing to identify itself with any object of the senses . . . or any state of our own minds, proclaims itself sheerly objective. (*SbJ*, 220–21)

In this way, Joy became a pointer not only to something beyond the self but to something beyond the world.

To say, therefore, that C. S. Lewis was surprised by Joy is to say that the experience he had mistakenly regarded as a state of the self turned out to be a desire for something else; that after savoring everything this world had to offer, he found that nothing truly satisfied him; and that this, together with the fact that his desire persisted, drove him to the conclusion that the real Object of his desire had to be something that transcends the world. This could only be God.

The overall argument goes like this:

(1)   Human experience provides us with a recurring desire so wonderful that we want it again and again.

(2)   It cannot be the experience itself, considered simply as an inner state, that we want, because every desire is a desire for something.

(3)   It cannot be a finite object that we want because no finite object fully satisfies us.

(4)   Yet the desire persists.

---

(5)   Therefore, there must be an infinite Object that can fully satisfy us. This Object is God.

The conclusion of the conversion story is, so to speak, as surprising as the surprise itself. After he became a Christian, Lewis "lost all interest" in Joy. Convinced that it had only been a "pointer" to something else that he had now discovered, he ceased to be preoccupied with it.

Lewis characterizes the Argument from Desire as empirical, based on experience. Walter Hooper reports that after Lewis's death he discovered among his papers an early draft of *Surprised by Joy* in which Lewis describes himself as "an empirical Theist" who arrived at belief in God "not by reflection alone, but by reflection on a particular recurrent experience."[5] But we need not resort to obscure documents. In *Surprised by Joy* itself Lewis repeatedly assures us that experience will not lead us astray and that the universe "rings true wherever [we] fairly test it" (*SbJ*, 177). The trouble, he thought, is that most people do not fairly test it, and so they remain in the dark about Joy's true object. It is important, therefore, to determine whether his argument really establishes what he thought it established.

Clearly Lewis is on solid ground in claiming that aesthetic experience is one of the important varieties of the experience he calls "Joy." Great (and even not-so-great) poetry and music can awaken within us powerful feelings that encourage us to believe we have gained temporary access to a dimension of reality that does not ordinarily manifest itself, that we have been vouchsafed an experience so charged with meaning that our daily lives seem humdrum and pedestrian by comparison. But what follows?

Lewis thought that anyone who took these experiences seriously and pursued each object of desire would discover that they do not ultimately satisfy. And from this he concluded without further ado that they are not what we really want. But this does not follow at all. The claim *Anything that does not ultimately satisfy us cannot be what we really wanted* may sound plausible when stated in so general a way, but it cannot survive the test of concrete examples. Would anyone seriously want to argue that the fact that Sam is hungry again four hours after breakfast proves that it is not food that he really wanted? Or that the fact that Jill is tired by 10:00 A.M. proves that it was not sleep that she really wanted? How, then, can such a conclusion follow in the case of our experiences of Joy? Why say that the failure of music or poetry to satisfy us fully proves that they are not really what we want? And why go on to claim that this, in turn, proves that what we really want is something else to which they are merely "pointers"?

Lewis was correct, of course, in claiming that every desire is a desire *for* something. But this is nothing more than an observation about the nature of desire. From this purely conceptual observation nothing follows about what really exists. All desires must have *grammatical* objects, but they need not have *real* ones. People desire all sorts of imaginary things. The existence of the object desired does not follow from the mere fact that someone desires it, not even from the fact that someone has a desire that nothing on earth can satisfy. From this fact alone we could just as well conclude that some desires cannot be satisfied.

Joy leads nowhere, and *Surprised by Joy* is wholly unconvincing as an attempt to demonstrate that there is a "road right out of the self" that points straight to God. So we are right back where we started—trying to account for a psychological state as yet unattached to any object whose existence has been empirically established.

As I have suggested, Lewis's writings contain a second way of trying to bridge the gap between Joy and its object. If we return to the 1943 preface to *The Pilgrim's Regress*, we find a claim which, although absent from *Surprised by Joy*, serves admirably as an additional step in the Argument from Desire. His claim is that *Nature does nothing in vain*. By this he appears to mean that for every natural desire, there is an object that can satisfy it.

In endorsing the view that nature does nothing in vain, Lewis identifies himself with the Natural Law tradition in philosophy, which has been embraced in one way or another by a distinguished line of thinkers extending from St. Thomas Aquinas and Richard Hooker all the way back to Aristotle and, in his own way, Plato. Archaisms aside, the following passage from Hooker's *Laws of Ecclesiastical Polity* could have been written by Lewis:

> For man doth not seem to rest satisfied, either with fruition of that wherewith his life is preserved, or with the performance of such actions as advance him most deservedly in estimation; but doth further covet, yea oftentimes manifestly pursue with great sedulity and earnestness, that which . . . exceedeth the reach of sense; yea somewhat the capacity of reason, something heavenly and divine, which with hidden exultation it rather surmiseth than conceiveth; somewhat it seeketh, and what this is directly it knoweth not, yet very intensive desire thereof doth so incite it, that all other known delights and pleasures are laid aside, they give place to the search of this but only suspected desire. . . . For although the beauties, riches, honours, sciences, virtues, and perfections of all men living, were in the present possession of one; yet somewhat beyond and above all this there would still be sought and earnestly thirsted for. So that Nature . . . doth plainly claim and call for a more divine perfection . . . since it is an axiom of Nature that natural desire cannot utterly frustrate.[6]

Here, then, is a new and perhaps more promising way of generating the desired conclusion.

When we look for Lewis's reasons for believing that nature does nothing in vain, however, we are in for a disappointment. Neither in *The Pilgrim's Regress* nor in *Surprised by Joy* does he explain why he thought this. Perhaps he agreed with Hooker that the claim was so obvious as to be axiomatic. If so, he was mistaken. As Bertrand Russell once observed, from the fact that you are hungry it does not follow that you will get food. Nor, he might have added, does it follow from the fact that you desire something this world cannot provide that your desire will be satisfied in some other world.

Only in *The Weight of Glory* does Lewis give us a reason for believing that nature does nothing in vain. After alluding to some "inconsolable secret" that all of us carry about within ourselves and that "hurts so much" that we "take [our] revenge on it" by calling it names like "Nostalgia, "Romanticism," and "Adolescence" (*WG*, 4), he offers one of those persuasive analogies that many readers find so irresistably apt. Perhaps with Russell's point in mind, he does address the objection that being hungry does not prove that we will get bread, but he declares that the objection misses the point:

> A man's physical hunger does not prove that man will get any bread . . . but surely [it] does prove that he comes of a race which repairs its body by eating and inhabits a world where eatable substances exist. In the same way, though I do not believe . . . that my desire for Paradise proves that I shall enjoy it, I think it a pretty good indication that such a thing exists and that some men will. (*WG*, 6)

The analogy underlying the inference we are being asked to draw here is that just as hunger proves that we inhabit a world in which food exists, so the desire for ultimate satisfaction is a "pretty good indication" that we inhabit a world in which spiritual beatitude is the destiny of at least some people. But this analogy is faulty. The trouble is not that Lewis's inference about desire does not follow from his claim about hunger, but rather that his claim about hunger is itself incorrect. The phenomenon of hunger simply does not prove that man inhabits a world in which food exists. One might just as well claim that the fear that grips us when we walk through a dark graveyard proves that we have something to be afraid of. What proves that we inhabit a world in which food exists is the discovery that certain things are in fact "eatable" and that they nourish and repair our bodies. The discovery of the existence of food comes not by way of an *inference* based on the inner state of hunger; it is, rather, an empirical discovery.

Properly understood, Lewis's analogy in fact serves to

establish precisely the opposite conclusion. Just as we cannot prove that we inhabit a world in which food exists simply on the ground that we get hungry, so we cannot prove that an infinite Object of desire exists simply on the ground that we desire it. The desire in and of itself proves nothing, points to nothing. For all we know, perhaps some desires *are* in vain. Inferences from our own psychological makeup to what actually exists, much less to what *must* exist, are fallacious. It follows that the version of the Argument from Desire found in *The Pilgrim's Regress* fares no better than that of *Surprised by Joy*.

Note what Lewis was trying to do. He wanted to establish that Joy had a real object, that it was not "in vain." His reasons for thinking this were, first, that Joy is a natural desire, and second, that every natural desire has a real object. But this is puzzling. How could Lewis have known that every natural desire has a real object *before* knowing that Joy has one? I can legitimately claim that every student in the class has failed the test only if I first know that each of them has individually failed it. The same is true of natural desires. On the other hand, if Lewis already knew that Joy had a real object before knowing the truth about natural desires in general, then the general claim becomes superfluous, for if he already knew that Joy had a real object, there would have been no gap between Joy and its object in the first place, and therefore nothing for an argument to bridge. Why, then, did Lewis put forth such an argument? Why try to prove what needs no proof?

It begins to look as if Lewis arrived at his belief that every natural desire has a real object on the basis of nonempirical considerations, that he has smuggled into his argument a covert metaphysical theory of desire about which we have not been informed. But then he was not an empirical theist after all. That being the case, his claim about natural desires has become true by definition: he has simply decided on *a priori* grounds that he will not call any desire "natural" unless it has a real object. Although such a procedure provides interesting information about his preferred linguistic usage, it should not be confused with an empirical argument for the existence of an infinite Object of desire. On empirical grounds, the Argument from Desire establishes nothing.

The claim that God is the ultimate Object of desire also invites theological scrutiny. The remarkable fact is that, in the light of Lewis's account of his own conversion, this claim appears to be false. In *Surprised by Joy*, he emphasizes that he did not immediately become a Christian after he became a theist. On the contrary, the moment he became convinced that the road right out of the self led straight to God, every trace of desire vanished. At this juncture, a resistance began to manifest itself that finally resulted in his being the most reluctant convert in all England.

But why? If the God of Christianity really was his heart's desire, the Object he had been pursuing unawares for all those years, why did Lewis draw back? Why did he describe this God as "Him whom I so earnestly desired not to meet"? Why did he experience only "unrelieved terror" at the thought that he had finally approached the source from which all those "arrows of Joy had been shot" at him since childhood? Why was "no desire at all" present when he was "dragged through the doorway" (*SbJ*, 230–31)?

Lewis's answer is that he had never dreamed that the search for Joy's object would lead him to God. Believing all along that he had been the agent in pursuit of something, he was quite unprepared for the discovery that he had in fact been the patient, that he had himself been the pursued. Once the exhilarating sensation of Joy had been replaced by a moral demand requiring nothing less than radical repentance, Lewis was no longer sure that he wanted to proceed any further along this route. To his dismay, he found himself recoiling from the discovery that a rich imaginative lifetime had encouraged him to believe he was eager to make. But this answer does not really own up to the question. If Joy's object really is God and if all desire is really desire for him, why when he was brought face to face with him did Lewis *cease* to desire him and search for a way of escape? Can the same Object that men want more than anything else also be the Object from which they flee the moment they are about to attain it?

Throughout *Surprised by Joy*, Lewis has very skeptical things to say about man's alleged search for God, likening it to the mouse's search for the cat. Such a remark reinforces the skepticism already apparent in *Miracles:*

> Men are reluctant to pass over from the notion of an abstract and negative deity to the living God. I do not wonder. . . .

The Pantheist's God does nothing, demands nothing. He is there if you wish for Him, like a book on a shelf. He will not pursue you. . . . The shock comes at the precise moment when the thrill of *life* is communicated to us along the clue we have been following. It is always shocking to meet life where we thought we were alone. . . . And therefore this is the very point at which many draw back—I would have done so myself if I could—and proceed no further with Christianity. An "impersonal God"—well and good. A subjective God of beauty, truth and goodness, inside our own heads—better still. A formless life-force surging through us, a vast power which we can tap—best of all. But God Himself, alive, pulling at the other end of the cord, perhaps approaching at an infinite speed, the hunter, king, husband—that is quite another matter. There comes a moment when the children who have been playing at burglars hush suddenly: was that a *real* footstep in the hall? There comes a moment when people who have been dabbling in religion ("Man's search for God"!) suddenly draw back. Supposing we really found him? We never meant it to come to *that*! Worse still, supposing He had found us? *(M,* 113-14)

This is a very effective passage. A great deal of nonsense has been written about man's search for God, and exposure of the more obvious silliness was always one of Lewis's specialties. Yet it is hard to see how this general skepticism is compatible with his view of God as the ultimate Object of desire. Either God is the ultimate Object of desire or he is not. If he is, then it makes no sense to talk about shrinking from him the moment he is found. If he is not, then we will not find our heart's desire by following Joy any more than mice will find theirs by pursuing the cat.

To this someone may retort, "But do we not often lose interest in the things we have desired once we have them?" Yes, we do. But Lewis himself has seen to it that this reply is irrelevant to the Argument from Desire. According to that argument, it is *earthly* objects that will sooner or later disappoint us because they are simply "pointers" to the true Object of our desire. All right. But then how can it be that Lewis ended up not wanting *that* Object either? If he drew back from the very Object he had been created to enjoy, of which all his previous earthly joys had been but tepid foretastes, what has become of the Argument from Desire?

Lewis thought that we drew back because we are sinners who

shrink from the demand for obedience. But this reply renders him vulnerable to the charge that he understood neither the Platonic theory of desire nor the biblical view of sin. The Platonic view knows nothing of the radical evil in man insisted upon by Christianity; it accounts for his pursuit of false objects by claiming that he is ignorant. The biblical view, on the other hand, knows nothing of the Platonic notion of desire; it accounts for man's pursuit of false objects by claiming that he deliberately and knowingly disobeys God. If our desire for God were really as strong and systematically operative as the Platonic view suggests, we could not be as wicked as the Bible claims we are. On the other hand, if we really are that wicked, our desire for God could not be as strong as the Platonic view claims it is. To say, with Lewis, that we desire God in his attractiveness but flee from his severe side is to give birth to a philosophical hybrid, a conceptual mongrel that lacks the authentic pedigree of either parent.

The routes of desire and repentance are not only based on incompatible views of God but on incompatible theories of human nature. There is no denying that the demand for radical repentance is what Christianity requires of every potential convert. But this requirement completely undercuts the Argument from Desire. Taken at face value, that argument tries to establish the existence of an infinite Object of desire on the basis of certain intensely Romantic experiences. The awkward fact, however, is that at the most crucial point those experiences are set aside and replaced by the very different experience of a moral demand that not only fails to establish the intended conclusion but establishes precisely the opposite one. The object arrived at is not desired at all. For Lewis thereupon to introduce elaborate qualifications about men fleeing from God because of their sin is to sabotage the argument he has invested so much effort in developing. Although a religious conversion was soon to follow, it was of a sort that the careful reader could have never guessed. Owing to the sudden turn of events precipitated by the cessation of his desire, Lewis had to be dragged in "kicking, struggling, resentful, and darting his eyes in every direction for a chance of escape"—peculiar behavior indeed on the part of an incurable Romantic who had just found his heart's desire!

The result is that the Argument from Desire has been completely derailed. This disconcerting spectacle prompts me to wonder just what bearing the experience of Joy did in fact have on Lewis's conversion. If God was not the Object of his desire, what was the point of talking about Joy at all? What difference would it have made to Lewis's conversion if Joy had never manifested itself in his life? Were the two even connected?

This unresolvable discrepancy between God as the Object of desire for whom men seek and God as the Moral Legislator from whom they flee results from Lewis's attempt to synthesize two fundamentally incompatable philosophical traditions. The first derives from Greek philosophy, the second from Judeo-Christian religion. *Surprised by Joy* is the record of Lewis's transparently unsuccessful attempt to hellenize Christianity—to interpret Christian theology in terms of the alien categories of Greek metaphysics. Of course, in this he had many predecessors. From the earliest days of Christianity there has been any number of apologists who have proclaimed that Christianity has not introduced something wholly new and unheard of into Western thought and who have viewed Greek philosophy as a *preparatio evangelica*. They never tired of congratulating the Greek philosophers for having gone as far as reason unaided by revelation could take them. In the considered opinion of this whole tradition of apologists, the fruit of pre-Christian speculation is considerable.

Lewis shared this view. He, too, defines the essence of religion as the thirst for and pursuit of an end higher than purely natural ends, in "the finite self's desire for, and acquiescence in, and self-rejection in favour of, an object wholly good and wholly good for it" (*GiD*, 131). He, too, believed that this thrist was present in paganism and that there was therefore a discernible continuity between Christianity and pre-Christian speculation:

> I could not believe in Christianity if I were forced to say that there were a thousand religions in the world of which 999 were pure nonsense and the thousandth (fortunately) true. My conversion, very largely, depended on recognizing Christianity as the completion, the actualization . . . of something that had never been wholly absent from the mind of man. (*GiD*, 132)

Christianity was for Lewis the realization or fulfillment of pre-Christian thought. The way had been paved not only by the Old Testament prophets but by Plato, Virgil, and Aeschylus as well.

What, then, of the exclusivism of Pauline theology, in which the urgent question "How can they believe in the one of whom they have not heard?" (Rom. 10:14) and the categorical denial that there is any "other name under heaven given to men by which we must be saved"? (Acts 4:12) have impelled countless missionaries to go into all the world to preach the gospel? Lewis's view is decidedly more mellow than St. Paul's. Such good men as Socrates, who never heard of Christianity, and John Stuart Mill, who heard of it but could not honestly believe it, were nevertheless seekers after truth. Although they did not believe, they were in "a state of honest ignorance or honest error" that will be "forgiven and healed" (*GiD*, 110-11).

The humaneness of Lewis's view is clearly preferable to the chop-licking attitude of such religionists as Tertullian and company who bubble with anticipation at the torments awaiting those who do not believe.[7] The suggestion that Greek philosophy was a preparation for the gospel is a lovely idea, as is the gentle opinion that honest ignorance and error will be forgiven and healed. But of course these sentiments cannot be taken seriously. There is not a shred of evidence in the Bible to support them, and there is plenty of evidence to the contrary. The concept of God as the universal Object of desire derives not from the Old or New Testaments but from Plato, and the biblical texts that contradict it are legion. The biblical view of man is not that of a creature sincerely bent on discovering its heart's desire and impeded only by an unfortunate ignorance that God is willing to overlook provided that one is a committed seeker of truth.

It was not Moses or Elijah or Jesus or St. Paul who declared that no one knowingly chooses evil recognized as such; it was Socrates.[8] The Christian gospel has as its purpose neither the satisfaction nor the setting in motion of man's natural desire for happiness. Its purpose is to persuade men to repent of their sins, and it does not look upon sin as the result of an unavoidable and regrettable ignorance. In setting forth the view that man is intended for fellowship with God, the biblical writers did not see themselves as merely underwriting a thesis that Greek philosophy had established on its own centuries ago. Nor does the biblical view picture human beings as desiring and groping for some good of which they have a dim awareness or "inkling"; it pictures them as at odds with God and in flight from him. We are fallen creatures whose relation to God is defined in terms of enmity, not aspiration. We love darkness rather than light. Unless we repent and believe, we will be cast into outermost darkness into the place prepared for the devil and his angels, where "the worm does not die" and where there is only perpetual "weeping and grinding of teeth" (Mark 9:43; Matt. 24:51).

The New Testament assesses neither the paganism of antiquity nor the unbelieving contemporary world as favorably disposed toward God in principle, lacking only an adequate idea of him. Those impressed by Joy have not sufficiently grasped the uniqueness that Christianity claims for itself or the degree to which it saw itself not as the extension but as the radical critique of the intellectual and spiritual bankruptcy of the ancient world. St. Paul did not note with astonished admiration that human wisdom had made remarkable progress toward the truth, borne aloft on the wings of desire, with reason making subtle distinctions at every turn. Nor did he diffidently suggest that revelation is required only to fill in a gap or two here and there. Instead, he propounded Christ crucified against all the vain efforts of human understanding and flatly declared that "the world through its wisdom did not know . . . God" (1 Cor. 1:21), that Christianity was "foolishness" to the Greeks (1 Cor. 1:23), and that God had seen fit to shame the wise by the foolishness of preaching (1 Cor. 1:27). The Pauline diagnosis of natural man differs radically from the Socratic. Man is carnal and reprobate. He has "exchanged the truth of God for a lie" and worships "created things rather than the Creator" (Rom. 1:22–25). Had not the prophets said the same thing? God, we are told, looked down from heaven to see whether there were any who loved truth and righteousness. What did he find? That although men were on the whole evil, there were always conspicuous exceptions such as Socrates and John Stuart Mill? No. He found that "There is no one righteous, not even one" (Rom. 3:10). Sin is not honest error but open rebellion. If man is characterized by any predictable, observable, and all-consuming desire, St. Paul was convinced that it is not a desire for God but the desires of a sinful nature (Rom. 1:27; Gal. 5:16–21).

In the Bible, then, the route to God is not that of desire or aspiration. We look in vain for a biblical counterpart to Joy. The psalmist declares that what God requires is not a diligent searcher but a broken and contrite heart. For St. Paul, not Joy but the Moral Law is the schoolmaster that leads the sinner to God. Christianity is not just one more version of self-realization ethics. To regard it as such is to misread Scripture and to reduce it to an espousal of the very notion of human aspiration that it is its purpose to expose as a ghastly delusion.

Such uncompromising biblical theses as these stubbornly resist the superficially attractive but fundamentally wrongheaded attempt to harmonize the Platonic concept of Joy with the biblical concept of sin, and any apologist who tries to have it both ways, and thereby salvage the best of both worlds, is doomed to fail. The Argument from Desire is shipwrecked not only on logical grounds but on theological grounds as well.

I have long regarded the Argument from Desire as an anomaly in Lewis's apologetic writings. Owen Barfield tells us that

> At a certain stage in [Lewis's] life he deliberately ceased to take any interest in himself except as a kind of spiritual alumnus taking his moral finals . . . and I suggest that what began as deliberate choice became at length . . . an ingrained and effortless habit of soul. Self-knowledge, for him, had come to mean recognition of his own weaknesses and shortcomings and nothing more. Anything beyond that he sharply suspected, both in himself and others, as a symptom of spiritual megalomania.[9]

This change in Lewis's behavior occurred about 1935, and it prompted Barfield to speak somewhat wistfully of "two Lewises: a friend and the memory of a friend."

But there are also two Lewises in the apologetic writings. One is the Lewis of *The Pilgrim's Regress* and *Surprised by Joy* who attached great importance to the inner state called Joy. Although Christian orthodoxy provided the theological scaffolding for his thought, he was thoroughly under the spell of Romanticism from the very beginning. Both books are informed by an undisguisedly Romantic impulse. In *The Pilgrim's Regress* he laments the fact that every finite object failed to satisfy his longings. He thought that we failed to grasp the true significance of these longings— namely, that they are "pointers" to a more adequate Object. Following Dante, he believed that even fallen men responded affectionally to God through poetry and beauty in general, which served as what Charles Williams called "God-bearing images."

As a Christian Romantic, Lewis was convinced that all men desire God, since all men desire happiness and true happiness can be found in God alone. Hence he thought that one effective way of leading people to Christianity is to awaken within them longings that God alone can satisfy. Although all human beings desire God, they seldom desire him knowingly. The connection between ultimate satisfaction and God is not so clear that we are unable to pursue other objects. Nor is it so obvious that the pursuit of these other objects has to take the form of open rebellion against God. Rather, we desire God unawares insofar as his goodness and beauty meet us on every hand in the things of this world. "Only by being in some respect like Him . . . has any earthly Beloved excited our love. It is not that we have loved them too much, but that we did not quite understand what we were loving" (*FL*, 190). Desire, as such, is blind. It is only as reason clarifies for us the true Object of our desire that we are in a position to see that it is God that we have been haltingly pursuing all along. "God will look to every soul like its first love because He is its first love" (*PP*, 147). Apart from the specific references to the God of Christianity, this much is pure Plato.

The other Lewis is the Lewis of *Mere Christianity* and the other apologetic books, the Lewis who cautions us that emotions and inner states are of no importance. Unless we can teach our moods "where they get off," we will quickly be reduced to the pitiful status of creatures "who dither to and fro," and our beliefs will really depend on "the weather and the state of [our] digestion" (*MC*, 123). In *Mere Christianity* it is precisely the Imagination that is said to give rise to the irrational doubts that reason must combat. The conflict is presented as a battle between faith and reason on the one hand, and emotions and the Imagination on the other.

Everyone who writes about Lewis dwells fondly on the fact that his writings exhibit a striking mixture of Romantic and Christian elements. Lewis himself acknowledged this. He regarded these elements as complementary and believed that in the end they converged in the same object. Part of the impact of *Surprised by Joy* is traceable to Lewis's tendency to describe his intellectual progress in a way that suggests that he had been led inexorably to God by sheer force of logic—as if, driven by Joy from one object to another while at the same time forbidden by reason from resting content with any finite object, he were enunciating a universal truth about human nature instead of just recording how he tried to reconcile the Romantic and dialectical elements of his own temperament.

What is not immediately obvious is that this mixture of Romantic and Christian elements prompted Lewis to make two incompatible responses to the claims of the Imagination. On the one hand, there was the orthodox Christian emphasis on sin, the corrupt heart, and the necessity of repentance: one must master one's moods and hold one's imagination in check by appealing to truths accepted on the basis of rational considerations. But this is only part of the story. On the other hand, and in spite of this theologically based polemic against the pernicious aberrations of the Imagination, Lewis's Romanticism assigned to the Imagination a function not only legitimate but indispensable. According to this view, it is precisely the Imagination that enables us to interpret our experience in a way that, far from calling Christian belief into question, leads straight to God as the only Object that can satisfy our longings. In order for *this* to occur, however, the entire emotional and imaginative experience of Joy must not be ignored but rather given its head.

Both Lewises cannot be right. Either that wonderful sensation of unsatisfied desire is "no mere neurotic fancy" but "the truest index" of our real situation, or, like the rest of our emotions, it is an irrational phenomenon and a true index of nothing. Contrary to what Lewis thought, the claims of Romanticism and reason are not complementary but contradictory. He never realized that taking Joy seriously was nothing but a preoccupation with one of those very inner states which, according to the Corrective, we ought to ignore. Anyone who consistently applied that Corrective would realize that the *feeling* of not being satisfied, the *craving* for something more, the *sensation* of intense desire, are of no importance. If inner states that seem to call religious belief into question are to be discounted, then, quite apart from what true faith may require, simple consistency demands that they be similarly discounted when they appear to lend support to those same beliefs. It follows that we must choose between the two Lewises, between the way of feeling and the way of fact, between subjective states and objective evidence.

To this someone may reply that Lewis *did* lose all interest in Joy. He *did* come to realize that the inner state of intense desire was of no importance. Yes, he did. But not until he had allowed it to do its work as a "pointer" to God. Of course no one continues to pay much attention to a pointer after discovering what it points to. The fact remains that if we heed Lewis's warnings about inner states, we will be forewarned against interpreting Joy as a pointer in the first place.

In *Surprised by Joy* Lewis tells us that as a young man he led what were for all practical purposes two separate lives: the life of Imagination and the life of the Mind. In my judgment, his writings reveal that he never adequately reconciled these two lives. In conferring legitimacy upon the very sort of inner state against which he so often warns us, he betrays that he is still making a two-fold response to the claims of the Imagination and thereby inadvertantly committing himself to two contradictory psychological theses, which in turn gives rise to two equally contradictory apologetic methods.

Consistently applied, the admonition to ignore inner states undercuts the religious thesis of *Surprised by Joy*. The lasting significance of the book is not the religious argument but the psychological advice that we ignore our inner states. Taken seriously, the Corrective constitutes as conclusive a demonstration as we could wish of the futility of making the elusive, narcissistic goal of personal satisfaction and fulfillment our all-consuming goal in life. The nagging feeling that we are not "fulfilled" or satisfied may indicate nothing more than the irrelevant fact that we have failed to conjure up the desired inner state. We should therefore not be misled into thinking that our present sense of emptiness is a true indication or index of anything. To ask "Is there no more to life than this?" is like asking "Am I having fun?" or "Am I spending enough time with my children?" Such questions invariably prompt negative answers to the extent that we count on the presence of a particular inner state. But this is just what we should not do and just where the Corrective can be of help.

The bewildering fact is that no one knew this better than Lewis. In his writings we observe the altogether remarkable phenomenon of one apologetic strategy coexisting quite comfortably with a contradictory strategy, not only unrecognized as such but defended with equal fervor. Paradoxically, we cannot grasp the genuine and permanent significance of *Surprised by Joy* until we have seen that it fails as an apologetic work and have seen why it fails. To endorse it as establishing some important truth about man's relationship to God is to betray that one has not absorbed the lesson that is there to be learned—namely, that Joy is itself one of the false Florimels.

What, then, of those individuals who know nothing of Joy, who look askance at the mention of "inconsolable longing," who neither have been nor want to be "stabbed" by this bittersweet sense of loss? Should the apologist try to awaken their latent desire? Is Joy really a salutary experience? The prelude to a momentous discovery? I do not think so. Perhaps those who are temperamentally insusceptible to its promptings are wiser than they know. Surely they are less prone to disparage such precious temporal goods as they are fortunate enough to enjoy for being poorer than some allegedly greater good for which they are still searching. Perhaps in rebuffing the advances of the Romantic apologist they reveal that they have learned not to make the delectable but self-defeating inner gesture.

It is perplexing that after so convincingly exposing the futility of trying to base a life on the shifting sands of our inner states, Lewis continued to try to base a religious apologetic on them. As *Surprised by Joy* builds to its emotional climax, he repeatedly chides himself for his "fussy attentiveness" to his inner states and announces that he has moved beyond his earlier obsession with Joy. But while none of us need be forever lamenting youthful mistakes, when we finally do put away childish things, we must do so once for all, as Lewis and his brother touchingly did when, as grown men, they together buried the chest containing the treasured toys of their childhood without succumbing to the temptation to raise the lid for one final parting glimpse. One should not, as Lewis tended to do with his treasured sensations, store them away for possible future use.

The pursuit of Joy is a childish thing, and Lewis's petulant complaint that he had tried everything and been disappointed every time only underscores its childishness. The self-important claim that reality is just not up to one's lofty standards is scarcely profound; it is simply adolescent disenchantment elevated to cosmic status, as it was when Lewis proceeded to assure us that one day something far more acceptable than a mere universe would be vouchsafed to chronic holdouts like himself. That in thus laying aside the Corrective and its hard-won psychological insight and resuming his quest for inner satisfaction he should have believed himself to be formulating an argument for the existence of God—this is one of the abiding ironies of his apologetic writings. To say this, of course, is to say neither that there is no God nor that there are no other reasons for believing in him. It is to say only that the Argument from Desire must be rejected together with the entire subjective method on which it depends. What remains is the far stronger objective method that the other Lewis advocates in his other apologetic writings. To that other Lewis I now turn.

Chapter Three

MORALITY

Surprised by Joy is an autobiography with a philosophical twist. In addition to telling the story of Lewis's conversion, it develops the thesis that man cannot be defined wholly in terms of nature and that all purely naturalistic views fail to account for our transcendental longings. Lewis employed this antinaturalistic argument on two other fronts: morality and reason. Just as desire is a "pointer" to God, so morality and reason give important clues about man, the universe in which we live, and what lies "behind" it. I will examine his view of morality in this chapter and his view of reason in the next.

Lewis's development of the Moral Argument for the existence of God is found in Book I of *Mere Christianity*. Not only is this Lewis's most evangelical book; it is also the clearest example of the style that made him famous. Here is the popularizer of Christianity at work: the unpretentious, no-nonsense Everyman's theologian. The tone is informal, the manner relaxed, the approach chatty. The most momentous questions are tackled in a winningly let's-see-if-we-can-make-sense-of-this fashion. For example, theologians say that Christ died for us and that his death washed away our sins. But, quips Lewis, the whole doctrine of substitutionary atonement is, on the face of it, a "very silly theory. If God was prepared to let us off, why on earth did He not do so?" (*MC*, 59). He proceeds with the confidence of an experienced guide thoroughly familiar with the terrain. His arguments have an economy and apparent cogency that seem to go straight to the heart of the matter. The only request, from one honest person to another, is for the reader to think things through.

Books I and II of *Mere Christianity*, entitled "Right and Wrong as a Clue to the Meaning of the Universe" and "What Christians Believe," were originally delivered in a series of installments over the BBC and first published in America under the provocative title *The Case for Christianity*. Lewis's purpose in this little book is undisguisedly evangelical, and its scope is enormous. Within the compass of less than fifty pages he attempts to prove the objectivity of morality, to refute ethical relativism and ethical subjectivism, to establish the existence of a Power behind the Moral Law, to show that atheism is too simple and theological liberalism too naive, to prove that Jesus is God and that orthodox Christianity is the only view that faces all the facts, and to offer some practical advice about how to deal with conflicting theories of the atonement—all this before wrapping things up with a resounding appeal to accept God's offer of salvation while there is still time.

It does not take long to realize that Lewis really thought that the evidence supports Christianity—not in the sense that there is *more* evidence in favor of Christianity than against it, but in the sense that there is *better* evidence for it. He believed that the case for Christianity is stronger than the case for atheism because Christianity can explain things that atheism cannot. One of those things is morality.

Mere Christianity opens with a discussion of people quarreling about morality. Someone says, "How would you like it if I did the same thing?" or "That's my seat. I was here first," or "Come on, you promised." Lewis thought we could learn a great deal by pondering such exchanges. First, we learn that the complaining parties are not just saying that they dislike the behavior in question; they are appealing to an objective standard of conduct that they expect the offenders to acknowledge. Second, the offenders usually do acknowledge it. Both groups seem to recognize a "Law or Rule of fair play or decent behaviour or morality" (*MC*, 17). These two facts, our knowledge of a Moral Law and the awareness that we do not keep it, are, for Lewis, "the foundation of all clear thinking about ourselves and the universe we live in" (*MC*, 21).

This Moral Law is different from what scientists call laws of nature. The laws of physics, for example, are nothing more than descriptions of how things in fact behave. They are not laws in the strict sense at all. There is probably nothing over and above the facts themselves. The word *law* might just be a manner of speaking. But this is not true of the Moral Law. In speaking about it, we are not describing how people in fact behave but how they *ought* to behave. For this reason, Lewis thought that in the case of morality there had to be something over and above the facts. Since the Moral Law is not simply a fact about human conduct, nor a "mere fancy," nor even a statement about how we would like people to behave, Lewis concludes that in the case of morality we are dealing with another kind of reality, a real law which none of us made, but which we found "pressing on us" (*MC*, 30). He believed that all those who deny this involve themselves in insuperable difficulties.

Some, for example, think that morality is nothing more than a "herd instinct" that manifests itself as a desire to help others. Against them, Lewis argues that we ought to help others even when we do not want to. Others hold that morality is merely a set of conventions that we learn from parents, teachers, and society generally. Against them, he argues that although we learn morality from others, it does not follow that it is just something that human beings have "made up." Still others believe that moralities differ so fundamentally from culture to culture that it is a mistake to speak of an objective Moral Law. Lewis rejects this contention as "a lie—a good, solid, resounding lie" (*CR*, 77). The moral teachings of the ancient Egyptians, Babylonians, Hindus, Chinese, Greeks, and Romans were in fundamental agreement. Furthermore, to say that there is no objective morality makes it impossible to claim that some moralities are better than others—that Christian morality is better than Nazi morality, for example. But we do want to claim this, and the moment we do, we are "comparing both with some real morality" and therefore presupposing the very objectivity we just denied.

According to Lewis, this objective Moral Law provides us with an important clue about the nature of the universe that enables us to reject materialism as an inadequate explanation of the facts. The materialist holds that matter and space "just happen to exist" and that the universe has "by a sort of fluke" just happened to produce human beings.

> By one chance in a thousand something hit our sun and made
> it produce the planets; and by another thousandth chance the
> chemicals necessary for life, and the right temperature,
> occurred on one of these planets, and so some of the matter

on this earth came alive; and then, by a very long series of
chances, the living creatures developed into things like us.
(*MC*, 31)

Lewis was convinced that this view reduces morality to an illusion. So much for materialism. On the other hand, there is the
religious view.

According to it, what is behind the universe is more like a mind
than it is like anything else we know. That is to say, it is conscious, and has purposes, and prefers one thing to another.
And . . . it made the universe, partly for purposes we do not
know, but partly, at any rate, in order to produce creatures
like itself . . . to the extent of having minds. (*MC*, 31–32)

Having set forth this tendentious contrast, Lewis briskly assures
his readers that he is in no way disparaging science (which he says
is "very useful and necessary"), but merely presenting the options
between which they must choose.

Before we choose, however, we must remember that no
matter how useful and necessary science might be, it has limits.
It is first of all confined to observable facts. As a result, it has
nothing to say about *why* anything exists or about whether there
is Something behind the facts. These are not scientific questions.
To answer them, we must employ a method different from that
of external observation.

Lewis, of course, held that there is a more reliable way of
answering these questions. The religious view teaches that there
is Something or Someone behind the observable facts. If this claim
is true, then obviously this Something or Someone cannot make
itself known "externally" as one of the facts. If it is to make itself
known, it must do so in some other way. According to Lewis,
there is only one thing in the entire universe that we know about
in a way other than external observation, and that is man. On
the subject of human beings, we have "inside information"
(*MC*, 33).

What is the content of this information? For one thing, we
know that we find ourselves under a Moral Law. This is significant, for if there is in fact Something behind the facts that cannot
reveal itself as one of the facts, this *internal* experience of moral
obligation is exactly the way in which we might expect it to com-
municate with us. In the one case in which there could be an af-

firmative answer to the question of whether there is anything behind the universe, the answer turns out to be Yes. Surely, Lewis thought, this ought to "arouse our suspicions" that there "is a Something which is directing the universe, and which appears in me as a law urging me to do right and making me feel responsible and uncomfortable when I do wrong" (*MC*, 34). Lewis did not, of course, think that this argument proves the existence of the God of Christianity, but he did think that it proves the existence of a Power behind the universe in general and behind the Moral Law in particular. It is in this sense that he thought right and wrong give us a clue about the universe. Reason can establish this much by itself. There is an objective Moral Law that we have broken, and in breaking it we have offended the Power behind it.

In Book II Lewis goes further. Convinced that he has established the existence of a Power behind the Moral Law, he proceeds to elucidate the nature of the God believed in by Christians and to explain how this God is related to that Power. In so doing, he tries to explain how Christianity can supplement and extend the knowledge we have already achieved "on our own steam."

Unlike some religions that teach that God is beyond good and evil, Christianity affirms that God is good. But a difficulty immediately arises. If God is good, why is there so much evil in the world? Before he became a Christian, Lewis had been perplexed by this problem. After all, Christianity teaches that God is not only good but omnipotent. If these claims are true, it seems that there would be no evil at all. If God is good, he should be willing to prevent evil; and if he is omnipotent, he should be able to prevent it. Yet there is evil. Hence God must either be good but not omnipotent or omnipotent but not good.

This is an objection of long standing; it has been advanced in one form or another by many religious skeptics. Lewis tried to answer it more fully in *The Problem of Pain* (which I will be discussing in Chapter 7). In *Mere Christianity*, however, he adopts a different strategy. Instead of replying to the objection, he claims that the skeptic contradicts himself in the very act of putting it forth.

According to Lewis, skeptics claim that the universe is cruel and unjust, and that the existence of evil casts doubt on the belief that the universe was created by a good and omnipotent God. Lewis grants that there is a problem here but proceeds to pose a corresponding difficulty for the skeptics: We do not call a line crooked unless we have some idea of a straight line. Similarly, if skeptics think that the universe is unjust, they must have some idea of justice. But where did they get that idea? What is its source? Since skeptics deny that morality is objective, consistency requires them to regard their idea of justice as "a merely human idea." But if they grant this, they can no longer claim that the universe really *is* unjust. Hence their case against Christianity collapses. On the other hand, if they claim that the universe really is unjust, they are appealing to the very objective standard they deny. Hence they contradict themselves, and their case again collapses. Atheism, therefore, is "too simple" (*MC*, 46).

Lewis then proceeds to endorse Christianity on the ground that it is *not* simple. Reality is never simple, he notes. The table before you seems simple, but a scientist will explain it in terms of "atoms, light waves, and the optic nerve." By the time he is finished, what you call "seeing a table" has become a very complicated affair. Christianity partakes of this complexity, and this is one of the things in its favor. It is the sort of religion you could have never guessed; it has "just that queer twist about it that real things have." *(MC,* 48). Christianity acknowledges the existence of evil, but it teaches that the world was created good and that mankind, even as we are today, retains the memory of how things ought to have been. The world has been spoiled by Satan and is now "enemy-occupied territory." Christianity itself is the story of how "the rightful king" has "landed in disguise" and is calling us to join in a "great campaign of sabotage" *(MC,* 51).

Remarks like these about enemy-occupied territory and its rightful king are neither rhetorical flourishes nor a merely picturesque manner of speaking. They are part and parcel of Lewis's apologetic. That this is so it can be seen by observing what he thought God had done about evil. First, God gave us conscience, that ineradicable sense of right and wrong. Second, he sent men "good dreams," those odd stories scattered throughout pagan religions about a dying God. Third, he spent centuries "hammering" into the heads of Jews what kind of God he was. But then came "the real shock." A man turned up among the Jews who claimed that he was God, that he had always existed, and that he would one day judge the living and the dead. Although these claims struck the Jews as blasphemous, one scandalized them more than anything else—namely, Jesus' claim to forgive their sins. Lewis sees their point:

> Unless the speaker is God, this is really so preposterous as to be comic. We can all understand how a man forgives offences against himself. You tread on my toe and I forgive you, you steal my money and I forgive you. But what should we make of a man, himself unrobbed and untrodden on, who announced that he forgave you for treading on other men's toes and stealing other men's money. Asinine fatuity is the kindest description we should give of his conduct. Yet this is what Jesus did. He told people that their sins were forgiven, and never waited to consult all the other people whom their sins had undoubtedly injured. He unhesitatingly behaved as if He was the party chiefly concerned, the person chiefly offended in all offences. This makes sense only if He really was the God whose laws are broken and whose love is wounded in every sin. In the mouth of any speaker who is not God, these words would imply what I can only regard as a silliness and conceit unrivalled by any other character in history. (*MC*, 55)

We must therefore make up our minds about Jesus. In addressing himself to this issue, Lewis set forth our alternatives in what has become one of his best-known and most-quoted passages:

> I am trying here to prevent anyone saying the really foolish thing that people often say about Him: "I'm ready to accept Jesus as a great moral teacher, but I don't accept His claim to be God." That is the one thing we must not say. A man who was merely a man and said the sort of things Jesus said would not be a great moral teacher. He would either be a lunatic—on the level with the man who says he is a poached egg—or else he would be the Devil or Hell. You must make your choice. Either this man was, and is, the Son of God: or else a madman or something worse. You can shut Him up for a fool, you can spit at Him and kill Him as a demon; or you can fall at His feet and call Him Lord and God. But let us not come with any patronising nonsense about His being a great human teacher. He has not left that open to us. He did not intend to. (*MC*, 55–56)

This is the Lord-or-lunatic dilemma: Jesus was either God or a lunatic. Since he was clearly not a lunatic, "I have to accept the view that He was and is God" (*MC*, 56).

In short, if we take morality seriously and ponder the claims of Jesus, we must conclude that the Power behind the Moral Law, whose existence can be established independently of the Bible, can plausibly be identified with the God who was incarnate in Jesus as revealed in the Bible. This is the case for Christianity.

Lewis's version of the Moral Argument does not depend only on the view that morality is objective; he also held that morality can be objective only if it is grounded in another kind of reality behind the factual reality observed by science. In a word, morality presupposes the supernatural. He rejects all naturalistic theories of morality on the ground that they reduce morality to an illusion and require us to hold that moral judgments are nothing more than expressions of taste or mere subjective preference. Lewis spelled out his view further in some of his theological and ethical essays. In *"De Futilitate,"* for example, he argues that if our sense of values is purely human—"a biological by-product in a particular species with no relevance to reality—then we cannot, having realized this, continue to use it as the ground for what are meant to be serious criticisms of the nature of things" (*CR*, 67). Indeed, "Unless we take our own standard of goodness to be valid in principle . . . we cannot mean anything by calling waste and cruelty evils" (*CR*, 69). He advances the same claim in "The Poison of Subjectivism":

> Either the maxims of traditional morality must be accepted as axioms of practical reason which neither admit nor require argument . . . or else there are no values at all, what we mistook for values being "projections" of irrational emotions. (*CR*, 75)

Lewis maintained that ethical subjectivism is not only false but has ominous consequences for our conduct:

> A man cannot continue to make sacrifices for the good of posterity if he really believes that his concern for the good of posterity is simply an irrational subjective taste of his own on the same level with his fondness for pancakes or his dislike for spam. (*CR*, 67)

It was precisely for this reason that he gravely warns that all subjectivistic ethical theories "lead to ruin." Accordingly, we must make a choice: either there is Power behind the Moral Law and right and wrong are real, or else the material universe is "the whole show," and morality is "inexplicable illusion" (*PP*, 22), a "mere twist" in the human mind (*PP*, 20), "mere subjective preference" (*CR*, 67).

Lewis was enamored of the view that neither naturalists nor ethical subjectivists are entitled to their moral judgments because they have no basis for them. He rejects all such theories on the ground that they cannot satisfactorily account for moral obligation. This unqualified rejection is surprising in view of the fact that he examines only two versions of the position he opposes, and only the weakest and most carelessly formulated ones at that: the view that morality is either a "herd instinct" or a mere subjective preference on the same level as a fondness for pancakes or a dislike for spam. This is irresponsible writing. To give vent to so ill-considered an opinion is to betray either that one knows next to nothing about ethical theory or that one simply chooses to ignore inconvenient points of view.

Not only does Lewis fail to consider many historically influential versions of ethical subjectivism, but he also bypasses without a word a host of *objectivist* ethical theories. From Socrates on, the history of Western thought has produced a series of sustained attempts to account for morality independently of the supernatural. The list is long and impressive: Platonism, Aristotelianism, Stoicism, hedonism, natural law theories, moral sense theories, self-realization theories, Kantianism, act utilitarianism, rule utilitarianism, general utilitarianism, act deontology, rule deontology, and so on. That Lewis did not have the opportunity to discuss these theories in detail does not justify his proceeding as if they did not exist.

Socrates, Plato, and Aristotle argued that actions are moral if they lead to happiness and thereby enable the moral agent to achieve "the good for man." John Stuart Mill claimed that an action is morally right if it produces "the greatest happiness of the greatest number." Hedonistic ethical theories base the distinction between right and wrong on the fact that certain actions lead to long-range intellectual and spiritual pleasure. Rule utilitarianism argues that one ought to do that which, when formulated as a general rule, will lead to the general good. Kant thought that moral imperatives forbid us to do anything we cannot consistently will as a universal law. Each of these theories attempts to set forth a way of determining within a shared rational framework what is right and what is wrong. Each vigorously denies that moral judgments are merely expressions of taste or merely personal preferences or *merely* anything else.

Lewis felt very free to accuse atheists of setting forth a version of Christianity suitable only for a child of six and then making *that* the object of their attack (*MC*, 47). He never tired of upbraiding his opponents for not bothering to trouble themselves with "the facts," and was perfectly capable of accusing others of having put forth "half-baked ideas" and "lies" (*MC*, 32)— even "good, solid, resounding lies" (*CR*, 77). No individuals should hazard to commit such allegations as these to print who are not very sure that they understand the positions they are denouncing and that they scrupulously avoid half-baked ideas themselves. Often enough Lewis did not take such pains. Although easily offended by superficial criticism of his own work, he exhibits a persistent tendency toward carelessness, inaccuracy, and oversimplification whenever he discusses opposing views.

Although some of Lewis's followers are inclined to view his withering equation of ethical subjectivism with such "irrational" matters of taste as a fondness for pancakes or a dislike for spam as yet another display of his sidesplitting wit, it seems to me that a different assessment is in order. No one with even a modest grounding in the history of ethics could settle for so crude a characterization. When Lewis proceeds in this precarious manner to "criticize" the view under consideration, his announced readiness to submit his judgments to the correction of wiser heads is not much in evidence. His polemical discussions are, in fact, seldom graced by accurate (much less charitable) interpretations. Rarely does he set forth the alternatives to his own view in philosophically recognizable form. His tendency is to rush into battle, misrepresent the opposition, and then demolish it. The demolition is often swift and the victory decisive, but the view refuted is seldom a position anyone actually holds.

A writer who in advocating his or her own theory finds it necessary to claim that every other theory reduces morality to an illusion had better examine every other theory and refute them one by one. Lewis chose not to do this. Although he claims that "uneducated people are not irrational" and that they can follow "quite a lot of sustained argument if you go slowly" (*GiD*, 99), there is little sustained argument in the Broadcast Talks. Nor did

Lewis heed his own advice about proceeding slowly. Throughout the talks, we find him scurrying over the terrain and constantly succumbing to the temptation to go for the big effects.

A few of his expositors have felt the force of this criticism. William Luther White tries to meet it as follows:

> There are, I think . . . reasons why Lewis sometimes appears to settle for simple answers rather than to explore the complexities and depths of issues. He occasionally warned his readers that he was oversimplifying an idea in the interests of clarity and brevity. While it may not satisfy professional theologians, this approach may be necessary to some extent when books are written for a large popular audience. . . . To be perfectly fair about it, an author can hardly be expected to hedge about his chief ideas with elaborate qualifications when they are being prepared for quick delivery to a mass audience.[1]

As a justification of Lewis's method, this will not do. *Of course* a popular author cannot be expected to cover in detail the entire history of philosophy, "hedging his subject with elaborate qualifications." But this "perfectly fair" defense of Lewis perpetuates the same oversimplification on which he himself relies. The fact is that a scholarly analysis of the entire history of Western thought on the one hand, and an all-but-complete disregard of the major ethical theories of the past 2,500 years on the other, do not exhaust the available options. It is true that Lewis does "occasionally" warn his readers that he is oversimplifying an idea, but he does not do so nearly often enough. My complaint about the Broadcast Talks is not that Lewis fails to be as thorough as his subject matter demands, but that he gives the impression of being thorough. The philosophically unsophisticated reader cannot fail to get the impression that Lewis *is* covering the ground, that he *is* doing justice to his material, and that he *is* compressing everything that needs to be said into highly compact but basically accurate form, when in fact he is not doing so at all. The desire to translate Christianity into language that uneducated people can understand, however admirable in itself, is not a sufficient justification for his travesty of the history of ethics.

Although Lewis's critics are often too volatile, a hard look at the contents of *Mere Christianity* reveals that they have found something worth complaining about. Nor is it widely known that the Broadcast Talks prompted some of Lewis's closest friends to make embarrassed apologies for him. Charles Williams ruefully observed that when he realized how many crucial issues Lewis had sidestepped, he lost interest in the talks.[2] Tolkien also confessed that he was not "entirely enthusiastic" about them and that he thought Lewis was attracting more attention than the contents of the talks warranted or than was good for him.[3]

One of Lewis's most serious weaknesses as an apologist is his fondness for the false dilemma. He habitually confronts his readers with the alleged necessity of choosing between two alternatives when there are in fact other options to be considered. One horn of the dilemma typically sets forth Lewis's view in all its apparent forcefulness, while the other horn is a ridiculous straw man. *Either* the universe is the product of a conscious Mind *or* it is a mere "fluke" (*MC*, 31). *Either* morality is a revelation *or* it is an inexplicable illusion (*PP*, 22). *Either* morality is grounded in the supernatural *or* it is a "mere twist" in the human mind (*PP*, 20). *Either* right and wrong are real *or* they are "mere irrational emotions" (*CR*, 66). Lewis advances these arguments again and again, and they are all open to the same objection. No matter how often he repeats the arguments, he never makes good his claim that an adequate theory of morality *must* be grounded in the supernatural.

Nor does he ever substantiate his charge that skeptics who complain that the universe is unjust are inconsistently appealing to the very objective standard that their view of the universe rules out. In order to claim that the universe is unjust, one need not, of course, be in possession of any transcendent standard of justice. Take a humbler example. The piano teacher who reproves a student for incorrect pedaling does not thereby invite a numbing dilemma. In order to distinguish incorrect pedaling from a standard of correct pedaling that he did not "invent" but that he nevertheless finds "pressing on him," the teacher need only point out that there are established practices for playing a keyboard instrument and that, in light of them, the student fully deserves criticism. Were the student to retort, "Either there is a transcendent standard of pedaling that exists independently of all pedalers or else the whole idea of correct pedaling is an illusion, a 'mere twist' in Beethoven's or Chopin's mind on the same level as a fondness for pancakes," we would not regard him as having made a telling point; we would give him up as hopeless. The same is true regarding moral standards. If Ruth claims that Bill's behavior is unjust, she might mean that it violates someone's rights, that it is wholly undeserved and unprovoked, or that it is unprincipled. Were Bill to respond by asking Ruth either to produce her transcendent standard of justice or else withdraw her claim, we would regard him as similarly, but more seriously, hopeless.

But Lewis was not content simply to argue that the moral judgments of ethical subjectivists are inconsistent with their general view of the world. He also claimed that ethical subjectivism has disastrous implications for moral conduct and that no one who holds such a theory can continue for very long to make sacrifices for the good of posterity. This is a different kind of claim. Whereas the former is a logical claim about what the subjectivist cannot *consistently* do, the latter is an empirical claim about what he cannot *in fact* do. I call it the Alarmist Thesis.

According to this view, the moral efforts of ethical subjectivists are doomed in principle because they are based on a theory that not only cannot sustain moral effort but that in fact undermines it. Two points are important here. First, no one can establish *by speculation* whether a theory such as ethical subjectivism has undesirable consequences for behavior: that is a factual question, and to answer it, we must look and see. Second, those who are determined to make such a claim had better be very sure that they understand ethical subjectivism. Lewis fails on both counts, as an examination of his most sustained "critique" of ethical subjectivism, set forth in *The Abolition of Man*, reveals.

Ordinarily if someone undertakes a critical examination of some theory, he or she consults an influential work in which it is powerfully formulated and rigorously set forth. In *The Abolition of Man* Lewis adopts a different strategy. For his critique of ethical subjectivism, he chooses an elementary textbook written by "two modest practising schoolmasters." He declines even to identify their names or the title of their unfortunate book, choosing instead to refer to them obliquely as "Gaius and Titius" and to their book as *"The Green Book."* At the same time, he "promises" us that "there is such a book and I have it on my shelves" (*AM*, 13).

This, then, is the object of Lewis's critique. As he formulates the view under attack, however, it is soon apparent that *The Green Book* proceeds at a very elementary level. What little it has to offer by way of a plausible version of ethical subjectivism is completely misunderstood by Lewis. Observe him at work. Two tourists are standing before a waterfall. One says, "That is sublime." Gaius and Titius comment that although this remark appears to be about the waterfall, it is actually about the feelings of the speaker. They add that this confusion is continually present in language. We often seem to be saying something about the world when in fact we are really saying something about our own feelings.

What is Lewis's reaction to this observation? Does he point out that the distinction is important? That it is essential to understanding a great deal of contemporary philosophical and semantic theory? That a voluminous body of literature is devoted to it? That it has significant implications for one's views on ethics, psychology, and theories of mental activity? No. Having quoted the remark as set forth in this textbook account, Lewis pounces on it and prophesies that any schoolboy who reads this passage will come to the conclusion that aesthetic and moral judgments are mere expressions of emotion and thus "unimportant" (*AM*, 15).

Ethical subjectivists do not, of course, claim that aesthetic and moral judgments are *mere* expressions of feelings or subjective preference. Nor do they regard such judgments as unimportant. They hold the very different view that moral judgments are based on feeling rather than on reason—that someone who claims that stealing is wrong, for example, is expressing disapproval of stealing and hoping to inculcate this same disapproval in others. They deny that moral judgments are assertions of fact not because they are hoping to abolish morality but because they want to emphasize its practical functions. Moral judgments are not descriptions but prescriptions, evaluations, recommendations: they guide conduct, influence choice, and express attitudes. But that is not to say that they are either irrational or based on mere preference. Those who put them forth are ready to argue in their behalf, willing to universalize or generalize them, willing to give reasons in support of them. In short, whatever version of ethical subjectivism its advocates might hold, they will not recognize it in the caricature singled out by Lewis for criticism.

In criticizing the position of Gaius and Titius, Lewis goes far beyond anything asserted or implied in the passages he quotes. Nowhere does he cite them as *saying* that moral values are "unimportant" or "irrational." These are Lewis's own inferences based on his misreading of what they did say. Nor does he give us any reason to believe that his ominous prophecy must come to pass. He simply states that "No schoolboy will be able to resist the suggestion brought to bear upon him by that word *only*" in the sentence "Moral judgments are not about the world but only about our feelings." But how can Lewis be so confident about what *no* schoolboy will be able to resist? Perhaps some of them would have had the good fortune of having been instructed by a teacher who understood ethical subjectivism.

Although Lewis announces at the outset of *The Abolition of Man* that he intends to examine "the philosophical credentials" of ethical subjectivism, he does nothing of the kind. Instead, he engages in a ferocious attack on the motives and personal character of the authors of *The Green Book*. They are "debunkers" of emotion, he says, committed to the view that moral judgments are "irrational"; whether they know it or not and whether they intend it or not, they are in fact debunkers of morality. Swept along by the momentum of his own prose, Lewis recklessly ascribes to Gaius and Titius views that they are nowhere shown to embrace and that a sober reading of the passages he quotes do not so much as suggest. He states that they are involved in "the questionable process of creating in others by 'suggestion' or incantation a mirage which their own reason has successfully dissipated" (*AM*, 31). They are "conditioners" who "undermine" the intellect and pave the way for the very consequences they claim to deplore: "In a sort of ghastly simplicity [they] remove the organ and demand the function. . . . [They] laugh at honour and are shocked to find traitors in [their] midst. [They] castrate and bid the geldings be fruitful" (*AM*, 35). It is an "outrage" that they should be regarded as intellectuals, for this pretense "gives them the chance" to say that whoever attacks them attacks intelligence. But they are wrong: "It is not excess of thought but defect of fertile and generous emotion that marks them out. Their heads are no bigger than the ordinary: it is the atrophy of the chest beneath that makes them seem so" (*AM*, 35).

As "evidence" for these abrasive claims, Lewis dwells on

what he was sure would become of the wretched schoolboys forced
to work their way through *The Green Book*. They would have
cut from their souls

> the possibility of having certain experiences which thinkers of
> more authority than [Gaius and Titius] have held to be gener-
> ous, fruitful, and humane. . . . Some pleasure in their own
> ponies and dogs they will have lost: some incentive to cruelty
> or neglect they will have received. . . . That is their day's
> lesson in English. . . . Another little portion of the human
> heritage has been quietly taken from them. . . . *(AM,* 20,
> 22)

Harsh words these. Especially in the view of the complete
misrepresentation of ethical subjectivism that precedes them. As
Lewis warms to his subject, it becomes increasingly doubtful
whether his own acquaintance with ethical subjectivism extends
beyond this textbook account.

The Abolition of Man cruelly reveals the excess of emotion
Lewis was capable of committing to print, his tendency to fall
on an opponent, to jeer at him, and to impute to him the worst
possible motives.[4] It also reveals the magnitude of his
misunderstanding of the view ostensibly under discussion.

As his spokesman for ethical subjectivism, Lewis might better have selected David Hume, who wrote that

> The notion of morals implies some sentiment common to all
> mankind, which recommends the same object to general ap-
> probation, and makes every man, or most men, agree in the
> same opinion or decision concerning it. It also implies some
> sentiment, so universal and comprehensive as to extend to all
> mankind, and render the actions and conduct, even of the per-
> sons most remote, an object of applause or censure, according
> as they agree or disagree with that rule of right which is
> established. . . .
>
> When a man denominates another his *enemy*, his *rival*, his
> *antagonist*, his *adversary*, he is understood to speak the
> language of self-love, and to express sentiments, peculiar to
> himself, and arising from his particular circumstances and
> situation. But when he bestows on any man the epithets of
> *vicious* or *odious* or *depraved*, he then speaks another
> language, and expresses sentiments, in which he expects all his
> audience are to concur with him. He must here, therefore,
> depart from his private and particular situation, and must

choose a point of view, common to him with others; he must
move some universal principle of the human frame, and touch
a string to which all mankind have an accord and sympathy.
. . . This affection of humanity . . . can alone be the
foundation of morals.[5]

Or he might have heeded the words of Edward Westermarck when
he said that

Ethical Subjectivism is commonly held to be a dangerous doctrine, destructive to morality, opening the door to all sorts of
libertinism. If that which appears to each man as right or good,
stands for that which is right or good; if he is allowed to make
his own law, or to make no law at all; then, it is said, everybody
has the natural right to follow his caprice and inclinations.
. . . To this argument may, first, be objected that a scientific
theory is not invalidated by the mere fact that it is likely to
cause mischief. The unfortunate circumstance that there do
exist dangerous things in the world, proves that something may
be dangerous and yet true. Another question is whether any
scientific truth really is mischievous. . . . I venture to believe
that this, at any rate, is not the case with that form of ethical
subjectivism which I am here advocating. . . . Ethical Subjectivism . . . does not allow everyone to follow his own
inclinations; nor does it lend sanction to arbitrariness and
caprice. Our moral consciousness belongs to our mental con-
stitution, which we cannot change as we please. We approve
and we disapprove because we cannot do otherwise. Can we
help feeling pain when the fire burns us? Can we help sym-
pathising with our friends? Are these phenomena less
necessary, less powerful in their consequences, because they
fall within the subjective sphere of experience? So, too, why
should the moral law command less obedience because it forms
part of our own nature?[6]

He might have even pondered the reflections of A. J. Ayer, who,
although he is not an ethical subjectivist, is often mistaken for one:

I hope that I have gone some way towards making clear what
the theory which I am advocating is. Let me now say what
it is not. In the first place, I am not saying that morals are
trivial or unimportant, or that people ought not to bother with
them. . . . Again, when I say that moral judgements are
emotive rather than descriptive, that they are persuasive expressions of attitudes and not statements of fact, and conse-

quently they cannot be either true or false, . . . I am not
saying that nothing is good or bad, right or wrong, or that
it does not matter what we do. . . . Finally, I am not saying
that anything that anybody thinks right is right; that putting
people into concentration camps is preferable to allowing them
free speech if somebody happens to think so, and that the contrary is also preferable if somebody thinks that it is.

[But] does not the promulgation of such a theory encourage
moral laxity? Has not its effect been to destroy people's confidence in accepted moral standards? . . . Such charges have
. . . been made, but I do not know upon what evidence. The
question how people's conduct is actually affected by their
acceptance of a meta-ethical theory is one for empirical investigation. . . . My own observations . . . do not suggest that
those who accept [my view] conduct themselves very differently
from those who reject it.[7]

Hume, Westermarck, and Ayer—thinkers of "more authority"
than Gaius and Titius—are unanimous in their belief that moral
values are important and perfectly rational. They have no intention of debunking morality. To anyone who has read their work
it is quite obvious that the refutation of ethical subjectivism cannot be accomplished by name-calling or grim forecasts of the sort
that fill *The Abolition of Man*.

But what of the matter of personal conduct? Did Lewis show
that the moral efforts of ethical subjectivists are doomed and that
they are, one and all, incapable of "great sacrifices for the good
of posterity"? No. If such claims are to stick, some evidence is
required. What would Lewis have said about Bertrand Russell,
who, while holding to a version of ethical subjectivism, spoke out
uncompromisingly against social evils of all kinds, often at great
personal cost: public ridicule, dismissal from teaching positions,
even jail sentences? Surely the behavior of such a person is enough
to cast doubt on Lewis's claim about what ethical subjectivists
"cannot" do.

We need not guess about his answer, for he has told us very
clearly. Having just laid it down that ethical subjectivists cannot
make sacrifices for the good of posterity, Lewis goes on to confess that he is "well aware" that many subjectivists do in fact
make "great efforts for the cause of justice and freedom." But
has he not contradicted himself? He did not think so. Here is his

"solution": morally earnest subjectivists "forget their philosophy. When they really get to work they think that justice is really good—objectively obligatory whether anyone likes it or not: they remember their opposite philosophical belief only when they go back to the lecture room" (*CR*, 67). But, as Russell himself once observed in another context, this way of arguing has all the advantages of theft over honest toil. Lewis tries to win a factual dispute by definition. When confronted with undeniable examples of ethical subjectivists doing exactly what he had said they could not do, he does not admit that he had been mistaken and withdraw his claim; he declares that they are not "really" subjectivists.

This strategy reminds me of an incident from the past. I once knew someone whose dog preferred lettuce to all other food. When I mentioned this to a friend, he refused to believe it. "Dogs can't eat lettuce," he protested. Yet when he finally observed the dog in question shamelessly devouring a bowl of lettuce, he admitted that he had been mistaken. But what if he had responded to the dog as Lewis responded to the subjectivist? What if he had said, "Well, I don't know what it is, but it's not a dog because dogs can't eat lettuce"? Clearly, we ought to abandon the Alarmist Thesis.

I turn next to Lewis's argument for the existence of a Power behind the Moral Law. Like the previous argument, it too is based on a contrast—in this case the contrast between the "blind" view of materialism and the "purposeful" view of religion. The argument goes like this:

(1)   If there is Something behind the facts observed by science, it cannot manifest itself externally as one of those facts. Hence either it must remain entirely unknown or it must make itself known in some other way.

(2)   We find within ourselves an internal command urging us to behave morally. Since this internal phenomenon cannot be observed by science, it provides us with exactly the kind of clue we would expect if there were Something behind the facts.

(3)   Therefore there is Something behind the facts that
            speaks to us through the Moral Law. This Something
            is the Power behind the Moral Law.

Taken at face value, this is a very poor argument, one that
can be disposed of with unusual speed. On any straightforward
reading, it commits the fallacy of affirming the consequent: "If
P, then Q; Q; therefore P." For example, "If you are to pass
this test, you will have to study very hard. You did study very
hard. Therefore you will pass this test." Alas, no. Similarly, "If
there is a Power behind the facts, it must reveal itself in some
way other than that of external observation; we are aware of
internal commands; therefore there is a Power behind the facts."
Again, no.

Furthermore, step two of this argument contradicts Lewis's
earlier endorsement of Christianity as the sort of religion you
could not have guessed. Surely he cannot claim on the one hand
that one of the reasons Christianity warrants our serious consideration is that it is unpredictable and presents us with the kind
of religion and universe we could have never guessed, and then
go on to suggest that another reason Christianity warrants our
serious consideration is that it offers us exactly the kind of religion
and universe we might have expected.

Lewis might have replied to the charge that he had committed the fallacy of affirming the consequent by saying that he did
not intend to assert that the Power behind the facts manifests itself
through the Moral Law, but only that this is a possible interpretation of morality. This reply, however, is incompatible with what
he claimed to be doing in the Broadcast Talks. We were supposed
to be finding out what we could establish about God "on our own
steam." Lewis habitually advances his argument with such expressions as the following: So "we are *forced* to believe . . ." (*MC*,
20); "we shall *have* to admit . . ." (*MC*, 30); "I now want to
consider what this *tells* us . . ." (*MC*, 31); "All I have got to
is a Something which is directing the universe . . ." (*MC*, 34);
"I am *forced* to assume . . ." (*MC*, 46); "I *have* to accept the
view that . . ." (*MC*, 56); and so on (emphasis mine). Anyone
who couches his argument in terms like these cannot fail to give
the impression of discovering important truths rather than simply casting about for a *possible* way of looking at things.

This is not a fussy point about terminology. It is a problem that plagues many of Lewis's arguments and infects his apologetic writings with a fundamental ambiguity. Too often readers must pause to ask themselves *exactly* what Lewis claims to have established and in exactly what sense he has done so. Has the existence of a Power behind the Moral Law been rigorously proved, or established as overwhelmingly probable, or established with reasonable certainty? Or have we only been given *some* reason for accepting this conclusion, which, while not "logically compulsive," is still "adequate"?

This ambiguity is regrettable for a second reason. It has the further and wholly unintended consequence of providing Lewis's disciples with a double standard for assessing his arguments. Their estimate of the cogency of those arguments seems to vary with the sort of criticism put forth. In response to the objection that Lewis does not really prove that the God of Christianity exists, they have typically pointed to his distinction between Faith-A and Faith-B. In response to the objection that he does not even establish the existence of a Power behind the Moral Law, they have replied that we must not take him too literally, that a logically "compulsive" proof is out of the question, that he was only claiming that his arguments are plausible, and that regarding the whole matter of God's existence proofs will only seem convincing to those who are already "favorably disposed" to them—a claim that would seem to imply that in the pursuit of truth it is not so much solid arguments as sunny dispositions that are decisive. On the other hand, Lewis enthusiasts do not typically urge these same cautions on those who fail to raise these sorts of objections to his arguments; on the contrary, in such company they are content to continue to think of him as the Apostle to the Skeptics.

This ambiguity is present in the Moral Argument itself. Granted, in presenting it Lewis specifically denies that he has proved the existence of the God of Christianity, but clearly he thought that he had proved the existence of a Power behind the Moral Law. Or did he?

On the one hand, his underlying logic suggests that he is setting forth a straightforward if-then argument, since if that is not the form of his argument, then there is no reason whatever that the mere fact of an internal moral command should "arouse our suspicions" to the point that we are "forced" to conclude that Someone is speaking to us through it. By itself, the psychological fact that we are conscious of an internal command suggests nothing beyond itself. Our "suspicions" will be aroused only if we grant two things: first, that an alleged Power "behind" the Moral Law can only reveal itself to us in some scientifically unobservable way; and second, that the internal command is one such way. These claims are precisely the ones Lewis wants us to accept. But this is also precisely the fallacy of affirming the consequent.

On the other hand, if Lewis is not setting forth a rigorous if-then argument, then of course he does not commit this fallacy—but neither will his argument "force" us to conclude anything on purely logical grounds. In that case, we are left with the mere psychological fact that we are aware of an internal command. From this alone nothing follows about the existence of anything.

There is also a religious objection to Lewis's version of the Moral Argument. He repeatedly insists that the Power behind the Moral Law cannot reveal itself within the universe. If he is right, then even if he does establish the existence of this Power, he cannot go on to identify it with the God of Christianity, for to claim that the God of Christianity cannot reveal himself within the universe is to be guilty of unorthodox theology. If he cannot, how could Jesus of Nazareth have been God incarnate? Furthermore, how can a deity presently reduced to such feeble, makeshift strategies as internal hints and voices be reconciled with the God who will one day come "crashing in" on the last day when the clouds shall be "rolled back as a scroll"? According to Christian theology, God *can* reveal himself publicly but chooses temporarily not to do so. Lewis simply sets orthodoxy aside in the interests of gaining a foothold for the Moral Argument.

In his haste to convince us that the Moral Law is the internal manifestation of a Power that can make itself known in no other way, Lewis skates out on thin ice. The teaching of historic Christianity plainly contradicts his claim. It does not support the contention that morality can be cited as the internal and scientifically unobservable manner by which some alleged Power finds it necessary to address us. Hence, Lewis's version of the Moral Argument fails again, on both logical and theological grounds. He does not show that there is a Power behind the Moral Law.

But even if he had shown it, and shown it conclusively in Book I of *Mere Christianity*, it would follow that the claims of Book II—that Jesus was God and that he will return on the last day—must be false. If the Power *cannot* reveal itself publicly within the universe, then Jesus cannot have been God incarnate, nor would he be able to return in any objectively visible way. On the other hand, if the Power *can* reveal itself publicly, then Lewis's assertion that the Moral Law is the only way in which it can manifest itself is simply wrong. Book II of *Mere Christianity* is therefore not a further development of the argument of Book I. On the contrary, Books I and II set forth two different and mutually exclusive cases for Christianity. Consequently, if Book II is to have any further claim on our attention, it must be regarded as independent of Book I. For the purposes of the discussion that follows, that is how I will regard it.

In Book II the reader is struck by Lewis's uncommonly tough-minded approach to the claims of Jesus. Although many of these claims shocked Jesus' contemporaries, none shocked them so directly as his claim to be able to forgive sins, and it is this claim that provides Lewis with his point of departure. There are many today who continue to reject Jesus' claim to be God but who are prepared to accept him as a great moral teacher. Lewis rejects this as an indefensible position on the ground that anyone who said the things Jesus said *and was not God* would not be a great moral teacher; he would be a lunatic. Since Jesus does not appear to have been a lunatic, Lewis concludes that "I have to accept the view that He was and is God" (*MC*, 56). The Lord-or-lunatic dilemma is yet another of Lewis's radical either/or, all-or-nothing arguments. What are we to make of it?

It would be pointless to become embroiled in the controversy surrounding the question of exactly who Jesus claimed to be or of precisely how, according to the four Gospels, he understood his messianic status. Some theologians have claimed that Jesus' claims about himself are not entirely consistent, but we need not put forth so strong a claim. It is enough simply to observe that his messianic claims have been variously interpreted. In light of this, Lewis's view that Jesus' claims were so clear as to admit of one and only one interpretation reveals that he is a textually careless and theologically unreliable guide.

Before asking whether Lewis is right about the Lord-or-lunatic dilemma, we shall consider what he meant by it. He apparently thought that if certain factual claims Jesus made about himself were false, a disastrous conclusion would follow about the truth, sanity, and reliability of his moral teachings. But why say that? Why should the fact that Jesus was wrong about who he was be enough to demonstrate that he was a "lunatic," a "mad-man," or a "megalomaniac, compared with whom Hitler was the most sane and humble of men" (*GiD*, 157)?

Perhaps Lewis thought that if Jesus' claims about himself were false, we would have to conclude that they were lies. But that does not follow either. We could simply suppose that although he sincerely believed that he was God, he was mistaken. This would bring us to the same problem: why should the mere fact that he was mistaken about himself have any implications for the soundness and acceptability of his moral teachings? Did Lewis think that if Jesus were not God, there would no longer be any reason for believing that love is preferable to hate, humility to arrogance, charity to vindictiveness, meekness to oppressive-ness, fidelity to adultery, or truthfulness to deception? Did he think that instead of forgiving our brother countless times (the biblical seventy times seven), once or twice would be plenty? That perhaps it is better to receive than to give? That stoning is obviously the proper way of dealing with adulterers? That we should not try to live peaceably with all men? Why would it follow from the fact that Jesus was not who he said he was that none of his teachings can be considered "sane"? Lewis failed to realize that the question of whether Jesus' factual claims about himself are true is wholly separate from the question of whether his teachings are sound. If we deny that Jesus was God, we are not logically compelled to say that he was a lunatic; all we have to say is that his claim to be God was false. The term *lunatic* simply clouds the issue with emotional rhetoric.

Some might be genuinely puzzled by the suggestion that Jesus could be sincerely mistaken in thinking that he was God. They might ask whether such a colossal error is not the kind that only a lunatic can make. Lewis himself encouraged such thinking when he said, "If you think you are God, there is no chance for you" (*GiD*, 158). But that is no answer. The sober answer to the ques-tion is No, this is not the kind of blunder that only a lunatic can make.

Theologians have long insisted that Jesus' messianic claims

must be viewed against the background of Jewish eschatology and the immanent expectation of the One who would deliver the Jewish nation. All devout Jews shared this hope. They believed that sooner or later someone would answer to the description of the promised Messiah—if not Jesus, then someone else. Consequently, the credentials of each claimant had to be investigated one by one. For those who proved deficient, the proper assessment was not "Another lunatic," but rather "This is not he for whom we look." Lewis's discussion suggests that all individuals of all times and places who say the kinds of things Jesus said must be dismissed as lunatics if their claims are rejected. But this overlooks the theological and historical background that alone makes the idea of a messianic claim intelligible in the first place.

The Jewish authorities rejected Jesus' claims for a number of reasons: many of them had known him as the carpenter's son, he had broken many of their laws, his teachings were not at all what they had expected, and he had been very critical of those in high places. But although they rejected his claims and were otherwise outraged by much of his behavior, they did not regard him as a lunatic; they regarded him as a blasphemer. Contrary to what Lewis thought, Jesus' claim to forgive sins does not fail to make sense if he is not God. All that is required for the claim to make sense is that he sincerely believe that he is God. The Jews recognized that he did in fact sincerely believe this, even though they did not. The claim made sense, but they rejected it. In rejecting it, however, they were fully aware that, viewed within the context of their own theology, the claims of Jesus were perfectly rational. They were precisely the sort of claims that *could have been* true. That is why they decided that he had to be done away with. And when they did dispose of him, it was not on the ground that he was a lunatic but on the ground that he was an imposter who had unfortunately gained a considerable following.

By insisting that anyone who rejects Jesus' claim of divinity is logically compelled to say that he was a lunatic, Lewis prevails by sending his readers into a state of shock while at the same time assuring them that their only hope of recovery lies in agreeing with him. That is not a philosophical argument but a psychological spell. In producing this admittedly powerful effect, he deprives his readers of numerous alternate interpretations of Jesus that carry with them no such odious implications. This fallacious strategy not only does violence to orthodox Judaism past and present but also impugns the intellectual and moral integrity of anyone whose theological opinions fall outside the purview of that question-begging touchstone of religious truth he calls "mere Christianity."

We must therefore emphatically reject the Lord-or-lunatic dilemma. Once its high-voltage psychological charge has been neutralized, it will no longer to be able to jolt us into supposing that we can remain unorthodox only by reviling a universally revered sage. It is perfectly legitimate to suggest that Jesus was a great moral teacher even though he was not God. Because of the manner in which it denies this obvious fact, the Lord-or-lunatic dilemma is the most objectionable of Lewis's many attempts to confront us with false dilemmas and to formulate non-exhaustive sets of options in emotionally inflammatory ways.

In his recent book *A Severe Mercy*, Sheldon Vanauken says of Lewis: "never was there a man who could so swiftly cut through anything that even approached fuzzy thinking."[8] Despite this fervent testimonial, I find Lewis's thinking in *Mere Christianity* considerably worse than "fuzzy." His use of the false dilemma is one particularly striking way in which he manages to give his arguments an appearance of cogency that they do not in fact have. Their apparent force depends on two conditions against which the reader should constantly be on guard. First, he consistently presents alternatives to his own views as being perfectly absurd and second, he consistently presents the absurd view as the only alternative to his own. The reader needs to be wary of such argumentation.

When Lewis or William Luther White justifies the popular approach on the ground that "if you are allowed to talk for only ten minutes, pretty well everything else has to be sacrificed to brevity" (*MC*, 74), he presents not a justification but an excuse. If that is true, why go on the air at all? Why not write a longer book in which "everything else" *can* be fully and fairly discussed? Although the need for brevity rules out exhaustiveness, it is not a license to set up straw men, produce false dilemmas, draw fallacious inferences, or argue from inconsistent premises. Anyone who finds that brevity is an obstacle to accuracy, fairness, and careful argumentation would be well-advised to avoid being brief.

Chapter Four

REASON

Man, declares Aristotle, is a rational animal. Although some have disputed the adjective while others shuddered at the noun, almost everyone is prepared to admit that man is capable of rationality. To be rational is to think, and to think is to possess reason. But what is reason? Recent philosophical discussions answer this question in a comparatively modest way, contending that to say that man possesses reason is to say that individuals are capable of having *reasons* for their beliefs and actions, that human behavior cannot be fully explained in purely causal terms, that evidence and arguments, purposes and intentions figure prominently in our conduct. Traditional theorists, on the other hand, put forth their claims in much weightier language and talk a great deal about Reason, by which they mean some unique faculty or "part" of man, some "organ" of truth that we alone possess and that distinguishes us "from the brutes." According to this view, the laws of thought have objective validity; to the extent that man's thought is patterned by these laws, human reason participates in a transcendent, cosmic Reason.

Lewis shared this traditional view. Just as our moral perceptions put us in touch with a reality behind the facts, he maintained, so the trust and confidence we repose in reason commits us to believing in a superior Mind. He believed human reason, then, to be yet another phenomenon that naturalism cannot explain and so he believed that it provides us with evidence for a third antinaturalistic argument. Although this argument appears in several of Lewis's shorter essays, it is set forth most fully in *Miracles*. I call it the Argument from Reason.

With characteristic boldness, Lewis suggests that naturalism can be refuted quite easily. In the third chapter of *Miracles*, entitled "The Self-Contradiction of the Naturalist," he sets out to do so, arguing along the following lines: naturalists think that nothing exists except nature. Nature is "the whole show," "the ultimate Fact," a self-contained and self-explanatory total system that goes on "of its own accord" (*M*, 15–16). Since every event within that system is caused by something else internal to it, nothing can claim independence from the system. Supernaturalists, on the other hand, believe that nature is not ultimate, that "One Thing" is "basic and original," and that all else is "merely derivative" (*M*, 17): they think that some things are independent of the total system called nature.

In a passage worth quoting, since I will be returning to its substantive content shortly, Lewis illustrates this contrast by way of a political metaphor. Naturalism gives us a "democratic" picture of reality, he suggests, while supernaturalism gives us a "monarchial" one:

> The Naturalist thinks that the privilege of "being on its own" resides in the total mass of things, just as in a democracy sovereignty resides in the whole mass of the people. The Supernaturalist thinks that this privilege belongs to some things or (more probably) One Thing and not to others—just as, in a real monarchy, the king has sovereignty and the people have not. And just as, in a democracy, all citizens are equal, so for the Naturalist one thing or event is as good as another, in the sense that they are all equally dependent on the total system of things. (*M*, 18)

The "One Thing" referred to here is God, of course, and Lewis tries to prove that he exists by arguing that naturalism is self-contradictory. The case for miracles depends on this thesis; indeed, it constitutes the philosophical backbone of the entire book.

If the naturalist is right, miracles cannot occur. There could, of course, still be extraordinary events. But no matter how extraordinary or unprecedented an event might be, a skeptic can always account for it by claiming to have been the victim of an illusion; and, said Lewis, if we are not supernaturalists, that is exactly what we will say. What we learn from experience depends on the philosophy we bring to it. It is therefore useless to appeal to experience before we have settled the philosophical question of whether miracles are possible.

In addressing himself to this question, Lewis deliberately eschews a method favored by some apologists. He does not collect a host of bizarre reports and then proceed to argue that since the character of the witnesses is blameless, we must accept their testimony as genuine and conclude that the events reported were in fact miracles that prove that God exists. He adopts the opposite procedure—and with good reason: no one will call an event a miracle who does not already believe in God.

The first order of business for Lewis, however, is to discredit naturalism. His general argument can be stated very briefly:

(1)   If naturalism is true, it must be possible to explain everything that happens in terms of the total system called *nature*.

(2)   But reason cannot be explained this way.

---

(3)   Therefore, naturalism is not true.

Since the crucial step in this argument is step two, we must examine it in some detail. Exactly why did Lewis think that reason could not be adequately explained in terms of nature? To answer this question, I must introduce a theory that may seem far removed from the subject of miracles but is nevertheless the foundation of Lewis's entire argument. It is a theory about how we acquire our knowledge. Although it flies in the face of common sense and has been rejected by most of the philosophers who originally proposed it, Lewis sets it forth without batting an eyelash:

> It is clear that everything we know, beyond our own immediate sensations, is inferred from those sensations. . . . Put in its most general form the inference would run, "Since I am presented with colours, sounds, shapes, pleasures and pains which I cannot perfectly control, and since the more I investigate them the more regular their behaviour appears, therefore there must exist something other than myself and it must be systematic." (*M*, 25)

This so-called "phenomenalistic" theory is a very unintuitive view for a popular apologist to endorse as the basis for sustained argument. Yet since Lewis not only accepts the theory himself but expects his readers to accept it too, we need to understand its implications. If this theory is correct, we never *directly* perceive material objects such as tables, chairs, cars, and buildings, or other persons such as our wives, husbands, friends, and children. What we *do* perceive are sense data—for example, colors, shapes, and sounds: not tables, but brown rectangular images; not apples, but red globular patches. So, whatever we might say in our unguarded moments, reflection requires us to correct these loose and imprecise ways of speaking, and to content ourselves with far more modest perceptual powers.

What, then, is the status of tables, chairs, cars, buildings, husbands, wives, friends, and children? The answer is a jolt to common sense: they are *inferred* entities. Lewis himself does not draw out these scandalous implications. Understandably, he confines himself to less unsettling examples, reminding us that we infer evolution from fossils and the existence of our own brains from what we find in the skulls of creatures like us. But he does nonetheless clearly accept the full-blown theory together with its curious implications. Even in *Mere Christianity*, in the course of explaining why Christianity is not simple, he assures us that the seemingly simple achievement of seeing a table is so complicated that it very quickly lands you in "mysteries and complications which you can hardly get to the end of" (*MC*, 46). What is hinted at there is set forth explicitly in *Miracles*:

> All possible knowledge . . . depends on the validity of reasoning. If the feeling of certainty which we express by words like *must be* and *therefore* and *since* is a real perception of how things outside our own minds really "must" be, well and good. But if this certainty is merely a feeling *in* our own minds and not a genuine insight into realities beyond them . . . then we can have no knowledge. Unless human reasoning is valid no science can be true. (*M*, 26)

But if we never directly perceive persons and things, it cannot be by our own immediate experience that we are justified in believing that they exist. Experience gives us only sense data, and our belief in persons and things does not follow from those sense data alone. In holding such beliefs, we go beyond what can be verified by experience.

It should now be clear why Lewis thought that the question of miracles is a philosophical rather than a factual one: he held that *no* factual questions can be settled by appeals to experience, that all factual beliefs depend on reasoning, and that it is therefore only by drawing inferences that we are justified in believing in the existence of anything—not only in miracles, but in tables, chairs, our families, and friends. It is not as if experience proves the existence of ordinary objects or events and that the troublesome case of miracles complicates our otherwise unproblematic picture of reality, he argues; that picture itself depends on the validity of inference. If reason is untrustworthy, we have no reliable picture of reality against which to consider the question of miracles. Unless we can trust reason as providing us with genuine knowledge, ordinary events will be no more probable than miracles.

Lewis's quarrel with naturalism is that it deprives us of this confidence.

> No account of the universe can be true unless that account leaves it possible for our thinking to be a real insight. A theory which explained everything else in the whole universe but which made it impossible to believe that our thinking was valid, would be utterly out of court. For that theory would itself have been reached by thinking, and if thinking is not valid that theory would, of course, be itself demolished. It would have destroyed its own credentials. It would be an argument which proved that no argument was sound—a proof that there are no such things as proofs—which is nonsense. (M, 26)

The naturalist thinks that there was a time when reason did not exist, that it was a latecomer on the scene, that minds are just one more product of the total system of nature. Lewis thought that if this were true, we would have to conclude that the workings of the mind cannot be rational. How could an irrational system give rise to rationality? Here the substantive content of his political metaphor comes into play. According to the naturalist's "democratic" picture of nature, in which every event is "as good as" every other, "the finest piece of scientific reasoning is caused in just the same irrational way as the thoughts a man has because a bit of bone is pressing on his brain" (M, 28).

In an effort to nail down this point, Lewis produces the following "rule": "*No thought is valid if it can be fully explained as the result of irrational causes*" (M, 27). If we consistently apply this rule, we will dismiss anything a person says the moment we discover that it can be accounted for in terms of irrational causes.

For example, if Sally thinks that a black dog is dangerous because she has often seen it muzzled, we will take her concern seriously, but if we discover that she thinks this only because she was once bitten by a black dog and has feared them ever since, we will realize that her belief has an irrational cause and dismiss it without further ado. The trouble with naturalism is that it does not allow us to make this distinction. If naturalists are to be consistent, Lewis argues, they will have to be committed to the view that *all* thoughts have irrational causes. If they are right, then "all thoughts are equal" and there is no way of distinguishing between those that are rational and those that are not. Hence, the naturalist

> will have to admit that thoughts produced by lunacy or alcohol or by the mere wish to disbelieve in Naturalism are just as valid as his own thoughts. What is sauce for the goose is sauce for the gander. The Naturalist cannot condemn other people's thoughts because they have irrational causes and continue to believe his own which have (if Naturalism is true) equally irrational causes. (*M*, 28)

Just as the consistent ethical subjectivist must admit that moral judgments are mere subjective preferences on the same level as a fondness for pancakes or a dislike for spam, so, according to Lewis, the consistent naturalist must admit that our factual beliefs are nothing more than "physiological or chemical reactions" produced by irrational causes and "no more capable of rightness or wrongness than a hiccup or a sneeze" (*GiD*, 137).

As always in his polemical passages, Lewis displays supreme confidence. We are repeatedly told what consistent naturalists "must admit," that their attempts to avoid Lewis's apparently decisive criticisms "won't do," and that there is "no escape" for them. In light of this confident finality, it is instructive to reduce Lewis's argument to its essentials and see exactly what is being claimed and why.

The case against naturalism turns out to be this: it "cuts its own throat," "refutes itself," and is "self-contradictory," because if it is true, then there is no such thing as truth, since nothing can be true that is the result of irrational causes. Hence, when naturalists claim that naturalism is true, they contradict themselves, for if it is true that *all* thoughts are the result of irrational causes, then the thought that naturalism is true must also be the result of irrational causes. So what the naturalists have really proved is that there is no such thing as a proof and that it is true there is no such thing as truth—which is nonsense.

Naturalists may, of course, try to avoid these difficulties by surrendering the claim to truth. They may say that it does not matter whether our beliefs are true, provided they are useful. But this maneuver, Lewis maintains, is fraudulent: "The claim [to truth] is surrendered only when the question discussed in this chapter is pressed; and when the crisis is over the claim is tacitly resumed" (*M*, 31). By which I gather that he means to say that naturalists are not only inconsistent but intellectually dishonest.

So much for naturalism. And the unfortunate naturalist is triumphantly placed on exhibit in Lewis's gallery of patronized blunderers alongside his caricatures of the Liberal Theologian, the Ethical Subjectivist, and the Uninstructed Romantic. Yet even naturalists have their redeeming qualities, he notes. Like ethical subjectivists, they sometimes "forget" their philosophy. That, says Lewis, is "their glory. Holding a philosophy which excludes humanity, they yet remain human. . . . They know far better than they think they know" (*M*, 46–47). Although naturalists hold a self-refuting theory, which Lewis does not hesitate to call "idiocy" (*GiD*, 274), they occasionally manage to make a true statement. Now and then they even blunder into doing what is morally right.

Having taken care of naturalism Lewis proceeds to draw the religiously relevant conclusion for which all this was the preparation: the collapse of naturalism entails that reason must have a "supernatural source" (*M*, 48). The Argument from Reason "follows rigorously" (*M*, 42).

Before stating his argument as set forth in *Miracles*, it will again be useful to consult the earlier essays. In "Bulverism" he sets forth our "only" alternatives: either naturalism, which leads to "sheer self-contradictory idiocy," or a "tenacious" belief in our powers of reasoning. With these the only options, no one will, of course, hesitate for very long. Once we have opted for this belief in the "powers" of reason, however, we will "have to grant" that there is "something transcendental or mystical about it." But what of that, Lewis asks, as if his patience has been taxed to the very limits. "Would you rather be a lunatic than a mystic?" (*GiD*, 274).

At least one kind of thought—logical thought—cannot be subjective and irrelevant to the real universe: for unless thought
is valid we have no reason to believe in the real universe. . . . I
conclude then that logic is a real insight into the way in which
real things have to exist. . . . We must [therefore] give up
talking about "human reason." In so far as thought is merely
human . . . it does not explain our knowledge. Where
thought is strictly rational it must be, in some odd sense, not
ours, but cosmic or super-cosmic. (*CR*, 63, 65)

Again:

The validity of rational thought, accepted in an utterly non-
naturalistic, transcendental (if you will), supernatural sense,
is the necessary presupposition of all other theorizing. There
is simply no sense in beginning with a view of the universe and
trying to fit the claims of thought in at a later stage. By thinking at all we have claimed that our thoughts are more than
mere natural events. (*GiD*, 138)

In short, confidence in reason commits us to belief in God.

Returning to *Miracles,* we find that Lewis's central contention is the same. Reason is independent of nature, and within
every human being there is an "area of activity" that goes on "of
its own accord" and according to its own laws—the laws of
thought. Yet to say that reason is independent of nature is not
to say that it is absolutely independent. It is not dependence qua
dependence but rather dependence on irrational causes that undermines the validity of reason. This is the basis for the Argument
from Reason, which proceeds as follows: no human being is
eternal, self-sufficient, or self-caused. Every person's reason
develops gradually from infancy, and even the adult's reason is
"interrupted" every night during sleep. From this it is evident
that no individual's reason can be "that eternal self-existent
Reason which neither slumbers nor sleeps." Yet if any thought
is valid, such a Reason must exist as the source of our own
"imperfect and intermittent rationality." Therefore human minds
"come into Nature from Supernature," and "each has its taproot
in an eternal, self-existent, rational Being, whom we call God"
(*M*, 36–37).

On February 2, 1948, less than a year after the publication
of *Miracles,* the British philosopher G. E. M. Anscombe, at her

own invitation, read a paper entitled, "A Reply to Mr. C. S. Lewis's Argument that 'Naturalism' Is Self-defeating" to the Oxford Socratic Club. Lewis responded, and an exchange followed.

Various people have commented on the outcome of this famous meeting. Humphrey Carpenter claims that Lewis was unprepared for the "severely critical analysis" to which his arguments were subjected, and reports that Anscombe's paper showed that his proof of theism was "severely faulty," and that most of those present shared the opinion that "a conclusive blow" had been struck against one of his "most fundamental arguments."[1] Anscombe herself is said to have responded to Walter Hooper's query about the encounter by "removing a cigar from her mouth only long enough to say, 'I won.' "[2] Some say that Lewis thought so too. Alan Bede Griffiths, for example, says that Lewis not only told him that Anscombe had "completely demolished" his argument but went on to complain that, since she was a Roman Catholic, she "might at least have provided an alternative argument."[3] Derek Brewer also recalls that Lewis had been "deeply disturbed" by the meeting and described it "with real horror," that his imagery was all of "the fog of war, the retreat of infantry thrown back under heavy attack," and that after the meeting, he was "miserable" and "in very low spirits."[4] Hugo Dyson went so far as to say that as a result of Anscombe's attack, Lewis "had lost everything and was come to the foot of the Cross," and Carpenter even suggests that after this bitter experience Lewis had "learnt his lesson" and wrote no more books on the subject of apologetics.[5]

Walter Hooper, on the other hand, predictably assures us that Lewis did not lose the debate, and claims that Lewis told *him* that he did not think so either. While Hooper does not deny that Lewis was "low and dispirited" about the meeting, he suggests a different explanation: this was not the result of Anscombe's arguments but of her "rather bullying quality."[6]

Fortunately, we are not reduced to the predicament of having to choose between one person's word and another's. There is independent evidence that casts doubt on Hooper's claim. In 1960 Fontana Books published a paperback edition of *Miracles* for which Lewis revised and expanded chapter three—the very chapter Anscombe had subjected to her devastating critique. Lewis had grown much more cautious. In the revised version he no longer accuses the naturalist of self-contradiction and is content to speak of the "cardinal" difficulty of naturalism.

Before turning to his revised argument, we need to take note of Anscombe's objections. She contends that Lewis had not shown that believing in naturalism is inconsistent with believing in the validity of human reason. She begins by rejecting his rule that "no thought is valid if it can be fully explained as the result of irrational causes." This "rule," she claims, fails to distinguish between *ir*rational and *non*rational causes. As examples of irrational causes, she cites "passion, self-interest, wishing to see only the agreeable or disagreeable, obstinate and prejudicial adherence" to one's views, and the like; as examples of nonrational causes, she cites such things as "tumours on the brain, tuberculosis, jaundice, arthritis," and so on.[7] Anscombe argues that Lewis's whole thesis is "specious" because it ignores the ambiguity of the words *why, because,* and *explanation* and because his equation of irrational and nonrational causes leads him to conclude that if a thought can be accounted for wholly in terms of causal laws, it must be invalid. Although she agrees that this is true of irrational causes, she does not think it extends to nonrational causes.

To show this, she examines Lewis's claim that naturalism destroys the distinction between valid and invalid reasoning. In response to his contention that according to the naturalistic hypothesis there could be no difference between the "finest piece of scientific reasoning and the thoughts a man has because a bit of bone is pressing on his brain," she argues that this simply does not follow:

> Whether [a person's] conclusions are rational or irrational is settled by considering the chain of reasoning that he gives and whether his conclusions follow from it. When we are giving a causal account of this thought, e.g. an account of the physiological processes which issue in the utterance of his reasoning, we are not considering his utterance from the point of view of evidence, reasoning, valid arguments, truth, at all; we are considering them merely as events. Just *because* that is how we are considering them, our description has in itself no bearing on the question of "valid," "invalid," "rational," "irrational," and so on.[8]

In short, Anscombe charges Lewis with having confused reasons and causes. She argues that the claim that a particular conclusion follows from a set of premises is in no way contradicted by the further claim that the assertion of the conclusion is a physical event that has a physical cause. Naturalistic explanations of human thought "have no bearing" on the validity of human reasoning. We are not interested in how one comes to have the thoughts that one has, but only in whether one's reasoning is valid. We are not searching for causes but grounds.

It follows that the claim of the naturalists that human reasoning can be accounted for in purely causal terms is not inconsistent with their belief in the validity of reasoning. When asked for reasons, we do not reply with causal explanations. If we have reasons for our beliefs, and if they are good reasons, and if they are our reasons, then our thought is rational, whatever subsequent causal statements some might proceed to make about us. The meaning of *because* in discussions of physiological causality involving the observation of regularities in our mental processes must be distinguished from the meaning of *because* in discussions of motives, reasons, and grounds. If I detect in my son passions or motives of self-interest that convince me that the reasons he has given, however good, are not *his* reasons in the sense that they do not explain why he believes as he does, then I rightly disregard his belief as having an irrational cause. But I do not do this when I discover that in addition to reasons for his beliefs there are also physiological causes. A causal explanation of a person's beliefs, says Anscombe, "only reflects on its validity as an indication, if we know that opinions caused in that way are always or usually unreasonable."[9]

A look at the Fontana edition of *Miracles* reveals that it was precisely these criticisms that prompted Lewis to rewrite the third chapter and to withdraw the charge of self-contradiction. (He also made some changes in terminology in the later chapters.) Like its disgraced predecessor, the revised argument begins with the claim that all knowledge is based on inferences from sense data and therefore depends on the validity of reasoning. Lewis again asserts (1) that if human reasoning is not valid, then we are left with the mere feeling of certainty rather than genuine knowledge; (2) that no theory is acceptable unless it enables us to account for the validity of reasoning; and (3) that naturalism must be rejected because it cannot provide such an account.

At this point, the major differences between the original and the revised arguments become apparent. Anscombe distinguishes between *ir*rational and *non*rational causes and argues that since naturalists explain reasoning in terms of the latter, they do not discredit its validity. Lewis grants the distinction but rejects her claim that an explanation in terms of nonrational causes does not discredit reasoning; he maintains that such explanations are as destructive of human reasoning as explanations in terms of irrational causes. The purpose of the revised argument is to show why this is so.

In the original version of the argument, Lewis distinguishes between a rational and an irrational fear of black dogs. He bases his argument on the rule that *"no thought is valid if it can be fully explained as the result of irrational causes."* In the revised argument, he quietly abandons this rule and replaces it with a very different claim that owes a great deal to Anscombe in terms both of substance and formulation.[10] "A train of reasoning," he argues, "has no value as a means of finding truth unless each step in it is connected with what went before in the Ground-Consequent relation" (M^2, 19). His examples have also changed. We hear no more of the black dog. Instead, he distinguished between the statements "Grandfather is ill today *because* he ate lobster yesterday," and "Grandfather must be ill today *because* he hasn't got up yet":

> In the first sentence *because* indicates the relation of Cause and Effect: The eating made him ill. In the second, it indicates the relation of what logicians call Ground and Consequent. The old man's late rising is not the cause of his disorder but the reason why we believe him to be disordered. . . . The one indicates a dynamic connection between events or "states of affairs"; the other, a logical relation between beliefs or assertions. (M^2, 19).

He next argues that in order for a chain of reasoning "to have value," it must proceed by means of the Ground-Consequent relation. The problem is complicated, he adds, by the fact that since every event has a cause, and since an act of thinking is an event, an act of thinking must also have a cause. This suggests that the two systems—Cause-Effect and Ground-Consequent— must apply simultaneously to the same series of mental acts. According to Lewis, this will not do. To resolve the difficulty, he argues that since one thought does not necessarily cause all the other thoughts that are related to it as consequents to ground, we must amend our account. Instead of saying that one thought can cause another by *being* its ground, we must say that one thought can cause another by being *seen to be* its ground. Given this distinction, he argues that acts of thinking are events, but events "of a special sort." They are about something other than themselves and hence can be either true or false. Acts of inference, then, are on the one hand psychological events that have causes, and on the other hand "insights into" or knowings of" something other than themselves.

> What from the first point of view is the psychological trans-
> ition from thought A to thought B, at some particular moment
> in some particular mind, is, from the thinker's point of view
> a perception of an implication (If A, then B). . . . And we
> cannot possibly reject the second point of view as a subjective
> illusion without discrediting all human knowledge. (M^2, 21)

Lewis thought that this account enabled him to regard inferences as "genuine insights" into the nature of reality. Although these "acts of knowing" have causes, it is a "unique mode" of causality: they are determined "solely by what is known" (M^2, 21). An "act of knowing" depends wholly "on the truth it knows" (M^2, 22). If these acts could be fully explained in terms of physical and psychological causes, they would cease to be knowledge. Hence, any theory that professes to explain reasoning without introducing these acts of knowing implicitly suggests that there is no such thing as reasoning. That is exactly the trouble with naturalism: It ". . . professes to be a full account of our mental behaviour; but this account, on inspection, leaves no room for the acts of knowing or insight on which the whole value of our thinking, as a means of truth, depends" (M^2 22).

According to Lewis, naturalists explain thinking in terms either of the doctrine of natural selection or of our individual psychological mechanisms, and neither account works. Although by natural selection men may have gradually become capable of making responses to external stimuli, these responses are the result of nonrational "conditioning." And if natural selection cannot account for the mental behavior we call reason, neither can our individual psychological makeup. It is, of course, true that repeated experiences of finding fire where we had seen smoke would "condition" us to expect fire whenever we see smoke. When expressed in a statement such as "If smoke, then fire," this is what we call an inference. But if *all* our inferences originate in this way, Lewis argues, they must all be invalid. His reasons for thinking this are very obscure. In order to avoid tendentious interpretation, I will quote the confusing passage in full.

> Such a process will no doubt produce expectation. It will train men to expect fire when they see smoke in just the same way as it trained them to expect that all swans would be white (until they saw a black one) or that water would always boil at 212° (until someone tried a picnic on a mountain). Such expectations are not inferences and need not be true. The assumption that things which have been conjoined in the past will always be conjoined in the future is the guiding principle not of rational but of animal behaviour. Reason comes in precisely when you make the inference "Since always conjoined, therefore probably connected" and go on to attempt the discovery of the connection. When you have discovered what smoke is you may then be able to replace the mere expectation of fire by a genuine inference. Till this is done reason recognises the expectation as a mere expectation. Where this does not need to be done—that is, where the inference depends on an axiom—we do not appeal to past experience at all. My belief that things which are equal to the same thing are equal to one another is not at all based on the fact that I have never caught them behaving otherwise. I see that it "must" be so. That some people nowadays call axioms tautologies seems to me irrelevant. It is by means of such "tautologies" that we advance from knowing less to knowing more. And to call them tautologies is another way of saying that they are completely and certainly known. To see fully that A implies B does . . . involve the admission that the assertion of A and the assertion of B are at bottom in the same assertion. The degree to which any true proposition is a tautology depends on the degree of your insight into it. $9 \times 7 = 63$ is a tautology to the perfect arithmetician, but not to the child learning its tables nor to the primitive calculator who reached it, perhaps, by adding seven nines together. If Nature is a totally interlocked system, then every true statement about her . . . would be a tautology to an intelligence that could grasp that system in its entirety. (M^2, 24–25)

What exactly is Lewis arguing here? That all inferences based on the fact that in the past two events have always been conjoined are *invalid* inferences? Or that they are not *inferences* at all? I cannot tell. The situation is not improved when he goes on to distinguish inferences from "genuine" inferences and expectations from "mere" expectations.

There is much more that is confusing in this passage. Did Lewis think that a tautology is simply a statement that is "completely" and "fully" known? Did he think that there are no differences between tautologies and factual statements? Did he not know that tautologies differ from factual statements not in the *degree* to which they are known (e.g. "completely" and "fully") but in the *way* in which they are known? Did he not know that tautologies are *a priori* and nonfactual and therefore irrelevant to any discussion about inductive inferences? Furthermore, what does he mean when he implies that some, or all, factual inferences depend not on past experience but on axioms? What are these "axioms"? And what does it mean to say that without them there can be no inferences at all but only expectations?

Since Lewis's revised argument against naturalism depends on this confused theory of inference, it is hard to pin the argument down precisely. Whatever he may have thought about inferences, expectations, and the differences between them, however, the revised argument begins to look more and more like the original outfitted with more cumbersome terminology. Not only that, but in the end Lewis reverts to his old thesis that naturalists give an account of human reason inconsistent with the claims they themselves make about it. Even in the revised argument, he concludes by accusing them not of a "cardinal" difficulty but of straightforward self-contradiction (M^2, 26–28). Despite its greater complexity and apparent inclusion of the distinctions Anscombe had insisted upon, the revised argument is not much different from the initial version.

Before examining the revised argument further, let us get our bearings. First, internal evidence from the Fontana edition of *Miracles* shows that Lewis granted Anscombe's distinction between irrational and nonrational causes. Second, the rule so important to the original argument, that "*no thought is valid if it can be fully explained as the result of irrational causes*," is laid aside in the revised argument. Third, throughout chapters three to five, the term *irrational* is replaced with *nonrational* whenever Anscombe's criticisms require it (see, for example, pp. 29, 30, 31, and 34 in the Fontana edition). Oddly, however, from page 39 on, *irrational* stands (see especially pp. 108–9). Apparently Lewis thought that the remaining *irrationals* did not matter or would not be noticed. This is puzzling. Having ostensibly granted Anscombe's criticisms and rewritten the offending passages at the most crucial juncture of his argument, he then proceeds as if these concessions had never been made—an approach that would seem to render him vulnerable to the same harsh charge he made against the naturalist: the substitution of *nonrational* for *irrational* is made only "when the question is pressed," but once the crisis has passed, the original claim is "tacitly resumed."

The objections Anscombe raised can be pursued further, and Lewis's revised argument does nothing to meet them. Lewis wrongly thought, and continued to think, that if human reasoning were "fully explicable" in terms of nonrational causes, it could not be valid. This reveals that although he granted Anscombe's distinction between irrational and nonrational causes, he failed to grasp its deeper import. His revised argument therefore boils down to this: we must distinguish between Cause-Effect and Ground-Consequent—Anscombe was right about that—but grounds and reasons are nevertheless physiological events and so they, too, must have causes. So the validity of reasoning is destroyed on this account too.

Lewis was wrong about this. To say that something is fully explicable in purely causal terms is only to deny that it is random, unintelligible, the result of "blind caprice." It is not to deny that other noncausal considerations are relevant or that they can provide complimentary explanations of a different logical type. Take the string quartets of Beethoven. There is a sense in which one would be on perfectly safe ground in claiming that they can be fully accounted for in purely causal terms. Beethoven, one might say, composed them because of an irresistible creative urge that allowed him to do nothing else even to the point of neglecting his health and business affairs. He was "driven" to compose music. In this sense, his string quartets are, in principle, fully explicable in terms of his psychological and temperamental makeup. *Fully* but not *merely*.

Merely is a word of which Lewis was inordinately fond, but it is a slippery one. He too often moved from "A is fully explicable in terms of B" to "A is explicable merely (simply, only) in terms of B." This is a logical error that obscures the fact that to say that it was Beethoven's creative urge that caused him to compose his string quartets is not to deny that they require further explication and analysis in terms of the principles of harmony, musical structure, part-writing, and so on. The musicologist who discusses the quartets in these terms can rightly claim to provide us with an explanation that explicates them as fully as can the psychologist who approaches them from the viewpoint of Beethoven's temperament. *Fully* means "exhaustively" *only from a particular point of view*. Hence the psychologist who claims to have fully explicated the quartets from the psychological point of view is not open to the charge of self-contradiction if he announces his plans to attend a musicologist's lecture on them. In music, as in psychology, the presence of nonrational causes does not preclude reasons. In fact, there is no limit to the number of explanations, both rational and nonrational, that can be given of why Beethoven composed his string quartets: he needed extra money, he was bent on convincing his critics that his deafness had not deprived him of his creative talent, he was trying to catch up with Haydn, he was obsessed with composing for string instruments, and so on. All these explanations "fully explicate" the composition of the quartets. But they are not mutually exclusive. They are not even in competition.

Lewis's failure to see this accounts for the fact that, having granted Anscombe's distinction between irrational and nonrational causes, he continued to think that in the final analysis reasons must themselves have causes and that this constitutes the "cardinal" difficulty of naturalism. It does not follow that he completely fails in his efforts to discredit naturalism. But his legitimate achievement must be assessed on a scale far less grand than he supposed. Although most naturalists do not claim that human behavior can be exhaustively explicated in terms of one set of explanatory categories, some do. Those who, for example, confidently assure us that our beliefs are simply the result of "conditioning," that we can never transcend our own cultural or economic or sociological framework, that our values are wholly traceable to the culture in which we find ourselves, while at the same time claiming that their own pronouncements somehow manage to avoid these otherwise universal limitations—such naturalists *are* refuted by Lewis's argument. The fact remains, however, that there are many other less naive varieties of naturalism. Against them, Lewis's argument has no force.

The revised argument against naturalism is open to other objections. The careful reader will have noticed Lewis's careless use of the terms *valid* and *validity*. It is clear to me from such usages that Lewis did not have a firm grasp of a number of the elementary principles of formal logic. He is given to using expressions such as "the necessities of thought" and fond of instructing us about what we are "forced" to conclude, but his account of reasoning in general and of validity in particular is confused and wrongheaded.

Lewis was in the bad habit of talking about valid *thoughts*. Although it would be pedantic to grumble about this in casual conversation, what purports to be a serious philosophical discussion of validity should avoid such imprecision. Thoughts are neither valid or invalid. The term "validity" does not apply to individual statements but to the logical process by which one statement is deduced or inferred from others. In a word, the term *validity* applies to arguments. If Lewis's general account of reasoning were acceptable, this would hardly be a point worth making, but his account is wrong, and this seemingly minor point is symptomatic of what is wrong with it.

Lewis maintained that all possible knowledge depends on the validity of reasoning. Although this claim may seem innocuous enough, it entails a fundamental and fatal confusion. Traditional logicians divide arguments into two kinds: deductive and inductive. A deductive argument is one in which the conclusion follows necessarily from the premises; if you grant the premises, you cannot deny the conclusion without contradicting yourself. For example, if you grant that all swans are white and that the creature before you is a swan, you must also grant that this creature is white. But the reason for this has nothing to do with swans. The conclusion of a valid deductive argument has nothing to do with the *truth* of the statements it contains. A deductive argument can be valid even if all the statements it contains are false—valid but not sound. To say that an argument is sound is to make a different claim. A sound argument is not only valid; it is an argument whose statements are true. But while the truth of the statements contained in an argument depends on the facts, the validity of the argument itself depends only on its *logical form*. The argument

> All swans are white.
> This creature is a swan.
>
> ---
>
> Therefore, this creature is white.

is valid only because *any* argument of the form

> All A's are B.
> This x is an A.
>
> ---
>
> Therefore this x is a B.

is valid. Lewis's claim that all possible knowledge depends on the validity of reasoning violates this elementary principle of logic. Not only is the fact that an argument is valid insufficient by itself to insure that its conclusion is true, but validity and truth are determined in wholly different ways. Knowledge (understood as truth) simply does not depend on validity. Validity is not a means to truth, as Lewis supposed; validity and truth are complementary— but distinct—means to soundness. It is a sound argument, not a merely valid one, that gives "genuine insights" into the world.

I anticipate the following objection: "You say that Lewis misuses the term *valid* but this charge depends on too strict a deductive interpretation of that term. You are overlooking the fact that the term *valid* is also used in a looser sense. To say that an argument or inference is valid in this sense is simply to say that it is correct, and it is perfectly proper to say that inductive arguments are valid in this sense. Furthermore, even if we do restrict ourselves to deductive arguments, is it not obvious that by *valid* Lewis meant 'sound'? Hence your argument against him reduces to a minor point about terminology."

If this objection is well-founded, we should be able to reformulate Lewis's view of validity so that it avoids the confusions I have mentioned. But we cannot. If we "correct" his claim that all knowledge depends on the validity of reasoning by substituting *soundness* for *validity,* we find that we can no longer say what Lewis wanted to say. What he wanted to show was that the attainment of truth depends crucially on the *rational* activity of inferring rather than on the *animal* activity of forming expectations. But he overlooked the fact that it is experience, not reason, that provides us with truths about the world. It is only because we already know some truths about the world that we can employ our "powers" of reasoning to deduce other truths from them.

Lewis maintained that statements based on experience cannot be true because they are arrived at by "conditioning," by the "animal" activity of noting similarities and "irrationally" coming to expect that the future will resemble the past. In thus presuming that the attainment of truth is dependent on valid inferences, he inadvertently commits himself to a theory of reasoning that guarantees that we can never have anything to reason about. His refusal to grant that inferences based on past experience can be valid (if he allows that they are inferences at all) leaves him with an unbridgeable gap between the *process* of reasoning on the one hand, and the *content* of reasoning on the other. The moment we admit a premise based on experience into our argument, we have made reasoning depend on what is, for Lewis, a nonrational cause. He did not see that if we refuse to admit such factual premises into our arguments, we can have no subject matter to reason about. This difficulty is easily avoided by distinguishing the validity of an argument from the truth of its premises. All we have to grant is that the truth of the statements contained in an argument are inductively inferred from experience and that on the basis of them we can deductively infer other statements. But this solution is not open to Lewis because when he rejects inductive inferences as a means to "genuine knowledge," he is left with the barren prospect of validity as our only road to truth. It is precisely this error that traps him in his empty view of reasoning.

It is interesting to note that although Lewis's use of the term *valid* commits him to the view that deduction is the only legitimate form of inference, all his examples in chapter three of *Miracles* are inductive. He speaks of inferring the Spanish Armada from the existence of historical documents, the theory of evolution from fossils, the existence of our own brains from what we find inside the skulls of creatures like ourselves, and fire from smoke. This is peculiar. His own theory of inference requires him to say either that these inferences are invalid or that they are not inferences at all. Perhaps his concessions to Anscombe about his use of the term *valid* are also symptomatic of his muddle about the differences between deductive and inductive reasoning. If so, we may perhaps be pardoned for asking why, when he revised his argument, he continued to use the term.

In an inductive argument, the conclusion never follows from its premises *necessarily* but only with some degree of probability. From the fact that in the past all observed crows have been black, we reasonably infer that future crows will be black too. Inductive inferences are genuine inferences. Lewis disagrees. According to him, even repeated instances of finding fire where we have seen smoke cannot yield inferences but only expectations. These expectations remain "irrational" because they result from "mere conditioning." Recall that for him *"whatever has been found together in the past will continue to be found together in the future"* is the guiding principle of animal, not rational, behavior. He argues that in order to advance from expectation (an animal activity) to knowledge based on inference (a rational activity), we must have "perceived a connection" between the two events that always occur together. But what could this connection be? Well, in speaking about his own example of fire and smoke, Lewis tells us that we must have discovered what smoke is. This is unhelpful. Either smoke is different from fire or it is not. If it is different, then even if we discover what smoke is, we would still not know why, having seen smoke, we are rationally entitled to infer fire, since simply to understand smoke more fully is not yet to have discovered the connection between smoke and fire. On the other hand, if smoke is not different from fire, if emitting smoke is simply part of what we mean by fire, then our inference becomes circular: if fire, then fire.

If Lewis is correct in saying that we must progress from the animal level of expectation to the rational level of inference, his theory must provide us with a way of distinguishing between the two. In this he fails once more. According to his view, the difference between expecting and inferring consists in the fact that we are not entitled to speak of inferences until reason infers "Since always conjoined, therefore probably connected" (*M*, 24). But what does *that* mean? Are we to take him as saying that uniform "animal" experience justifies us in drawing a cautious inference? If so, how would such a mental state differ from an expectation?

To say only that expectation is an animal activity while inference is a rational one is no answer at all. I hear the dinner bell, conclude that it is time to eat, and walk straight to the dining room table. My dog sees me pouring food into his bowl, concludes that it is time to eat, and runs straight to the back porch. Does Lewis want to deny that the dog has drawn an inference, even a correct inference? How could he deny this? By explaining its behavior in terms of "conditioning" perhaps? The dog has inferred nothing, he might argue; it has simply come to expect that certain events are invariably conjoined with others in its experience. But this reply presupposes the very distinction it is intended to explain. Nor is it helpful to remind us that the subject in question is only a dog. We know what it is. What we want to know is whether it is capable of drawing inductive inferences, and, if not, how its behavior is to be accounted for. One thing is clear: no matter how hard Lewis pushes the idea of expectation and withholds the coveted term "inference," the fact remains that the dog is on the back porch eating its dinner. Linguistic preferences aside, what so sharply distinguishes the dog's behavior from mine that we are "forced" to say that while my presence at the table is the result of an inference, the dog's presence on the back porch is the result of a mere expectation? Why not just say that we both inferred something? Inductive inferences should not be contrasted with expectations for the very good reason that they *are* expectations. Whereas in a deductive argument one infers a conclusion on the basis of a perceived logical connection between statements, in an inductive argument the inference is based neither on any logical connection between statements nor on any necessary factual connection between events. An inductive inference is based solely on the past conjunction itself—on the recognition that it has always been so.

It follows that Lewis's view of reason as a "power" of perceiving necessary factual connections is wrong—not because he failed to discover those connections but because there are none. We ought therefore to reject his theory of reasoning, grant that our well-founded inductively based expectations are one particular type of inference, and conclude that the drawing of such inferences, far from being unfavorably contrasted with reasoning, is part of what we mean by it. To those who thereupon skeptically inquire with what justification we think it rational to believe that fire will burn or that where there is smoke there will be fire, we may simply reply that we think this on the basis of past experiences. If the doubters are still not satisfied, we can only ask them what alternatives they have in mind and what improvements they would like to suggest. It does not follow that we are thereby reduced to "blind faith" in reason. The fact is that we do *not* "trust" reason about matters of fact. For empirical truth, we rely wholly on our senses, on our undisputed ability to discover constant and regular conjunctions.

To say this, of course, is not to deny that there is another sense in which we do repose enormous confidence in our reasoning abilities. But this confidence is confined to *a priori* contexts: logic, mathematics, and other purely formal subject matter. In these areas, reason can draw conclusions that are absolutely necessary and that can be denied only on penalty of self-contradiction. But these conclusions do not give us "genuine insights" into the natures of things. This legitimate confidence is limited to formal inferences, internal consistency, and the analytical unpacking of the meanings of words and concepts. The fact that I can infallibly infer that if my next-door neighbor is a bachelor, he is unmarried; that if A is taller than B and B is taller than C, then A is taller than C; that "Mozart is dead" and "Mozart is not dead" cannot both be true; and that "C. S. Lewis is mortal" follows from "All men are mortal" and "C. S. Lewis is a man" in no way commits me to believing in some cosmic Mind that alone can guarantee that these inferences are valid and thereby rescue them from being explained in terms of irrational causes such as "a bit of bone pressing on my brain."

All other objections aside, however, there remains yet another difficulty with Lewis's argument that is more fundamental than those we have already considered. Any account of how we come to have expectations about the future based on how things have behaved in the past presupposes that we have reason to believe that things other than ourselves do in fact exist. If we have no reason for believing this, all questions about their behavior become wildly premature. If we accept Lewis's sense-data theory, however, we are left without any reason to believe in the existence of the external objects. So let us begin from the beginning and see exactly why the argument presented in *Miracles* breaks down at the very outset.

Recall that Lewis's case against the naturalist depends on the view that we never directly perceive objects. This is a strategically ingenious way for him to begin, for it enables him to argue that no event, miraculous or otherwise, can be established through appeals to experience alone. But the strategy backfires. It is not the naturalist who discredits human reasoning but Lewis himself. We can see that this is so by returning to his account of how by means of "valid" inferences from sense data reason provides us with "genuine insights" about the world. Anyone who begins by placing us in so severe a subjective predicament must provide us with a way out. Lewis does not. Let us ask him *how* we can validly infer that things besides our sense data do exist. Here we need to improve on his terminology. Let us follow his advice, though not his practice, and substitute *veridical* for *valid*. The question, then, is this: Given the unfortunate fact that we perceive only such sense data as, say, brown rectangular patches, how can we know that the inferred entities we call tables actually exist outside our own minds and that they are the causes of our sense data? In short, *how* are we justified in regarding our sense data as veridical, as putting us "in touch with" objectively existing things?

Lewis offers only one argument for believing that these momentous inferences are justified, and it is a bad one: the more we investigate the colors, sounds, and shapes presented to us by our senses, the more regular their behavior seems to be. "Therefore," he argues, "there must exist something other than [ourselves], and it must be systematic" (*M*, 25).

Therefore? It is striking that Lewis does not require of his own theory what he requires of the naturalists'—namely, that it provide us with genuine knowledge about the world rather than with an account of how our minds "happen to work." Granted, the more we investigate our sense data, the more regular *they* seem to be. But this tells us nothing about what, if anything, exists beyond them, much less about what "must" exist "in a systematic way." Here Lewis is caught in the act of appealing to the criterion of "mere regularity"—the very criterion of "animal" behavior that he everywhere else haughtily rejects as inadequate to the requirements of rationality. But if he can legitimately base his entire argument on this criterion, his case against the naturalist collapses. If "mere regularity" entitles him to draw the momentous conclusion that other things exist, surely it entitles the naturalist to draw the much weaker conclusion that the future behavior of these things will be similar to what it was in the past. In ridiculing the naturalist for employing this criterion, Lewis is again trying to have it both ways.

Deprived of his inconsistent appeal to the criterion of regularity, Lewis is left with no justification whatever for making inferences from sense data to actually existing objects. It is not as if every time in the past that we had certain brown and rectangular sense data, we later found real tables corresponding to them and that we are therefore justified in inferring that this will continue to be true in the future. According to Lewis's argument, no such situation could ever arise. We never see tables. It follows that the only regularity his theory entitles him to talk about is the regularity between his present and past sense data. On the basis of this, however, he can infer only that his future sense data will be like his past sense data. All he can rightfully claim, therefore, is that "the finest piece of scientific reasoning" differs from nonsense because of the purely psychological fact that the two parties have different sets of sense data.

So far as the attainment of truth is concerned, being hopelessly confined to contemplating one's own sense data is hardly an improvement on having one's thoughts generated by a bit of bone pressing on the brain. In neither case is the mind "set free" from "the huge nexus" of nonrational causation (M^2, 27). If we restrict ourselves to what Lewis has actually shown, as opposed to what he claims, we can have no genuine knowledge at all. We remain confined to observing regularities among our sense data from which not even minimally "animal" expectations about the world can arise—a humble station indeed and one that discredits the credentials of reason as thoroughly as Lewis would have us believe naturalism does.

Although writing as a champion of reason in an age gone mad and claiming to confront us with alleged "necessities of thought" that "force" us to reject naturalism and acknowledge that believing in the validity of reason commits us to believing in God, Lewis betrays again and again that he seriously misunderstood the very reasoning process that naturalism is said to discredit and that he claims to be defending. Lewis understood naturalism and the issues it raises no better than he understood ethical subjectivism. Just as ethical subjectivists neither say nor are committed to saying that moral judgments are on the same level as fondness for pancakes or a dislike for spam, so naturalists neither say nor are committed to saying that they have reduced reasoning to the level of "hiccup or a yawn." Like the gods of the heathen, Lewis's straw men have eyes but they see not; ears have they but they hear not; neither speak they through their throats. The genuine naturalists of which they are caricatures, however, can respond briefly and conclusively: "We do not believe what you say we believe, so whomever you are refuting, it is not us."

One cannot read *Miracles* and doubt for a moment that Lewis is enjoying himself at the naturalists' expense. But his celebration of the defeat of naturalism is premature. Again and again his "refutation" depends on the shaky foundation of the straw-man argument and the false dilemma. *Either* hold the absurd view that the feeling of certainty we express by such words as "therefore" and "must be" is a "mere feeling in the mind," *or* grant that reason provides us with "genuine insights" into reality, he demands. *Either* hold the absurd view that there is no such thing as inference, *or* grant that reason is independent of nature. *Either* hold the absurd view that we are reduced to "animal expectations," *or* grant that the ability of reason to perceive connections enables it to escape from the web of causal necessity in which nature remains forever trapped. *Either* hold the absurd view that you are yourself absolutely independent and self-sufficient, *or* grant that your ability to think commits you to believing in a God who is Reason itself. As with the Lord-or-lunatic dilemma, these alternatives are simply not exhaustive. Intermediate positions remain open to us. Naturalism is one of them.

Chapter Five

UNBELIEF

Lewis's arguments for believing in God are unsound. They establish the existence of neither an infinite Object of desire nor a Power behind the Moral Law nor a cosmic Mind. Since it is on these arguments that his "case for Christianity" depends, the case fails. Before turning to other matters, however, I want to linger a little longer over the phenomenon of unbelief and raise two questions: first, how does Lewis portray unbelief; and second, how does he portray the unbeliever?

I concluded my discussion of naturalism by observing that few people are guilty of the blunders that Lewis attributes to the naturalist. This leads to a more general complaint about his polemical tactics. His arguments against ethical subjectivism, naturalism, and atheism imply that such points of view are nothing more than silly. If Lewis's account of them is correct, it is incredible that any reasonable person would hold them. It is as if he wants us to conclude that unbelievers are fools. Of course he never comes right out and says so, and I am sure that he would have dismissed such a suggestion as absurd. But I am not interested in empty reassurances about what Lewis "really" thought, "would have said," or actually told one of his close friends.

In claiming that Lewis implies that unbelievers are fools, I am neither indulging in idle speculation about his personal attitudes nor drawing rash inferences about his state of mind as he wrote his books; I am making a straightforward claim about what actually appears in his writings, quite apart from what he or anyone else might wish to endorse as his "official" view of unbelief. Official views on such subjects are notoriously unhelpful. What we find throughout Lewis's polemical passages is a characteristically tongue-in-cheek manner of proceeding, a palpable delight in setting forth his opponent's case in the weakest possible form, an unmistakable sense of intellectual amusement, a superior air of patiently dispelling nonsense and putting the embarrassed opposition to flight. The style is the man, and it is precisely these characteristics that enliven Lewis's prose and mark it as his alone. The result is that his arguments are reinforced by a powerful psychological undercurrent that not only provides the reader with a distorted account of the view under attack but also shapes his attitudes toward those who hold it.

As early as 1958 Kathleen Nott complained bitterly about the "general emotional tone" of Lewis's writings, by which she meant an "offensive vulgarity" that prompted him to "go out on all the street corners and among the booths and side-shows [to] challenge all comers" combined with the sort of "knowing quality" of being one of the elect common to those Christians "preoccupied with sin rather than with charity."[1] My point is different. I do not fault him for being an orthodox Christian. Nor do I expect him to be emotionally neutral about atheism and other views that he considers false. But I do expect him to be fair. My complaint is that almost invariably he is not. Although in a paper entitled "On Obstinacy in Belief" he once soberly assured an Oxford University audience that the evidence is "mixed" to such a degree that neither the theist nor the atheist can be accused of "irrationality or absurdity" (*WLN*, 20–21), his typical manner of proceeding reveals a strikingly different attitude. His apologetic writings abound with passages in which this judicious tone is wholly absent. If we piece together the most representative of them, what emerges is a highly unflattering composite portrait of the unbeliever as fool.

The Pilgrim's Regress remains our most fertile source. Here Lewis explicitly refers to himself before his conversion as a "fool" who had at one time or another embraced all sorts of false views that many unbelievers still hold. As examples of the foolishness he left behind, he cites the sort of understanding of religion that is based on what anthropologists have to say about it. You will recall that anthropologists are described as people who go around to "backward villages" in order to collect "odd stories" that "country people" tell (*PR*, 36). What is the implication of this if not that the sociology of religion is the work of fools? The same description applies to unbelieving scientists whose method consists of making guesses that, if made often enough, become knowledge (*PR*, 37)—a view of science that resurfaces in Lewis's account of human reasoning in *Miracles*. Again, John, the main character of *The Pilgrim's Regress*, journeys through "darkest Zeitgeistheim" where he encounters the "nonsense" of a host of ludicrous "modern" intellectual blunderers, including Mr. Enlightenment, Mr. Sensible, Mr. Sigismund, Mr. Mammon, and Master Parrot. Since none of these folks are particularly acute or illuminating, John becomes temporarily disconsolate. On the brighter side, he soon makes the acquaintance of Wisdom, from whom he "learns" a great deal: that atheism is a form of wish fulfillment (*PR*, 73), that modern man does not want to be bothered by the facts (*PR*, 87); that all human beings, unknown to themselves, really desire God; and that even their most depraved lusts are a testimony not only to this fact but to the even more astonishing fact that in the very act of fleeing from God a person proves that it is God whom he or she is seeking (*PR*, 179–80).

It is futile to point out that Lewis came to have reservations about this book, for these same caricatures appear in all of his books and in equally blatant form. The only difference is that in the later works the references are scattered and so their impact is diffused. Collectively, however, they present the same attitudes of the earlier work. In *Mere Christianity*, for example, we learn that atheists are like ostriches: they keep their heads in the sand in order to avoid facing facts that damage their position. One of the issues they most fervently ignore is the Lord-or-lunatic dilemma, because only in this way can they persist in their "patronizing nonsense" that Jesus was nothing more than a great moral teacher. They refuse to acknowledge that anyone who rejects his claim to be God must accept the "absurd" alternative that he was a lunatic on the level of a man who claims that he is a poached egg (*MC*, 56).

It is noteworthy that in *Mere Christianity* there is not one word about the "mixed" quality of the evidence for theism. Instead, those who have doubts about Christianity are ridiculed as pitifully unstable creatures who "dither to and fro" and whose beliefs are dependent "on the weather and the state of [their] digestion" (*MC*, 124). We are told that atheism is "too simple," that like materialism it is "a boys' philosophy," "a philosophy for the nursery" (*R*, 55). What is the implication of this if not that atheism and materialism are childish errors that are easy to refute and unworthy of the rational man? Such facile comments as these are hard to reconcile with the sober tone of "On Obstinacy in Belief," in which Lewis insists that when men differ about God there is no need to suppose "stark unreason" on either side, that whoever is wrong, "we must suppose that their error is at least plausible" (*WLN*, 21, 18). Was not Lewis again trying to have it both ways: confiding to a sophisticated Oxford University audience that atheism has a certain plausibility while assuring the general reader that it is really quite silly?

Turning to *Surprised by Joy*, we find that a young atheist "cannot guard his faith too carefully," that danger "lies in wait" on every side, and that a successful adherence to atheism depends on being very selective in one's reading (*SbJ*, 226, 191). We are again assured that atheism is a form of wish-fulfillment and informed that in its "modern" forms it has "come down in the world" and now "dabbles in dirt" (*SbJ*, 226, 139). Finally, we discover that atheists are not committed inquirers, that they merely "play at" religion, and that their minds reel "in a whirl of contradictions" (*SbJ*, 115).

What is even more striking than the censoriousness of these utterances is the fact that Lewis makes no real effort to substantiate them. How can such bellicose outbursts count as serious assessments, much less be brought under the rubric of that obligatory charity to which Lewis so often directed us when he was in a different mood? We have already observed him acknowledging in the 1943 preface to *The Pilgrim's Regress* that in certain passages he had "lost his temper." But does he not do so again in *Surprised by Joy*? And does he not predictably do so whenever he argues against views he finds unacceptable? It is one thing to engage in committed polemical argument; it is something else to accuse unidentified opponents of deliberately ignoring facts, of consciously exercising selectivity in their reading, of playing at religion, of dabbling in dirt, and of other equally serious intellectual and moral offenses.

In *Miracles* we learn that naturalists contradict themselves and reduce human reasoning to an involuntary response "like a hiccup, yawn, or vomit." In "*De Futilitate*" and "The Poison of the Subjectivism" we discover that ethical subjectivists hold that moral judgments are "mere tastes" and "personal preferences" on the same level as a fondness for pancakes or a dislike for spam. In *The Abolition of Man* we are assured that the heads of these so-called intellectuals seem large only because they have allowed their chests to atrophy. Sometimes they are a laughingstock, as when, having just mocked patriotism, they are shocked to discover traitors in their midst. Lewis mockingly implores those subjectivists who have destroyed his reverence for conscience on Monday not to expect to find him still "venerating" it on Tuesday (*M*, 47). In "Bulverism" we are assured that naturalists prefer "sheer self-contradictory idiocy" to a belief in the powers of reason. Atheists tell lies (even "good, solid resounding lies"), believe the universe came into existence by a fluke, modify their self-contradictory claims only when compelled to do so, and dishonestly revert to them the moment the crisis has passed. In *The Problem of Pain* atheists are said to "part company" with "half of the great poets of the human race," to "close their eyes" to the experience of the numinous, to regard morality as a "mere twist" in the human mind, and to reject the testimony of their own childhoods. They do not know what they "really" want, "worship sex," are "duped" by fashionable "climates of opinion," prefer Hell to God, "cut themselves off" from the common ground of humanity, "remain barbarians," misunderstand love, overlook the obvious, and fail to see that their conduct is incompatible with the views they hold.

Clearly, Lewis's procedure in his apologetic writings requires us to assess his uncharacteristically conciliatory and respectful remarks about unbelievers in "On Obstinacy in Belief" as embodying something more like what Thomas Hardy once called a "conviction put on for the occasion" than what the Psalmist had in mind when he spoke of a lamp to the feet and a light to the pathway.

How can it be that Lewis's convinced expositors not only fail to find these passages objectionable but fail even to mention them? A possible answer lies in the fact that as a Christian apologist, Lewis defends views that many of his readers already accept or are strongly predisposed to accept. The simple fact is that it is gratifying, not to mention fun, to find one's own views set forth as more intellectually defensible than those of the opposition. To hear a view one repudiates rejected as false is not nearly so satisfying as to hear it ridiculed as a ludicrous muddle. This is especially relevant to the case at hand, for Christians have often enough been targets for abusive criticism. But the tendency is not confined to religion; it is a commonplace in politics and in every academic discipline. Most of us tend to seek out and identify with compatriots who will provide us with that sustaining bond of reciprocated intimacy within which, safely snuggled together, we and like-minded colleagues can collectively marvel at, while at the same time lamenting, the seemingly endless varieties of intellectual folly to which others are prone. In *Surprised by Joy* Lewis candidly owns up to the us-against-the-world attitude he and his brother had consciously adopted at a very early age. How easy it is, while reading Lewis, for readers to feel that they have been invited into that select circle, have been offered an invitation to become "one of us." Pleased with a sense of belonging, such individuals who then come upon Lewis treating unbelievers in the manner I have just documented need not be understood as shamelessly approving of unfairness and caricature but as witnessing the twentieth century's chief apologist fighting the good fight.

This, I have said, is one explanation of the scarcity of complaints about Lewis's tactics among his followers. But I do not think it is the best one. There is a much simpler way to explain why so many of Lewis's readers fail to find his polemics objectionable. The people to whom he primarily addresses himself are — not trained in philosophy; they are on the whole simply not in a position to recognize his distortions, omissions, and oversimplifications. Few of them will have made any serious investigation of ethical subjectivism, naturalism, or materialism. In fact it seems likely that the vast majority of Lewis's readers are in the unenviable position of having to take his word for what these views teach. They must simply trust him and assume that his accounts are accurate and responsible. In light of his authoritative demeanor and effective prose style, it is little wonder that he is able to convince them that Christianity's chief intellectual rivals are absurd and that he has demolished them. Indeed, the passages I have singled out for criticism are the very ones these readers typically regard as so unforgettably "effective."

But Lewis's polemical discussions are seldom accurate or fair. In saying this, I am not, of course, suggesting that he is malevolently perpetrating a fraud, but I am claiming that the dozens of examples I have culled from his books demonstrate that when it comes to expounding philosophical positions he is very unreliable.

How would Lewis have responded to the charge that he

indulges in polemical excesses? We do not have to guess. *Surprised by Joy* contains the answer: "The key to my books is Donne's maxim, 'The heresies that men leave are hated most.' The things I assert most vigorously are those that I resisted long and accepted late" (*SbJ*, 213). The "key" in question here is, of course, psychological. It serves to shed light on both the views Lewis "hates" (the term is significant) and on the views he accepts. Although I have no desire to scrutinize Lewis from a psychological point of view, something needs to be said about this key.

First, Lewis's talk of being a "reluctant convert" starts wearing noticeably thin after a while. Who, after all, would be *reluctant* to abandon the absurd views he ascribes to subjectivists, naturalists, and atheists? Second, consider Donne's maxim itself. For the sake of argument, let us grant the psychological generalization it expresses. Let us say that it is true that all of us really do come to hate the views we once embraced but now consider false. Exactly what secret interpretive doors is this key supposed to unlock? Surely it is not a justification for misrepresenting those views. Perhaps Lewis would have been more successful in controlling himself if he had taken greater pains to insure that he understood the views that so enraged him. In the end, of course, it is irrelevant whether Donne's maxim is true or false. What does matter is whether the atheistic views against which Lewis so energetically protests are accurately and honorably presented. Clearly they are not.

W. Norman Pittenger once published a critique of Lewis as an apologist in which he rebukes him for his "vulgarity." As examples, he points to Lewis's use of the Lord-or-lunatic dilemma, his "inept" likening of the Trinity to a cube, his "crude" use of the Pauline metaphor of the church as the body of Christ, his "sub-Christian" understanding of miracles, and his tendency to set up and knock down straw men.[2]

Lewis's "Rejoinder to Dr. Pittenger" contains an ominous remark that should be pondered carefully by anyone who wants to come to terms with his sometimes facile arguments and reckless accounts of opposing positions. In response to the specific charge of vulgarity, he reminds Pittenger that he had written "*ad populum*, not *ad clerum*" (*GiD*, 182)—for the masses, not for theologians and philosophers. "If it gets across to the unbeliever what the unbeliever desperately needs to know," he said, "the vulgarity must be endured" (*GiD*, 182). Clearly, if there are arguments in favor of Christianity, the unbeliever needs to know about them. But Lewis's writings reveal that he thought the unbeliever needed to accept the *conclusions* of those arguments even more "desperately" than he needed to understand the arguments themselves. How else are we to interpret the following comment about evangelizing the masses?

> The actual attack . . . may be either emotional or intellectual. If I speak only of the intellectual kind, that is not because I undervalue the other but because, not having been given the gifts necessary for carrying it out, I cannot give advice about it. But I wish to say most emphatically that where a speaker has that gift, the direct evangelical appeal of the "Come to Jesus" type can be as overwhelming today as it was a hundred years ago. . . . I cannot do it: but those who can ought to do it with all their might. I am not sure that the ideal missionary team ought not to consist of one who argues and one who . . . preaches. Put up your arguer first to undermine their intellectual prejudices; then let the evangelist proper launch his appeal. (*GiD*, 99)

Karl Barth once said that belief cannot argue with unbelief; it can only preach to it. Here Lewis advocates a strikingly different method: let belief argue with unbelief for as long as it can, and if it fails, then let it preach to it. Could it be that his conviction that the conclusions of the arguments are more important than the arguments themselves is what accounts for his willingness to set forth alternatives by relying on caricatures and straw-man arguments? If so, then perhaps he believed that such tactics, while reprehensible by the first standard, are by the second perfectly acceptable.[3] In any event, once we realize that according to Lewis the apologist's task is to undermine intellectual *prejudices*, the cat is irretrievably out of the bag. We are no longer in the arena of responsible debate in which honest inquirers discuss the "mixed" quality of the evidence.

Lewis's portrait of unbelief not only decisively undercuts his criticisms of opposing views but also undermines his defense of Christianity. If he had been content simply to set forth arguments in support of his own views, he would have encouraged his readers to examine those arguments on their own merits. But he was determined to argue against non-Christian views. Although his prose style is often brilliant and his rhetoric calculatingly persuasive, the philosophical content of his arguments is consistently disappointing. An apologetic such as Lewis's runs the risk of making Christianity appear to be little more than the best of a bad lot. Certainly it would be a dubious triumph if Christianity were to prevail over opposing views solely by default, but the case is even worse if it manages to prevail only over poorly defended versions of those opposing views. That is why it is so important to take the trouble to find out what those other views really are. Since Lewis's arguments fail, we will sooner or later have to reconsider what arguments Christianity is in fact up against.

Chapter Six

COUNTEREVIDENCE

An apologist who does not ask us to accept Christianity if our best reasoning tells us that the weight of evidence is against it would appear to be wedded to the facts for better or worse. If the evidence if favorable, we may believe confidently; if it is mixed, we ought presumably to believe more tentatively; if it is unfavorable, we will have to abandon our beliefs altogether. In short, it would seem that Lewis's concept of rational religion requires that we proportion our beliefs to the state of the evidence at any given time. In fact, however, this was not his view.

Although Lewis owns that there is a sense in which the evidence has a direct bearing on whether it is rational to believe in God, he also insists that there is another sense in which it is perfectly rational and even meritorious to persist in one's beliefs not only in the absence of favorable evidence but even in the face of contrary evidence. Does Lewis hedge on this issue? I think not, and in what follows I will attempt to explain why.

In order to understand Lewis's position we must take note of two crucial points: first, he makes a sharp distinction between the way individuals *initially* assent to Christianity and the way they *later* assent to it; and second, he maintains that the evidentialist requirement (viz., that it is rational to believe something only if the evidence supports it) applies only to the former. Thus, when he says that he does not ask anyone to accept Christianity whose best reasoning suggests that the weight of evidence is against it, he is speaking to the unbeliever; when he says that one must hold fast to one's beliefs whatever the evidence, he is speaking to the believer. He does not ask anyone to accept Christianity without evidence, but he does ask those who have accepted it to stand fast in their beliefs.

Although Lewis's most sustained discussion of the problem of contrary evidence appears in one of his later essays, "On Obstinacy in Belief," he also touches on the issue in *Mere Christianity,* in which volume he goes to great lengths to distinguish contrary evidence from something else with which it is often confused—namely, moods. Not only in the religious life but elsewhere, he argues, we must often stick to our beliefs in spite of how things seem. For example, someone who knows perfectly well that surgeons do not start operating until their patients have been anaesthetized may nevertheless be overcome by a "childish panic" upon being wheeled into surgery. In such cases the reaction is not triggered by the discovery of new evidence against doctors; such doubts arise not from reason but from emotion and the imagination. Since they are irrational, they should be ignored.

Turning from worries about overeager surgeons to the difficulties involved in living the Christian life, Lewis reminds his readers that people often entertain doubts about God not because new contrary evidence requires them to do so but because of an analogous sort of childish panic, because of a "mere mood." He maintains that a distinction must therefore be drawn between *genuine* difficulties, which are traceable to "real new evidence" against Christianity, and *apparent* difficulties, which are traceable to our emotions. Faith is, in part, "the art of holding on to things your reason has once accepted, in spite of your changing moods" (*MC*, 123).

Lewis sets forth the same view more dramatically in *The Screwtape Letters*, in which his fictional character Screwtape, a devil recently promoted to an administrative position in Hell, writes to a novice instructing him in the fine art of undermining faith:

> Humans are amphibians—half spirit and half animal. . . . As spirits they belong to the eternal world, but as animals they inhabit time. This means that while their spirit can be directed to an eternal object, their bodies, passions, and imaginations are in continual change. . . . Their nearest approach to constancy, therefore, is undulation—the repeated return to a level from which they repeatedly fall back, a series of troughs and peaks. . . . As long as [man] lives on earth, periods of emotional and bodily richness and liveliness will alternate with periods of numbness and poverty. (*SL*, 36–37)

The tempter's apprentice is advised that these "undulations," wisely used, will keep him well-stocked with raw materials the diabolical potential of which can hardly be exaggerated. They provide endless opportunities for confusing the Christian who easily forgets that God relies more on the troughs than on the peaks.

> It is during such trough periods . . . that [the creature] is growing into the sort of creature He wants it to be. Hence the prayers offered in the state of dryness are those which please Him best. . . . Our cause is never more in danger than when a human, no longer desiring, but still intending, to do [God's] will, looks round upon a universe from which every trace of Him seems to have vanished, and asks why he has been forsaken, and still obeys. (*SL*, 39)

As in *Mere Christianity*, this apparent absence of God is traceable to a psychological state—a "mere mood." What superficially appears to be counterevidence that calls religious belief into question is in fact nothing more than a trough, an emotional low point. Properly instructed believers can foil the devil and thus "escape the tempter's snare" simply by reminding themselves of the Law of Undulation. During such periods they must practice what the later Lewis calls "obstinacy" in their beliefs.

At the same time, Lewis freely acknowledges that not all doubts can be explained in terms of our moods, that some arise because of (at least apparently) contrary evidence that gives rise to "real new reasons" against Christianity, and that these "have to be faced" (*MC*, 123). The following question can therefore no longer be postponed. Let us suppose that I have accepted Christianity on the basis of what I thought was solid evidence. Granted, I may then persevere in my beliefs in the face of "mere moods," but how should I respond to contrary evidence? Lewis does not deal with this question explicitly in *Mere Christianity*, but he does in his later essay on obstinacy.

He begins with the skeptic's charge: whereas "the scientific attitude" requires us to proportion our belief to the evidence, the benighted Christian must disregard evidence and continue to believe no matter what. Belief in God is therefore irrational.

It will come as a surprise to no one to learn that Lewis rejects the charge. Interestingly, however, he does so not only on the ground that it is unfair to the Christian but that it is unfair to the scientist as well. Scientists, he declares, are not concerned with believing things but with finding things out. They are trying to escape from belief into knowledge, and it would not occur to them to use the term *believe* with regard to what they have found out. In trying to find things out, the scientist will of course employ hypotheses, but a hypothesis is not a belief. Before performing an autopsy, a medical examiner may say "I believe that the victim was poisoned"; afterward, he or she simply says that the victim was poisoned. The autopsy has not provided stronger evidence for believing this; on the contrary, it has provided sufficient evidence to go beyond belief to knowledge.

Of course Lewis grants that, unlike the scientist, the Christian does have beliefs, but he suggests that this dissimilarity is nothing to worry about. He tries to account for it by calling attention to two facts about the Christian's beliefs. The first is that the religious meaning of the term *believe* differs significantly from the nonreligious meaning, which denotes weak (sometimes very weak) conviction—for example, "Where is Tom?" "Gone to London, I believe." For the Christian, however, *believe* denotes a conviction so strong that in terms of subjective certitude it is "hardly distinguishable" from the certitude of knowledge. Although the believer does not claim to have a demonstrative proof of God's existence, the "mere formal possiblity of error" does not lead to doubt. Accordingly, Lewis defines *belief* as "assent to a proposition which we think so overwhelmingly probable that there is a psychological exclusion of doubt, though not a logical exclusion of dispute" (*WLN*, 16).

Second, as I have already indicated, Lewis holds that there is a fundamental difference between the way a person initially assents to "the Christian propositions" and the way he assents to them later.[1] Regarding the initial assent, he reaffirms what he says in *Mere Christianity*: "So far as I know it is not expected that a man should assent to [the Christian] propositions in the first place without evidence. . . . At any rate, if anyone expects that, I certainly do not" (*WLN*, 17). But how should one assent to them *later*? Lewis was characteristically forthright. It is true, he said, that "in a sense" Christians do recommend a certain discounting of apparently contrary evidence:

> It is here that the charge of irrationality and resistance to evidence becomes really important. For it must be admitted

at once that Christians do praise such adherence as if it were
meritorious; and even, in a sense, more meritorious the stronger
the apparent evidence against their faith becomes. (*WLN*, 21)

Yet he did not think that this was irrational, because after conversion, belief in God is no longer a hypothesis. Those who have
become Christians no longer believe in God experimentally or
tentatively—until new contrary evidence turns up to force them
to reassess or even abandon their religious beliefs. Since their
beliefs no longer depend wholly on the evidence, Christians must
practice obstinacy.[2] They are no longer simply faced with an argument that demands their assent; they are confronted by a Person
who demands their trust. At this point, the "logic of speculative
thought" gives way to the "logic of personal relations" (*WLN*,
30). Faith-that (Faith-A) gives away to faith-in (Faith-B).

While the favorably disposed reader might find this account
perfectly satisfactory, it will likely strike the skeptic as suspect—
and Lewis knew it. That is why he immediately proceeded to
develop the dubious concept of the "logic of personal relations"
in the hope of showing that it was "the logical conclusion" of
the initial assent.[3] After conversion, he declares, Christian belief
is not belief *without* evidence, but rather belief that *goes beyond*
evidence. In the case of a hypothesis, to ignore the slightest bit
of contrary evidence is "foolish and shameful": it must be ex-
posed to every test; every doubt must be invited (*WLN*, 22). But
such treatment is inappropriate in the case of one's personal relationship to God and to one's relationships to others generally.
Here we do not, and should not, proportion our beliefs to the
evidence. The nature of personal relationships requires that we
take in stride certain facts that seem damning to the detached
observer.

> To love involves trusting the beloved beyond the evidence, even
> against much evidence. No man is our friend who believes in
> our good intentions only when they are proved. No man is our
> friend who will not be very slow to accept evidence against
> them. . . . The suspicious man is blamed for a meanness of
> character, not admired for the excellence of his logic. (*WLN*,
> 26)

This, of course, is true. Once convinced of the rationality of a
belief or of the rightness of a decision, a person should not be
at the mercy of every fluctuation of the evidence. Rational com-

mitments should be neither lightly undertaken nor cavalierly withdrawn. One does not rethink one's marriage vows each time a new problem looms on the horizon. One says "I do," not "Perhaps," or even "I'll try."

Certainly, according to Lewis, nothing less should be involved in a person's commitment to God. Here, too, trust beyond the evidence is a central ingredient.

> If human life is in fact ordered by a beneficient being whose knowledge of our real needs and of the way in which they can be satisfied infinitely exceeds our own, we must expect *a priori* that His operations will often appear to us far from benefi- cent and far from wise, and that it will be our highest prudence to give Him our confidence in spite of this. (*WLN*, 24–25)

Hence, if there are good reasons for believing in God, it might indeed be rational to remain obstinate in the face of a great deal of contrary evidence.[4] In that case, what the skeptic calls irra- tionality, the believer will call "waiting on the Lord." "Though he slay me, yet will I serve him," declares Job—surely not a man insufficiently impressed by contrary evidence. Like the bride and groom, new converts anticipate difficulties. But having been forearmed with the information that God moves in mysterious ways, they decide to trust him. In the words of a well-known hymn,

> When through fiery trials thy pathway shall lie
> My grace all-sufficient shall be thy supply.
> The flame shall not hurt thee. I only design
> Thy dross to consume and thy gold to refine.

Even believers like Lewis, whose distaste for hymns was exceeded only by his horror of religious verse, will readily admit that such words were not penned by some breezy Christian enjoying an ex- hilarating ride on the glory train. They emerge from the dark night of the soul, those times when God seems absent, even nonexistent. Yet Christians are not to be faithless but believing. Those who are quick to doubt are not commended for proportioning their belief to the evidence; they are rebuked for their lack of faith.

Lewis sees a close parallel between the trust of one person in another and the trust of a person in God. Just as it would be wrong to insist that our relations with other people be governed by the bogus requirement of proportioning belief to the evidence, so it would be wrong to insist that our religious beliefs be governed by it. The so-called "scientific" attitude ought not to be pressed in the religious case any more than it can in the others. *All* trust, loyalty, allegiance, and commitment go beyond the evidence. Insofar as we are willing to trust our wives, husbands, friends, children, and associates, we all practice "obstinacy" every day, and so, he argues, there is no reason why it cannot also be practiced in religious contexts. For the skeptic to single out religious belief as if it alone violates an otherwise universally recognized requirement is simply perverse.

> The saying "Blessed are those that have not seen and have believed" has nothing to do with our original assent to the Christian propositions. It was not addressed to a philosopher enquiring whether God exists. It was addressed to a man who already believed that. . . . It is a rebuke not to scepticism in the philosophic sense but to the psychological quality of being "suspicious." It says in effect, "You should have known me better."

> Our opponents, then, have a perfect right to dispute with us about the grounds of our original assent. But they must not accuse us of sheer insanity if, after the assent has been given, our adherence to it is no longer proportioned to every fluctuation of the apparent evidence. They cannot of course be expected to know on what our assurance feeds, and how it revives. . . . (*WLN*, 28–29)

Lewis concludes his essay with the observation that in the face of contrary evidence, the believer's situation is "rendered tolerable" by two facts. First, Christians continue to receive favorable evidence—some of it in the form of external events such as answered prayers and some of it in the form of a "knowledge by-acquaintance of the Person we believe in, however imperfect and intermittent it may be" (*WLN*, 25). Second, Christians understand why they are required to trust God beyond the evidence; they believe that God wants to create a personal relation between himself and us and that complete trust is an essential ingredient in that relation. Since after conversion belief in God is no longer a hypothesis, it follows that it is no longer a speculative question either. In fact, it is no longer a *question* at all.

It is by means of this extended argument that Lewis tries to deal with the problem of contrary evidence. Whether the distinction between the "logic of speculative thought" and the "logic of personal relations" can withstand scrutiny, whether the concept of obstinacy continues to be intelligible beyond a certain point, and whether these ruminations in fact served to provide Lewis with an account of God's goodness that could sustain him when he was plunged into the deepest "trough" of his own life— these are the questions that will occupy us in the remaining chapters.

Chapter Seven

PAIN

If God were good, He would wish to make His creatures perfectly happy, and if God were almighty, He would be able to do what He wished. But the creatures are not happy. Therefore God lacks either goodness, or power, or both. (PP, 26)

Thus Lewis restates the argument that many religious skeptics regard as the most powerful objection to Christianity ever put forth.[1] Evil can exist only if God is either unwilling or unable to prevent it. If he is unwilling, he is not good; if he is unable, he is not omnipotent. Evil does exist. Therefore God is either good but not omnipotent or omnipotent but not good. It follows that the God believed in by Christians does not exist. Although most philosophers call this the Problem of Evil, Lewis calls it the Problem of Pain. He took this objection very seriously. Not only does he devote an entire book to it, but he also abandons his usual strategy of setting up and knocking down straw men. In fact, he formulates the skeptic's argument so forcefully that in order to reply he found that he had to retreat.

The Problem of Evil raises the tangled subject of the connection between God and morality. Few subjects have so predictably divided Christians as this one and the important philosophical issues related to it. Since the view Lewis ostensibly holds is one that many Christians reject, we should be clear about both positions at the outset.

Although some Christians are deeply disturbed by the Problem of Evil, there are, and always have been, others who hardly give it a thought.[2] Whether we see evil as a problem depends largely on what we mean when we call God good. Christians have differed about this for centuries. One school of thought, which

I will call the Platonic view, holds that the term *good* when applied to God cannot mean something radically different from what it means when applied to men. According to their view, God's goodness must be defined in terms of ordinary moral standards. Although his goodness may differ in some respects from human goodness, it must still be *recognizable* as goodness or else the term *good* will be emptied of all content.

This view was originally set forth by Plato. In his dialogue *Euthyphro* he poses the following question: Are things good because the gods command them, or do the gods command them because they are good? For example, is truthfulness good only because the gods have commanded it, or do they command it because it is good? Plato embraces the second alternative and argues that the distinction between good and evil cannot be based on the arbitrary commands of the gods; on the contrary, the gods themselves recognize that certain things are good and others evil, and issue their commands accordingly. Christians who follow Plato on this point agree that morality cannot be based on divine commands and, consequently, that morality does not depend on religion.

The other school of thought bristles at this analysis. I will call it the Ockhamist view, after the fourteenth-century Christian philosopher William of Ockham, who set it forth in very unflinching terms. According to this view, when we talk about God's goodness, we must be prepared to give up our ordinary moral standards. The term *good* when applied to God *does* mean something radically different from what it means when applied to human beings. To suppose that God must conform to some standard other than his own sovereign will is to deny his ultimacy. God is bound by nothing and answerable to no one. He is not under any moral constraint to command certain actions and forbid others. He does not, for example, forbid murder because it is wrong; it is wrong because he forbids it. If God would command us to murder, then *that* would be our duty, just as it was the duty of Abraham to sacrifice Isaac, of Elijah to slay the prophets of Baal, and of Joshua to slaughter the Canaanites right down to the last woman and child. Some Ockhamist Christians have even gone so far as to say that God could have reversed the entire moral law and made virtues not only of murder but of adultery, theft, coveting, and bearing false witness. As Ockhamist John Calvin puts it, "The will of God is the highest rule of justice; so that what he wills must be considered just . . . for this very reason, because he wills it."[3] And one contemporary Calvinist, Gordon H. Clark, surpasses even Ockham and Calvin on this point: "God . . . cannot be responsible for the plain reason that there is no power superior to him: no greater being can hold him accountable; no one can punish him . . . ; there are no laws which he could disobey."[4] Unlike the Platonic Christian, the Ockhamist Christian thinks that morality *is* based on divine commands. What God commands is good by definition. Plainly, no one who believes this will have any problems with evil.

First impressions to the contrary, it is hard to unravel Lewis's position on this issue. There are, of course, numerous passages scattered throughout his writings in which his allegiance to the Platonic view is forcefully and unambiguously expressed. With Plato and Hooker, and against Ockham, Johnson, and Paley, he "emphatically embraces" the Platonic view (*PP*, 100). The Ockhamist alternative could easily lead to the "abominable" conclusion that charity is good only because God arbitrarily commands it and that he might have commanded us to hate him and one another. Indeed, *The Problem of Pain* contains one of Lewis's rare attacks on a doctrine held by other Christians—the Calvinist doctrine of Total Depravity, according to which human standards of good are "worth simply nothing." Lewis denounces this doctrine and declares that such a view could turn Christianity "into a form of devil worship" (*PP*, 37–38, 66–67). Similarly, in his essay "On Ethics" he asserts that morality is not based on God's commands and that those who believe this "are deceived" (*CR*, 55). Christianity, he maintains, presupposes morality and does not require us to reverse our moral standards or to resign ourselves to the fact that our "black" may be God's "white." Lewis agrees with Hooker that "they err who think that of the will of God to do this or that there is no reason besides His will" (*PP*, 100), and asserts that "if [God] is not (in our sense) 'good' we shall obey, if at all, only through fear—and should be equally ready to obey an omnipotent Fiend" (*PP*, 37). The Ockhamist view, held by certain "terrible theologians," cannot be rejected too vigorously, he argues, for it makes of morality "a mere toss-up" and of God "a mere tyrant"; it would "be better . . . to believe in no God and to have no ethics" than to hold such a view (*RP*,

61). In fact he states that according to the book of Job it is the man who accepts our ordinary standards of good and evil and "hotly criticizes" divine justice in terms of them who receives God's approval, and that those who "palter" with moral standards in their attempt to "justify" God's ways to man are reproved (*CR*, 70).

In spite of these well-known passages, however, Lewis's real view is more elusive. If, with his convinced followers, we confine ourselves to such remarks as these, we will call him a Platonist pure and simple, but in doing so we will have overlooked his actual arguments, in which he radically qualifies his apparent Platonism and arrives at a very different position.

Our first clue is found early in *The Problem of Pain*. Having set forth the religious skeptic's argument and its conclusion that we must deny either God's goodness or his omnipotence, Lewis immediately makes an unexpected concession. Speaking of the Problem of Evil, he says, "The possibility of answering it depends on showing that the terms 'good' and 'almighty,' and perhaps also the term 'happy' are equivocal: for it must be admitted from the outset that if the popular meanings attached to these words are the best, or the only possible, meanings, then the argument is unanswerable" (*PP*, 26). This ominous remark signals the first of a series of retreats by Lewis from his professed Platonism.

At this point, I should perhaps allay possible suspicions that I am going to end up claiming that Lewis was really an Ockhamist. I am not. What I do insist on, however, is that by the time his argument has run its course he no longer claims that God's goodness is recognizable in any ordinary sense. On the contrary, he suggests that we can call God *good* only if we are prepared to assign a new meaning to the term. And the situation becomes even more desperate when we realize that he is asking us to accept new definitions of *omnipotence* and *happiness* too.

Lewis prefaces his discussion of God's goodness with some remarks about his omnipotence. To say that God is omnipotent is to imply that he can do everything, that all things are possible with him. But the terms *everything* and *possible* are slippery. An omnipotent God can no more do everything than an omnivorous animal can eat everything. The terms *possible* and *impossible* have two meanings, which Lewis explains as follows. To say that it is impossible for me to see the street from where I am now sitting is to say that this is impossible unless I change my position. Lewis calls this a "relative" impossibility. It arises only because the facts happen to be as they are. On the other hand, to say that it is impossible to see the street so long as I remain where I am and the intervening building remains where it is is to say that this is impossible given the nature of space and human vision. Lewis calls this an "absolute" or "intrinsic" impossibility. Such impossibilities are impossible under all conditions, in all worlds, and for all agents—including God himself.

This distinction is familiar to all students of philosophy, but Lewis's exposition of it is muddled. The fault is traceable partly to his lack of clarity and partly to the fact that his examples are ill-chosen. He is attempting to distinguish between two kinds of impossibilities: factual impossibilities and logical impossibilities. Let us consider factual impossibilities first. There are all sorts of things that we can imagine ourselves doing even though we cannot in fact do them—flying unaided, for example. Such impossibilities involve no contradiction; we are simply physically unable to do them. This is not true of logical impossibilities, which do involve contradictions. For instance, I cannot draw a round square—not because I lack the necessary skills or have not practiced hard enough, but because the concept itself is self-contradictory. Not even God can draw a round square. To say this, however, is not to deny his omnipotence.

Following St. Thomas Aquinas, Lewis defines omnipotence as the power to do everything except that which involves a contradiction: "You may attribute miracles to [God], but not nonsense. . . . Meaningless combinations of words do not suddenly acquire meaning simply because we prefix to them the two other words 'God can.' It remains true that all *things* are possible with God: the intrinsic impossibilities are not things but nonentities" (*PP*, 28). This distinction between factual and logical impossibility provides Lewis with a reply to the religious skeptic who claims that evil in the form of pain and suffering disproves the existence of a good and omnipotent God.

Having made this distinction, Lewis goes on to propose two theses. First, not even Omnipotence can create a society of free souls without at the same time creating an independent and "inexorable" nature (*PP*, 29). In advancing this claim Lewis is not saying that it was logically impossible for God to have created the world differently. Considered as bare possibilities, things could have been created with properties and characteristics quite unlike those they presently have. He is saying that the creation of free creatures "necessitates" a stable world with a "fixed" structure because the possibility of significant choice presupposes a world with predictable consequences. In such a world not all states of matter will be equally agreeable to the wishes of any given person. If fire comforts at a certain distance, it will burn if that distance is reduced. Hence, even in a perfect world there would be the necessity for those danger signals that the nerves of our bodies transmit. It follows that when religious skeptics demand that God should have created *both* a free creature *and* a world lacking a fixed or inexorable structure, they are demanding a logical impossibility.

Human life depends on a "field" or "world" common to all, and matter can serve as such a field only if it has a fixed nature: "If a 'world' or material system had only a single inhabitant it might conform at every moment to his wishes—'trees for his sake would crowd into a shade.' But if you were introduced into a world which thus varied at my every whim, you would be quite unable to act in it and would thus lose the exercise of your free will" (*PP*, 31–32). Lewis does not hold that the fixed nature of matter entails that evil in the form of pain and suffering must actually exist, but it does entail that such evil be inescapably present as a possibility.

Lewis's second thesis is that in creating human beings as free agents, God created creatures who could abuse their freedom. They could, for example, exploit the fixed character of matter in order to harm others. The fixed character of wood which enables me to use it as a beam for a house also enables me to use it for hitting someone else over the head.

> We can, perhaps, conceive of a world in which God corrected the results of this abuse of free will by His creatures at every moment: so that a wooden beam became soft as grass when it was used as a weapon, and the air refused to obey me if I attempted to set up in it the sound waves that carry lies or insults. But such a world would be one in which wrong actions were impossible, and in which, therefore, freedom of the will would be void. (*PP*, 33)

A world "continually underpropped" by remedial divine intervention would hardly be a world at all.

To sum up, it is Lewis's argument that the unavoidably "fixed" natures of things together with the equally unavoidable possibility of man's abuse of his freedom bring into actual existence the evil inherent in any world as a possibility. If we ask why in that case there should be free creatures at all, Lewis's answer is that it would have been logically impossible for God to have created a rational-moral agent such as man who was not free. So God took a "risk." He created a society of free creatures who could by disobeying him actualize the possibility of evil, but whose freedom was at the same time the only condition under which they could voluntarily turn to him. The "risk" is therefore justified because of this higher good which it alone makes possible.

Having discussed God's omnipotence, Lewis turns next to his goodness. He begins with a complaint. By *good*, he declares, "people nowadays" mean little more than "lovingness," just as by *love* they mean only the desire to see others happy (*PP*, 39–40). When they proceed to ask how a good God can allow suffering, they fail to realize that their question betrays a lamentably watered-down concept of goodness. Lewis asserts that the Problem of Evil arises only among those who attach trivial meanings to the words *good* and *love*. This error results from the common but false assumption that man is at the center of things and that our daily wants, needs, and desires take priority over all other considerations. Lewis tells us that what many people want is "not so much a Father in Heaven as a grandfather in heaven—a senile benevolence who, as they say, 'liked to see young people enjoying themselves,' and whose plan for the universe was simply that it might be truly said at the end of each day, 'a good time was had by all' " (*PP*, 40). He admits, of course, that few would formulate their theology in precisely those terms but at the same time, he is convinced that a view very similar to it "lurks" in the back of their minds. Since no good can come of anything reduced to "lurking" somewhere behind the scenes, the first item on Lewis's agenda is to expose it as sentimental rubbish.

In the course of correcting this presumed trivialization of the meaning of the word *good* Lewis hastens to assure his readers that he does not claim to be an exception, and that he too "should very much like to live in a universe . . . governed on such lines.

But since it is abundantly clear that I don't, and since I have reason to believe, nevertheless, that God is Love, I conclude that my conception of love needs correction" (*PP*, 40). His disclaimers made, Lewis moves with astonishing speed. Although there is kindness in love, when the two are separated, kindness inevitably becomes indifferent to its object, even contemptuous of it. Kindness "merely as such" cares nothing about whether its object becomes good or bad, but only about whether it is happy and escapes suffering. Kindness thereby fails to recognize that "it is bastards who are spoiled: the legitimate sons . . . are punished. It is for people whom we care nothing about that we demand happiness on any terms: with our friends, our lovers, our children, we are exacting and would rather see them suffer much than be happy in contemptible and estranging modes" (*PP*, 41). If God is good, his goodness must by definition be something more than mere kindness. He is not a "senile benevolence." Indeed, he has paid us "the intolerable compliment" of loving us "in the deepest, most tragic, most inexorable sense" (*PP*, 41). People find this love intolerable because they expect him to be content with them as they are. But he cannot be. Man is a "spoiled species," "vermin," a "horror to God and himself" (*PP*, 85, 67). As a result, God's goodness and love are "impeded and repelled" by us (*PP*, 48).

It follows for Lewis that the difficulty of reconciling human suffering with the existence of a good and omnipotent God arises only if we attach trivial meanings to the words *good* and *love,* only if we forget God's original intention in creating man, only if we fail to recognize that through disobedience man has frustrated that intention, and only if we ignore the fact that in spite of our disobedience God continues to recall us to himself.

Lewis suggests that one way in which God continues to recall us to himself is by seeing to it that we are never fully content in this world. In language reminiscent of the Argument from Desire, Lewis writes:

> The settled happiness and security which we all desire, God withholds from us. . . . It is not hard to see why. The security we crave would teach us to rest our hearts in this world and oppose an obstacle to our return to God: a few moments of happy love, a landscape, a symphony, a merry meeting with our friends, a bathe or a football match, have no such tendency. *(PP,* 115)

But what if these gentle remainders fail, as they almost invariably must, given the likes of the "vermin" with whom God is forced to deal? In that case, more desperate remedies are in order. The infliction of pain and suffering may be one of them. Lewis asserts that this is not only compatible with God's goodness and love, but that it is demanded by them.

Since the proper good of a creature consists in the voluntary surrender of its will to its Creator, he argues, and since we are "rebels" whose self-wills are "inflamed and swollen with years of usurpation," this process of self-surrender is difficult. It is, in fact, a "kind of death." The "bitter, prolonged rage at every thwarting," the "burst of passionate tears," the "black, Satanic wish to kill or die rather than to give in" that characterizes us as children merely takes a more subtle form in adults (*PP*, 91). That is why God must break us by inflicting suffering. We will not surrender so long as we labor under the illusion that all is well. The purpose of pain and suffering is to shatter this illusion. Pain is "God's megaphone" (*PP*, 95). He must make our lives less agreeable by removing all false sources of happiness. This does not show that God is evil; on the contrary, it is just here, where his providence seems most cruel, that the divine humility deserves the most praise. If God were proud, he would not so resolutely pursue creatures who prefer everything else to him. But he is not proud; "He stoops to conquer" (*PP*, 97). The creature's illusion must be shattered for the creature's sake. Far from counting against the goodness of God, pain and suffering are evidence *for* it. Like good parents, God would rather see us suffer, even suffer much, than be happy "in contemptible and estranging modes." In short, when one scratches beneath the surface of things, pain and suffering prove to be the logical corollaries of God's love—part of the "compliment" he has paid us. It is only because we are sinners in flight from him that we find the compliment "intolerable."

A number of objections have been put forth in response to this argument of Lewis's. Some insist that God could have created human beings in such a way that they always freely chose the good, and that therefore the mere fact that they were free would not entail the possibility of evil.[5] Others claim that the existence of avoidable evil cannot be justified simply on the ground that it constitutes the only condition for the attainment of higher goods such as the voluntary turning of a creature to its Creator.[6] Still others point out that, at best, arguments like Lewis's account only for evils directly or indirectly traceable to man and leave unexplained others that predate him or are not traceable to him at all.[7] Finally, some argue that empirical observation reveals that the response to pain and suffering is often not a return to God but a defection from the faith, and that therefore God's purpose of recalling individuals to himself by sending them affliction is constantly frustrated.[8] I do not want to avail myself of any of these arguments, for regardless of their validity, they do not begin to point out the serious problems in Lewis's argument.

The claim that not even Omnipotence can create the kind of world the skeptic has in mind depends for its plausibility on the mistaken assumption that certain facts that are true of our world are necessarily and "inexorably" true of *any* world. Of course fire burns *given the way things are now*. But an omnipotent God is bound neither by the present properties of matter nor by the causal laws now in operation. He could have created the universe in any way he saw fit. Man could have been created without the capacity for pain or with a much higher pain threshold. While the resulting creature would have been different from us, it would in no way have had to be self-contradictory. We can therefore grant Lewis's general claim that any world must have *some* "fixed" character without having to grant his specific claim that things must have their present characters. Their natures could vary enormously without undermining in the slightest the permanent "neutral field" that Lewis insists is necessary in order for there to be a world at all.

Furthermore, it is simply not true that if God had created the world differently, he would have ruled out the possibility of human freedom. Those who try to account for the existence of evil by appealing to the concept of free will habitually imply that freedom is an all-or-nothing affair, that men are either wholly free or not free at all. They fail to recognize that human freedom is necessarily restricted, a matter of degree. No one is wholly free. But the mere fact that we are not free to do some things is in no way incompatible with our being free to do other things. However God might have created the world, some freedom would have been eliminated because certain actions would have been ruled out. For example, God created men without wings, but we do not complain that we have been deprived of the freedom to fly unaided. Why, then, should we complain that if God had created us without pain receptors, we would have been deprived of the freedom to feel pain and of the possibility of being perfected by suffering? No doubt, if we could fly unaided, we would be able to perform more evil actions than are possible now. Hence, the fact that we cannot fly unaided deprives us not only of our freedom to fly but also of our freedom to do all the additional evil acts we could have done with our increased speed and mobility. By creating us unable to fly unaided, therefore, God arbitrarily restricted the number of evil acts we could perform. Since this is so, and would remain so *however* he had created us, why did he not restrict still further the evils we can presently do? It cannot be argued that this would have deprived us of complete freedom, for God has already done that.

The whole issue of free will in the all-or-nothing sense is a red herring. Since any world God creates necessarily rules out some actions and thereby deprives men of some freedom, would not a good and omnipotent God create a world in which there was just that degree of evil required for men to be free? And are not the evils of our world far in excess of that minimal requirement?

Such a world would also contain much less pain and suffering. Recall Lewis's remark about the wooden beam. If I were to hit you over the head, as things are now, it would hurt considerably. To prevent this, however, God need not intervene by altering the structure of matter and making the beam "soft as grass." Why not just make you in such a way that it does not hurt? Or hurts less? For that matter, why should there be any pain at all? These suggestions involve no contradictions. Since they do not, Lewis's definition of omnipotence as the power to do everything except that which involves a contradiction is irrelevant. Nothing I have said requires any flouting of the laws of logic. So, since logical impossibilities alone provide insurmountable obstacles to omnipotence, what is the problem? If God could have created things differently, why didn't he? Whatever answer one gives, it cannot be Lewis's. His own examples undercut his thesis. All of them show very clearly that it *is* logically possible for God to cause trees to crowd together to form a shade and for wood to become soft as grass. If that is so, what is there to prevent fire from producing a pleasant sensation at all distances? Lewis cannot say that we need pain receptors because it is the nature of fire to burn and the nature of man to be capable of feeling pain. Given two things between which there are "relative" impossibilities, all Omnipotence has to do is change the nature of those things or, better still, foresee the problem before creating them. If these proposed alterations of the "fixed" natures of things really offended against the laws of logic, Lewis could not have made use of the delightful examples scattered throughout his discussion of omnipotence. In fact, he has made a good start on providing us with an imaginative glimpse of the kind of world that the skeptic has in mind. Is it not reasonable to think that a good and omnipotent God would have carried such a project to its completion? What the skeptic wants to know is why he has not done so.

Here someone might reply, "If God had removed all pain from the world, he could no longer shatter our illusion that all is well and thereby succeed in recalling us to himself. For that to occur, pain is necessary." But can God not shatter men's illusions without inflicting pain? Is Omnipotence limited to a single option? Well, only if all others either involve a logical impossibility or deprive human beings of their freedom. And do they? Clearly not. God could have created human beings in such a way that they would have returned to him as the result of many other things: boredom, frustration, noise, depression, and so on. He need not have sent pain; he could simply have withheld pleasure. There are, of course, two replies to this. One is that we are so fallen that we would prefer any amount of boredom and frustration to God. The other is that even if these other things did succeed in bringing us back to God, it would not be as the result of a free choice. We would simply have had no alternative. A world as depressing and frustrating as all that would have coerced us into returning to God.

What if we grant for the sake of argument that the kind of world I have just described would deprive men of their freedom. Does Lewis's solution avoid this? Consider the case of truly hard-core sinners who will not turn to God except in response to pain—prolonged and excruciating pain. What if they finally do turn to God as a result? Will they have done so freely? No. An analogy may help. I ask you for information that I know you possess.

You refuse. So I inflict pain on you until you tell me everything I want to know. Have you imparted this information freely? No you have not. It was the pain that brought you to terms. The same is true of the pain-racked sinners who finally turn to God as a result of their pain. Put it this way. Why would a good and omnipotent God create free creatures with real alternatives from which to choose and then by the infliction of pain and suffering systematically attempt to nullify their options in the hope of restricting them to the one desired? In such a state of affairs, it would be idle to speak of free choice. This remains true despite Lewis's remarks about the divine humility. Most of us, he declares, would not have one another on such terms, but God will, and this reveals how he "stoops to conquer." This fine phrase may easily obscure the nature of the terms in question. They are causal terms. It is not as if pain-racked people freely decide to repent and return to their Creator. They are compelled to do so. Lewis gives this away himself without realizing that he is thereby sawing off the branch on which he had been sitting. He cheerfully assures us that God is prepared to accept sinners "who prefer everything else to Him." But if I prefer *everything* else to God, how can anyone say that I have freely chosen him? You might as well claim that I freely choose to hand over my money at gunpoint.

Like deathbed conversions or promises made in foxholes under heavy shelling, such "turnings to God" are suspect. Behavior like this cannot plausibly be described as the result of a free choice. In such cases, we have been reduced to a single alternative, and one alternative is not an alternative at all. If the concept of a grandfather in heaven who wants nothing more than to see us enjoying ourselves trivializes the meaning of the term *good,* surely the concept of a God who deprives us of every available alternative so that we will freely turn to him equally trivializes the meaning of the term *free.*

Turning from omnipotence to goodness, one is struck by Lewis's eagerness to strip the terms *good* and *love* of their usual connotations and to replace them with severer meanings. Everyone will, of course, immediately grant that parents often "correct," "chastise," and "punish" their children, and that, at least to the child, love often *appears* to be different from "mere kindness." But it by no means follows that parents would rather see their children "suffer much" than be happy "in contemptible and estranging modes" (*PP*, 41). It is hard to know what Lewis is driving at here. What "modes" does he have in mind?

Perhaps he simply meant that many parents would rather see their children suffer much than do what is morally wrong. To take an example from the time Lewis was writing *The Problem of Pain*, it seems reasonable to suppose that many parents in Nazi Germany might have preferred to see their children stand up to their government in protest of its "contemptible and estranging" policies of race hatred, even if such a protest led to imprisonment or worse, rather than see them capitulate to (and thus help to perpetuate) such political evil.

At the same time, it seems doubtful that this is all that Lewis meant. His primary contention in this context is not that heroic suffering is better than decadent happiness, but rather that many things we ordinarily regard as good are not good at all and that God cannot therefore be faulted for failing to keep us well supplied with them. This, of course, is a dangerous doctrine. And it becomes even more dangerous when I begin visiting my children with my own version of the intolerable compliment in order to ensure that they have what is "really" good for them rather than what they want. One thing is certain in any case: were I to become "exacting" with them in Lewis's awful sense, I am confident that they would not rejoice in their newly acquired discovery that I "really" loved them. Nor do I believe that such a failure to rejoice would be a sign of some juvenile deficiency in them. When love is seen as intolerable, two assessments are always possible: the recipient may be infantile and impossibly self-willed, or the parental overtures may not in fact be manifestations of love.

Lewis, of course, faults the recipient. These self-indulgent people, he says, want a grandfather in heaven, a senile benevolence who caters to their every need and spoils them rotten with good things. Is Lewis right about this? In certain moods such a prospect does seem rather attractive, but are we to suppose that this is an accurate description of the settled attitude of the entire human race? And that it justifies Lewis in invoking the Consuming Fire that somehow deigns to love such incorrigible adolescents? Or is he just having more fun "exposing" the ridiculous theology that "lurks" in the minds of "most people"?

It is perhaps worth observing that many diligent and morally earnest men and women whose lives are undone by pain and suffering do not fall into this facile category. Wanting the best for one's family and working hard to achieve it are not quite the same as wanting a grandfather in heaven. Nor does living one's life by trying to honor one's long-term commitments warrant the following sort of characterization:

> My own experience is something like this. I am progressing along the path of life in my ordinary contentedly fallen and godless condition, absorbed in a merry meeting with my friends for the morrow or a bit of work that tickles my vanity to-day, a holiday or a new book, when suddenly a stab of abdominal pain that threatens serious disease, or a headline in the newspapers that threatens us all with destruction, sends this whole pack of cards tumbling down. At first I am overwhelmed, and all my little happinesses look like broken toys. Then, slowly and reluctantly, bit by bit, I try to bring myself into the frame of mind that I should be in at all times. . . . And perhaps, by God's grace, I succeed, and for a day or two become a creature consciously dependent on God. . . . But the moment the threat is withdrawn, my whole nature leaps back to the toys; I am even anxious, God forgive me, to banish from my mind the only thing that supported me under the threat. . . . God has had me for but forty-eight hours and then only by dint of taking everything away from me. Let Him but sheathe that sword for a moment and I behave like a puppy when the hated bath is over—I shake myself as dry as I can and race off to reacquire my comfortable dirtiness, if not in the nearest manure heap, at least in the nearest flower bed. *(PP,* 106-7)

Unburdened of this "confession," Lewis goes on to declare that is why "tribulations can never cease" until God sees to it that we are "completely remade."

How could Lewis so flippantly generalize from his own condition to that of the human race as a whole? The prior question, of course, is whether that was how Lewis really behaved. Were his apologetic books and all those thousands of letters to correspondents from the four corners of the earth really written during abdominal attacks and reluctantly sandwiched between wanton dashes to manure heaps and flower beds? I cannot believe it. Passages such as this one contain nothing more than ingenuous posturing. I will therefore ignore this "contentedly fallen and godless" caricature that Lewis has substituted for real men and women and try, amid all this mirth, to conduct a serious inquiry into how pain and suffering are supposed to shatter our illusions and thereby reveal a loving intention on the part of their sender.

Following most philosophers and theologians, Lewis divides evils into two kinds: moral evils, which are traceable to man's abuse of freedom, and natural evils, which are not. Notice first that most if not all moral evils are our own fault. "It is men, not God, who have produced racks, whips, prisons, slavery, guns, bayonets, and bombs," he says, and it is "by human stupidity" that we have poverty and overwork (*PP*, 89). One can only marvel at the brevity with which Lewis solves problems even when he is not handicapped by strictly enforced time limits. As for racks, slavery, guns, bayonets, bombs, and all the rest, it would seem that not even Omnipotence can eliminate them. Such remedial intervention, in addition to depriving us of our freedom, would be bad for us; it would amount to no more than the sentimental indulgences of a "senile benevolence," a grandfather in heaven. Men would, of course, be happier if God intervened, but their happiness would then be of that spurious and reprehensible variety that revolts Lewis.

Concerning natural evils, which are not traceable to men, Lewis appears to be of two minds. Sometimes he is content to say that God allows these evils, but that they originate with Satan and his hosts. (He notes in passing that there is no evidence against the existence of devils, just a "climate of opinion" unfavorable to belief in them.)[9] But the main argument of *The Problem of Pain* is much bolder: God does not just allow evils; he sends them. They are his "instrument" *(PP,* 93). It follows that, contrary to what we had been led to believe earlier, God does not work within the limits imposed by the "fixed" and "inexorable" natures of things after all. Lewis's view of divine goodness requires him to affirm the very thesis that his view of divine omnipotence has required him to deny: God *does* constantly intervene in the world by performing the very remedial actions that were earlier ruled out.

This brings us to the Shattering Thesis. According to Lewis, God sends us pain and suffering in order to shatter our illusions and recall us to himself. Many dispute this claim. For the sake of argument, however, I want to accept it in order to see what happens if it is consistently applied.

Lewis endorses the Shattering Thesis without qualification. He does not claim that *some* pain is inflicted in order to recall its victims to God; he claims that this is true of all pain. Since all men have drifted from God, all must be recalled. Some will, of course, respond more quickly than others—either to mild pain or possibly even to gentle, nonpainful experiences such as Joy. But what of the more difficult cases? Clearly sterner measures are required for them—such as the infliction of pain.

But this view runs into trouble with the facts. Some people who do not suffer seem far from God while others who do suffer seem close to him. There are flourishing atheists and terminally ill believers. Yet if we accept Lewis's argument, we must conclude that those who suffer only appear to be close to God but in fact are not—otherwise why do they suffer? We must also conclude that those who do not suffer only appear to have drifted from God but in fact have not. Furthermore, the more you suffer, the further from God you are; and the less you suffer, the closer you are. Finally, the more you suffer, the more God loves you, and the less you suffer, the less he loves you, since it is those we love that we punish and those to whom we are indifferent that we allow to be happy in contemptible and estranging modes.

Some may protest that it is presumptuous to draw these inferences, but how can we avoid them? Lewis's thesis is that pain is God's instrument for recalling to himself those who have drifted away. If he had wished to qualify his thesis, surely he would have done so. Since he did not, we must accept it as it stands. I agree, of course, that my inferences are outrageous—not only absurd but heartless. But that is exactly the point. The fact that everyone, religious or not, recoils from applying Lewis's theory reveals better than anything else what is wrong with it. The trouble is not that it fails to explain anything; on the contrary, it explains so much that we are loath to apply it to the very cases it was designed to illuminate. Although someone may claim to accept the theory on some rarified theological plain, it cannot be taken seriously in real cases. Only so long as one talks idly about Suffering rather than sufferers; about "fallen creatures" rather than wives, husbands, children, and friends; about abstractions like "illusions" and "compliments" rather than those utterly concrete persons to whom our lives are fully committed does such an argument seem plausible.

Try spending the night in the children's ward of a hospital or an afternoon among the terminally ill. Try persuading yourself that in feeling compassion for those hopeless creatures for whom life holds in store no merry meetings with their friends, no moments of happy love, landscapes, symphonies, football matches, or baths, whose lives are over—in some cases before they have even begun—try persuading yourself that in feeling compassion for them you are attaching trivial meanings to the words *good* and *love*.[10] Finally, try convincing yourself that this tragic sea of sufferers lying there without hope, in some cases even without friends, are to be accounted for in terms of illusions that still need shattering. In such immediate contexts Lewis's abstract pontifications begin to seem not only callously inappropriate but morally repugnant.

We have already observed Lewis declaring that the lesson of the book of Job is that God reproves those who "palter" with ordinary moral standards in an attempt to justify his ways to man, and that he approves of those who accept these standards and, in terms of them, "hotly criticize" divine justice. This is most peculiar. What we find in *The Problem of Pain* is a paradigm of such paltering. In this book, there is not a trace of criticism of divine justice on the basis of ordinary moral standards. On the contrary, revised standards are constantly being pressed upon us. Lewis even warns us at the outset that he will be asking us to accept new meanings for every crucial term he plans to discuss—and all of this in a sustained effort to do what God is alleged to reprove us for doing: justifying his ways to man!

Meanwhile, whatever became of Lewis's professed Platonism, of those moral standards that we are told belief in Christianity does not require us to lay aside? Where is that *recognizable* goodness we were promised? How is obedience to a Being who can, but does not, eliminate avoidable suffering different from obedience to "a cosmic Fiend"? How is Lewis's view with its new meanings for *good* and *love* different from the Ockhamist view he deplores? In *The Problem of Pain* we are confronted with an apologist emphatically endorsing a view that he almost immediately lays aside in favor of a position that differs only semantically from the one he claims to reject. By the time he has finished, our "black" *has* become God's "white," and moral standards *have* been reversed. What we call suffering, Lewis calls having our illusions shattered. What we call happiness, Lewis calls self-indulgence. What we call a moral outrage, Lewis calls a compliment. What we call kindness, Lewis calls indifference. What we call cruelty, Lewis calls love.

No one has written more forcefully about the requirement of recognizable divine goodness and the ordinary meanings of ethical terms than John Stuart Mill, that "honest doubter" whose inability to believe, Lewis speculates, will be "forgiven and healed":

> If in ascribing goodness to God I do not mean what I mean by goodness; if I do not mean the goodness of which I have some knowledge, but an incomprehensible attribute of an incomprehensible substance, which for aught I know may be a totally different quality from that which I love and venerate . . . what do I mean by calling it goodness? and what reason have I for venerating it? . . . To say that God's goodness may be different in kind from man's goodness, what is it but saying, with a slight change of phraseology, that God may possibly not be good? To assert in words what we do not think in meaning, is as suitable a definition as can be given of a moral falsehood. . . . If, instead of the "glad tidings" that there exists a Being in whom all the excellences which the highest human mind can conceive, exist in a degree inconceivable to us, I am informed that the world is ruled by a being whose attributes are infinite, but what they are we cannot learn, nor what are the principles of his government, except that "the highest human morality which we are capable of conceiving" does not sanction them; convince me of it, and I will bear my fate as I may. But when I am told that I must believe this, and at the same time call this being by the names which express and affirm the highest human morality, I say in plain terms that I will not. Whatever power such a being may have over me, there is one thing which he shall not do: he shall not compel me to worship him. I will call no being good, who is not what I mean when I apply that epithet to my fellow-creatures; and if such a being can sentence me to hell for not so calling him, then to hell I will go.[11]

Mill's forthright refusal to worship a being to whom the ordinary meaning of *good* does not apply should not be piously dismissed as an unprecedented display of human wickedness, for it is nothing but a reaffirmation of Lewis's own expressed unwillingness to worship an "omnipotent Fiend" who is not good *in our sense* (*PP*, 37). The fact is that Lewis's professed Platonism leads straight to the conclusion that Mill so rigorously draws. To avoid it, he has to redefine all of his crucial terms. Language has to be overhauled in the interests of the religious beliefs he is determined to salvage. It is Mill who really champions the Platonic view that Lewis claims to hold but in fact abandons the moment his theology requires him to do so.

The following dilemma can therefore be formulated: either Lewis is a Platonist or he is not. If he is, then he should insist upon the ordinary meanings of ethical terms and draw whatever conclusions about God's goodness they require. If he is not, then he is of course free to redefine ethical terms in any way he sees fit. But in redefining them, he is no longer operating within our shared moral vocabulary; and the more he assures us that his revised meanings convey "deeper" insights, the more he reveals that he is again trying to have it both ways.

Chapter Eight

FIDEISM

Lewis believed that the weight of the evidence is in favor of Christianity and that it is only for this reason that the apologist can rationally ask anyone to accept it. This view is rejected by most contemporary American and British philosophers of religion on the ground that the very attempt to evaluate religious claims in terms of empirical evidence is mistaken in principle and betrays a deep misunderstanding of religious belief. In their opinion, Lewis was an old-fashioned apologist saddled with an outdated method. It is worth the effort to work at understanding what is at issue here, for only then can we see where Lewis stands in relation to the contemporary debate. We must therefore turn from his writings to a brief survey of the course of recent Anglo-American philosophy.

Traditional philosophers had debated the truth-claims of the Christian religion. Believers had set forth arguments in the hope of establishing these claims, and unbelievers had responded with counterarguments designed to undermine and refute them. Neither party to the discussion ever doubted for a moment the apparent truism that Christianity is either true or false. The only question was: Who is right, the believers or the skeptics?

All this changed very abruptly in 1936 when A. J. Ayer published a little book entitled *Language, Truth and Logic,* in which he set forth the main tenets of the school of philosophy known as Logical Positivism. There had, of course, been positivists of sorts before, but the Logical Positivism of Ayer was not just a new name for old ways of thinking. Although based on the views of the eighteenth-century empiricist David Hume, it embodies a radically new set of doctrines. It is "positivistic" in that it regards the empirical and observational method of science as the paradigm of, and basis for, all genuine knowledge. It is "logical" in that it conceives of philosophy as the analysis of language in general and of meaning in particular. Ayer himself was convinced that most traditional disputes between philosophers had been as unwarranted as they were unfruitful. Unlike the natural sciences, which make constant progress and bring about significant advances in human knowledge, philosophy appeared to him to have made little progress since its beginnings in Greece more than two thousand years ago. Ayer diagnosed these depressing symptoms quite simply. The illness that afflicted philosophy was not caused by the fact that philosophical problems are more difficult than scientific problems but by the fact that philosophers had never been able to agree on a satisfactory method. The cure prescribed by *Language, Truth and Logic* involves massive surgery.

Ayer's fundamental criticism of previous philosophers is not that their views are false. His charge is more serious. He maintains that their views are worse than false; they are meaningless. What was needed, he thought, was a criterion that would enable us to determine which statements are empirically meaningful and express genuine propositions, and which are not. The criterion he proposed is the now-notorious Verification Principle:

> We say that a sentence is factually significant to any given person, if, and only if, he knows how to verify the proposition which it purports to express—that is, if he knows what observations would lead him . . . to accept the proposition as being true, or reject it as being false.

What happens if this condition is not satisfied? Ayer did not hesitate to tell us:

> If, on the other hand, the putative proposition is of such a character that the assumption of its truth, or falsehood, is consistent with any . . . future experience, then . . . it is . . . a mere pseudo-proposition. The sentence expressing it may be emotionally significant . . . but it is not literally significant.[1]

Unverifiable statements are meaningless, nonsensical. Since no sense experience is relevant to determining their truth-values, they are not statements at all, but pseudo-statements. They have no factual content. They say nothing.

With the Verification Principle as his logical scalpel, Ayer began to operate. His plan was to eliminate metaphysics and thereby remove the diseased tissue from the body of philosophy. If what remained was almost unrecognizable, it would at least be healthy. By a metaphysical statement Ayer meant a statement that appears to assert some important truth about the world but is in fact unverifiable and therefore only contributes to the vast accumulation of nonsense that the human race has managed to produce in the name of philosophy. When confronted with any sentence that purports to assert a fact about the world, he argued, we must ask whether it is empirically verifiable. If it is, well and good. If not, then it is a metaphysical statement and must be rejected forthwith.

> The metaphysician . . . does not intend to write nonsense. He lapses into it through being deceived by grammar. . . . It is true, however, that although the greater part of metaphysics is merely the embodiment of humdrum errors, there remain a number of metaphysical passages which are the work of genuine mystical feeling. . . . But, as far as we are concerned, the distinction between the kind of metaphysics that is produced by a philosopher who has been duped by grammar, and the kind that is produced by a mystic . . . is of no great importance: what is important to us is to realize that even the utterances of the metaphysician who is attempting to expound a vision are literally senseless. . . . [2]

The implications of this principle for religious language are grim. Since statements about God cannot be empirically verified, such religious utterances as "God exists" or "God loves the world" are dismissed as pseudo-statements. Ayer minces no words: Since the theist "says nothing about the world, [he] cannot be justly accused of saying anything false. . . . It is only when [he] claims that in asserting the existence of a transcendent God he is expressing a genuine proposition that we are entitled to disagree with him." The theist who claims this is deceiving himself. "Those philosophers who fill their books with assertions that they intuitively 'know' this or that religious 'truth' are merely providing material for the pyschoanalyst."[3] Claims about God can be neither believed nor disbelieved, because they are neither true nor false. Since its claims are meaningless, theism does not so much as achieve the dignity of being an error.

Ayer's critique of religious language elicited a great deal of discussion. Few found his analysis wholly convincing, and many repudiated it altogether. At the same time, a survey of the philosophical journals of the next several years reveals that *Language, Truth and Logic* did manage to unsettle many whom it had failed to convince. In review after review, one detects a marked impatience with Ayer coupled with a jittery eagerness to be rid of the Verification Principle without having shown what was wrong with it. Apologists grew fond of assuring their opponents as well as one another that religious claims are verifiable on a "deeper" level of experience than the merely empirical, although no one seemed entirely clear about what this level is nor particularly helpful in explaining how one might go about defending such a claim.

Collectively these reactions signaled that all was not well within the citadel of Christian apologetics. Although Ayer could not be tolerated for a minute, he had nevertheless scaled a wall that one would have thought too foolhardy to risk. What? The language of religion nonsensical? The claim seemed too bizarre to take seriously. Yet Ayer seemed correct in saying that statements about God could not be empirically verified. To abandon the empirical content of religious language thus seemed as necessary as it did unsatisfactory. It was frankly embarrassing to find oneself reduced to logically suspect allusions to some "deeper" level of experience. Such rhetoric rendered one vulnerable to the charge of having been the unwitting victim of a pious delusion, and indeed suggested that all religious belief might simply be neurotic.

Apologists hardly had time to catch their theological second wind before Antony Flew launched an even more numbing critique of religious language. Unlike Ayer, who had insisted that religious language be verifiable, Flew contented himself with the requirement that it be falsifiable. Whereas Ayer had made verifiability the criterion of meaningfulness as such, Flew set forth the Falsification Criterion as the criterion of *empirical* meaningfulness. He did not claim that religious language is wholly meaningless, only that it is factually meaningless. Since a correct understanding of "Flew's Challenge" depends on a careful reading of the *ipsissima verba* of the original argument, it is necessary to quote his much-quoted words once more.

But let us confine ourselves to the cases where those who utter [religious] sentences intend them to express assertions. . . . Suppose then that we are in doubt as to what someone who gives vent to an utterance is asserting, or suppose that, more radically, we are sceptical as to whether he is really asserting anything at all, one way of trying to understand (or perhaps it will be to expose) his utterance is to attempt to find what he would regard as counting against, or as being incompatible with, its truth. . . . And if there is nothing which a putative assertion denies then there is nothing which it asserts either: and so it is not really an assertion. . . . Now it often seems to people who are not religious as if there was no conceivable event or series of events the occurrence of which would be admitted by sophisticated religious people to be a sufficient reason for conceding "There wasn't a God after all" or "God does not really love us then." Someone tells us that God loves us as a father loves his children. We are assured. But then we see a child dying of inoperable cancer of the throat. His earthly father is driven frantic in his efforts to help, but his Heavenly Father reveals no obvious sign of concern. Some qualification is made—God's love is "not a merely human love" or it is "an inscrutable love," perhaps—and we realize that such sufferings are quite compatible with the truth of the assertion that "God loves us as a father. . . ." We are reassured again. But then perhaps we ask: what is this assurance of God's (appropriately qualified) love worth, what is this apparent guarantee really a guarantee against? Just what would have to happen . . . to entitle us to say "God does not love us" or even "God does not exist"?[4]

The challenge may be expressed as follows: Any statement that puts forth a genuine truth-claim about the world must satisfy the requirement of falsifiability—that is, it must exclude something; there must be some fact or set of facts that, if shown to be true, would count against the truth of the statement and force the speaker to withdraw it as mistaken. If this requirement is not satisfied, if nothing could conceivably count against the statement, its factual content will quickly evaporate.

Flew argues that religious believers systematically violate the falsification requirement by their unwillingness to allow anything to count against their assertions. But they pay an enormous price. Their statements are thereby qualified so thoroughly that they eventually die "the death of a thousand qualifications." To believers who insist that nothing could ever bring them to deny that God loves the world and that they will continue to assert this no matter what happens, Flew replies that this is not an admirable profession of faith but a plain demonstration of the fact that statements such as "God loves the world" have no factual content. By making their statements unfalsifiable, believers see to it that they become vacuous.

What would you make of an insurance agent who told you that although your policy did not provide for collisions, for injuries sustained in collisions, for vandalism, or for theft, you were nevertheless fully covered? Would you not ask, "What is the difference between *that* kind of 'coverage' and no coverage at all?" The same problem arises for someone who asserts that God loves the world, but then goes on to explain that this does not mean that there will be no more war, cancer, spinal meningitis, floods, earthquakes, plane wrecks, rapes, or epidemics. Such a claim suffers the same fate as that of the insurance agent. We must again ask, "What is the difference between *that* kind of 'love' and no love at all?"

The response to Flew was mixed. To some, he had simply dethroned A. J. Ayer as the English-speaking world's most obnoxious philosopher; and like Ayer before him, Flew and his criterion were roundly denounced. The Falsification Criterion was reviled as a thinly disguised version of Logical Positivism "outfitted in new clothes" and pronounced "reductionist" in intent.[5] Flew himself was pilloried for having "rigged the rules of the game," for having "ignored" the conceptual complexity of religious language, and for being "content" to use John Wisdom's suggestive Parable of the Gardener, on which his analysis had been partly based, for his own (apparently dark) purposes.[6] Not since the days of *Language, Truth and Logic* had a philosopher been so widely suspected of being up to no good and made the object of such overt and unpropitiable ferocity. It is a mark of his personal (albeit nonreligious) stature that Flew never saw fit to reply to his religious critics in kind. "By their fruits shall you know them" remains a bitter secular truth.

There were also many sober responses to Flew's Challenge. But these were the most surprising of all. Instead of a series of counterarguments defending the factual content of religious language, the initial response took the form of a straightforward concession. Almost in unison, numerous Anglo-American apologists abandoned traditional methods of defending the faith and, following R. M. Hare, acknowledged that, on the ground he had marked out, Flew was "completely victorious." Accordingly, the logically suspect claim that religious language consists of empirically meaningful assertions was quietly withdrawn. Thus deprived of its cognitive status, it appeared that religious language had suffered a deathblow.

No appearance was ever more misleading. Almost overnight a new apologetic was born. It is no exaggeration to say that Flew's application of the Falsification Criterion of meaning to religious language provided the stimulus for a species of philosophical theology without precedent in the entire history of philosophy. From its very inception, the new apologetic movement was a self-consciously post-Flew phenomenon, a philosophical countermovement whose many and otherwise widely divergent participants discovered a common identity in their shared belief that the meaningfulness of religious language could only be elucidated by abandoning its fact-stating character and appealing to a host of startling conceptual innovations. The new apologists gave every indication of having perceived that desperate remedies were in order, and the unsuspecting philosophical public was shortly given notice that the true religious believer does not intend to be stating facts or to be making empirical assertions, and that to suppose otherwise is simply to betray an incorrigible descriptivist obsession. In working out these unpromising claims, the new apologists turned to the writings of J. L. Austin and Ludwig Wittgenstein, neither of whom had written directly on religious subjects but whose work nevertheless seemed to provide the conceptual tools required for this wholesale rehabilitation of religious language.

Austin had made a great deal of the "descriptive fallacy"— the misguided tendency to think that the truth-stating function of language is its only or even its most important function. In a series of influential papers, he offered detailed analyses that show that language actually functions in diverse ways and that its descriptive or truth-stating function is only one among many.[7] One of Austin's most significant discoveries was that we not only *say* things with words but *do* things with them too. When used in appropriate circumstances, certain linguistic expressions constitute the performance of actions. He had initially focused his attention on the performative function of language and had spoken of "performative utterances." By this he meant locutions that *in our act of uttering them* constitute the performance of the action indicated by the verb. To say "I promise" is to promise; to say "I baptize" is to baptize. In his later investigations, Austin paid less attention to performative verbs and concentrated on what he called "speech-acts." This broader notion includes not only performative utterances but many other types of linguistic performances. To perform a speech-act, it is not necessary to perform the specific action indicated by the verb; the same verb may be used to perform a variety of actions. For example, to say "I know" in response to your daughter's report that the cat is dead could be the speech-act of comforting her, of acknowledging that your worst fears had just been confirmed, of imploring her to spare you the heartbreaking details, or even of indicating that you wish to read the newspaper without interruption. Austin demonstrated that we do many things with words in addition to stating facts, and that an utterance that is not descriptive can still be perfectly meaningful.

Impressed by Austin's philosophical techniques, R. B. Braithwaite was one of the first to apply them to religious language.[8] It is a mistake, he argues, to think that religious statements are descriptive. Those who want to make empirical facts relevant to the meaning of religious statements but at the same time maintain those statements in the face of contrary evidence are indulging in "double-think." They want religious statements to be factual but irrefutable. This is now known to be a blunder. Most "educated believers at the present time" no longer think that God's existence is subject to empirical tests or that belief in God involves evidence. They have long ago given up the fact-stating function of religious language.

In explaining how religious statements do function, Braithwaite shifts to what he thought to be the more solid ground provided by moral statements, the function of which is not to state facts but to guide conduct. Since it is by appeal to this function that we establish the meaningfulness of moral statements, we need only assimilate religious statements to moral ones and we will have saved the day. This is exactly what Braithwaite does. The "primary use" of religious assertions is "to announce allegiance to a set of moral principles," he argues. So to say "God loves the world" is not to make a factual claim about the deity; it is to perform the speech-act of announcing one's intention to live an agapeistic life. Although such an announcement has its roots "in the Christian story," it is "not necessary . . . for the asserter . . . to believe in the truth of the story. . . . What is necessary is that the story should be entertained in thought. . . . [The Christian] need not believe that the empirical propositions presented by the stories correspond to empirical fact."⁹

R. M. Hare put forth another equally nondescriptivist analysis. He, too, rejects the view that religious language consists of empirical assertions, and argues that philosophers must fasten upon some other logical feature if they are to account for its meaning. He concludes that the meaning of religious language is to be found in the attitudes (he calls them "*bliks*") it enables a person to adopt.¹⁰ His discussion of St. Paul's conversion reveals how far he was prepared to go in order to purge religious language of every trace of the descriptivism then in disgrace.¹¹ Although it seems natural to suppose that St. Paul's conversion would have required him to change some of his factual beliefs, Hare assures us that this was not so. It is true, of course, that before his conversion St. Paul thought Jesus was an imposter whereas afterward he thought he was the Son of God, but Hare contends that this change did not involve any of his factual beliefs.

Upon hearing this, the "uneducated" believer may pardonably wonder what did change when St. Paul was converted. According to Hare, it was his attitude. Before his conversion, St. Paul already knew all of the facts about Jesus: that he was born in Bethlehem, that he had twelve disciples, that he suffered under Pontius Pilate, that he was crucified, and so on. His conversion did not consist in the acquisition of further facts in light of which he found it necessary to exchange his false belief about Jesus for a true one; rather, it consisted in adopting a different attitude toward the facts with which he was already acquainted. Similarly, when Simon Peter said, "Thou art the Christ, the Son of the living God," he was not stating a fact about Jesus; he was not *saying* something, but *doing* something—namely, performing the speech-act of worshiping.

As more and more of these jarring elucidations of religious language were put forward, it began to look as if the practitioners of this kind of philosophical analysis preferred *any* account of religious language, no matter how bizarre, to a factual one. Willem Zuurdeeg describes religious language as "convictional" and the believer as one who assumes a convictional "stance." For Donald Evans, religious language is the language of "self-involvement." And T. R. Miles, arguably the most logic-intimidated of them all, counsels the believer to take the way of silence broken only by an occasional parable.[12]

While these sought the aid of Austin, others turned to Wittgenstein. G. E. M. Anscombe reports that Wittgenstein once remarked of his later philosophy that "Its advantage is that if you believe, say, Kant or Spinoza, this interferes with what you believe in religion, but if you believe me, nothing of the sort."[13] This characteristically compressed remark suggests that being a follower of Wittgenstein is compatible with being a religious believer. Informed sources report that Wittgenstein himself was not a believer, although Norman Malcolm observes that "there was in him, in some sense, the *possibility* of religion" and that he "looked on religion as a 'form of life' . . . in which he did not participate, but with which he was sympathetic and which greatly interested him."[14] Biography aside, many of the new apologists took Wittgenstein's remark about religion as a corollary of his views about the nature of philosophy in general, according to which philosophical analysis is a purely descriptive enterprise. Its purpose is not to impose any single criterion of meaning upon language as a whole, but by means of patient conceptual investigation, to elucidate the ordinary uses of language and the various "logics" peculiar to the diverse modes of human discourse that Wittgenstein called "language games." In a word, according to Wittgenstein, meaning is use.

Whether or not the new apologists were correct in believing that their elucidations of religious language can be legitimately derived from the writings of Wittgenstein, they themselves were convinced that their views were genuine extensions and applications of his thought. It was precisely for this reason that Kai Nielsen soon dubbed their position "Wittgensteinian Fideism."[15]

Like their Austinian counterparts, the Wittgensteinian fideists reject the view that believers employ religious language to put forth empirical assertions that must satisfy the requirement of falsifiability. It is true, of course, that believers often seem to

employ it in this way; but we must not jump to conclusions. Instead, we must follow Wittgenstein's advice that we look to see
whether they do in fact employ it in this way. Claiming to have
thus investigated, the fideists came to the conclusion that believers
do not use religious language in this way, and thus that such
language is not descriptive. Religious language, they suggested,
has its own "grammar," which must be distinguished from that
of other modes of human discourse, such as the scientific, in which
empirical evidence is of crucial importance. According to the
fideists, traditional apologists had been confused on this point.
They had proceeded on the mistaken assumption that in order
to defend Christianity as rational, one has to appeal to empirical
evidence, to "the facts," which must be understood as providing
some objective justification of or foundation for religious belief.
They did not realize that just as there is no single criterion of
meaning common to all significant statements, so there is no single
paradigm of rationality common to all inquirers. Whether
religious belief is meaningful depends on your views about meaning; whether it is rational depends on what you mean by rationality. Furthermore, the fideists held that traditional apologists had
assumed that in setting forth proofs for the existence of God, they
already knew what the term *God* meant. But this overlooks the
fact that the meaning of this term can only be learned within the
religious "form of life." For all these reasons, the fideists argued,
it is not only impossible but wrongheaded to try to provide a
philosophical "foundation" for religious belief independent of
the "language game" or "form of life" in which it finds its natural
expression. Religion neither has nor needs a justification. Religious
language is a language game that, by virtue of the fact that it is
played, constitutes an internally coherent and self-justifying mode
of discourse. Hence Wittgenstein, too, was pronounced an ally
in the campaign against the linguistic skeptic.

The success of these "ground-shifting" strategies was not
notable. Quite apart from the question of whether the writings
of Austin and Wittgenstein do in fact lend their immediate and
unqualified support to such views, the price to be paid for holding
them is excessively high. Flew himself marveled at the apparent
ease with which the new apologists surrendered the distinctively
Christian content of the language of faith. It was not long before
similar protests were recorded by equally disgruntled believers who

found themselves at one with the skeptic in thinking that these conciliatory and *ad hoc* metareligious defenses are dubious not only as plausible explications of Austinian and Wittgensteinian philosophical techniques but also as satisfactory explications of the logical character and content of religious language itself.

Surely these protests are justified. Whatever Braithwaite's "educated" believers might make of the views of the fideists, the ordinary believer can make nothing of them. They simply are not elucidations of what the man in the pew means when he uses religious language. This poses a severe difficulty to which the new apologists remained puzzlingly insensitive. You cannot very well deny that religious language makes sense from without and then proceed to account for it from within in a way that is so at variance with the beliefs and linguistic practices of those very insiders whose religious language you claim to be analyzing that they uniformly reject what you say out of hand. Much less can you defend yourself by invoking Wittgenstein's dictum that one must look to see how religious language actually functions in its natural home—unless, of course, you are prepared to affirm the self-defeating principle that the very insiders whose linguistic usage embodies the paradigm of authentic meaning for which you are searching are themselves hopelessly confused. But surely such a view would herald a return to the very kind of philosophical analysis against which Wittgenstein himself had protested. In that case, the fideists would not be offering descriptive elucidations of how believers *in fact* use religious language; instead they would be offering prescriptive and revisionist proposals about how believers *ought* to use them.

Little wonder, then, that John Passmore rebukes certain admirers of Wittgenstein who "desire to be uncritically religious without ceasing to be critically philosophical," or that Dallas High laments the rise of "a whole new rash of nonsense and simple-mindedness" in contemporary discussions of religious language.[16] But it is Flew himself who puts forth the most damaging criticism of all when he points out that anyone whose religious belief neither involves nor is even intended as involving assertions about a personal Creator is surely "not a Christian at all."[17]

This charge, one of Flew's most fundamental objections to such proceedings, is designed to bring out the fact that insofar as the views of the fideists rule out such truth-claims as "God exists" and "God loves the world" they are adequate neither to the expression nor the preservation of the content of their own religious utterances. This is not only too high a price to pay; it is precisely the price one cannot pay if the term *believer* is to retain its meaning. If in saying "God loves the world" you do not intend to assert anything true, why say it at all? To this, one of Braithwaite's "educated" believers might retort that one says such things not to state facts but to comfort people. This, too, is puzzling. Surely people will be comforted by being told that God loves the world only if there really is a God who loves the world. According to the view before us, however, this distinction cannot be made; one cannot *assert* that there is a God who loves the world. In saying "God loves the world," one is only announcing the way of life he or she intends to follow. I cannot help thinking that the ordinary believer would have severe difficulties with this. Would not the troubled person in the pew who was temporarily comforted by hearing that God loved the world feel more than a little cheated if the "educated" believers, laughing hollowly, were pressed into admitting that, in saying this, they had only intended to announce their own intention to live an agapeistic life? Could there be a more misleading way of making this announcement? If this is how religious language functions, why use it at all?

On the other hand, Stanley Cavell speaks of the salutary religious effect of the Wittgensteinian recovery of Kierkegaard's insight that faith can be defended only from within and that religious believers who fail to grasp this will only help to deliver their faith "bound and gagged into the hands of philosophy."[18] D. Z. Phillips also strives mightily to provide an authentically Wittgensteinian account of religious language, and in one book after another reaffirms the fideist principle that the demand for an independent justification of religious belief is unintelligible.[19]

It is precisely this issue to which Norman Malcolm addresses himself in a curious paper entitled "Is It a Religious Belief That God Exists?"[20] Malcolm argues that belief that God exists is *not* religious, and he attempts to dispose of troublesome locutions such as "God exists" and "I know that God exists" by arguing that these are statements that philosophers make, that they do not occur within the religious language game, and that all attempts to prove that God exists involve an *abuse* of religious language. The question of God's existence makes sense only as a reply to skeptical doubts, but these doubts never arise within the religious language game; within it, the existence of God is assumed as a matter of course. Furthermore, according to Malcolm, Christians do not believe that God exists; they believe *in* God. Evidence in the philosopher's sense plays no part "in workaday religious instruction and practice." Hence, belief in God can be held in such a way that no fact of experience can falsify it. Questions about God's existence and the empirical evidence for it put in their appearance "only when language is idling."

What began, therefore, as a fundamentally defensive maneuver that struck many as little more than a series of bizarre attempts to salvage some shred of meaning from the cognitive wreckage of religious language soon came to be seen as a collection of penetrating new insights into its "real" logic. The day came when the new apologists gratefully acknowledged that Ayer and Flew, far from being the enemies of religious language, had merely underscored the urgent need for rethinking the logic of religious language and had thereby provided the occasion for recognizing that the empirical analysis of religious language had been a colossal blunder. After the dust had settled, religious philosophers reread *Language, Truth and Logic* and discovered that Ayer himself had pointed out that his view of religious language "accords with what many theists are accustomed to say themselves."[21] Had Ayer and Flew deprived religious language of its empirical character? So be it. Henceforth their critiques would be borne in mind and religious language would be reinterpreted in the light of them. With the tables thus turned, the debate between believers and skeptics assumed a new form. The typical post-Flew believer joined the skeptic in rejecting traditional apologetic methods. As a result, the few remaining traditional apologists, such as C. S. Lewis, found that they had come under attack not only from their time-honored opponents, the skeptics and the atheists, but from many fellow believers as well.

Which side of this controversy would Lewis have taken? The question suggests that he was unfamiliar with the issue and that therefore no confident answer can be given. Both conjectures are false.

It cannot, of course, be denied that Lewis did not directly participate in the contemporary religious debate, nor that many of his colleagues dismissed him on the ground that his apologetic method was hopelessly out of touch with the kind of philosophy then in favor at Oxford. But this charge loses its sting when one realizes what being *in* touch with Oxford philosophy required of an apologist. I am not referring to the writings of Austin and Wittgenstein themselves, nor am I in any way minimizing the importance of the revolution in philosophy they produced; I am speaking only of the religious ends for which their writings were employed by the new apologists. It was Lewis's commitment to traditional apologetics that distanced him from the contemporary debate. He was looked upon as a curiosity, a relic from the past who, partly out of ignorance and partly out of an unconcealed delight in holding unpopular opinions, insisted on defending Christianity by means of a discredited apologetic method. Even his friend and fellow believer Austin Farrer ruefully observed that although Lewis was a "bonny fighter," he had not kept up with developments in philosophy, that he had "dropped out of the game."[22]

What game? The contemporary apologetic game the counters of which had been provided by the conceptual tools of the new school of linguistic philosophy associated with Austin and Wittgenstein. Lewis's refusal to assimilate and employ these methods prompted Farrer to see him as a dropout, someone who stubbornly insisted on proceeding as if the crisis precipitated by Ayer and Flew had never occurred. This is a very unfair criticism. Until his death Lewis continued to play the same apologetic game he had always played, maintaining that Christianity must be either true or false. Before Ayer and Flew, he had believed the language of religion to be empirically meaningful; after them, he believed it still. Lewis refused to play by the new rules not out of sloth or ignorance but out of conviction. Farrer's glum appraisal obscures the fact that even if Lewis had diligently pored over each new development in the religious debate, there is every reason to believe that he would have continued to defend Christianity in traditional terms.

If anyone had dropped out of anything, it was the new apologists, who had abandoned the view that Christianity involves truth-claims that can be defended on empirical grounds. Lewis was convinced that the content of Christian faith does not unproblematically lend itself to the techniques of the new apologists, and he regarded their innovative analyses as but the most recent examples of the whittling process he had deplored from the very beginning. Although by 1963 the arena was mostly deserted, Lewis was still playing as hard as ever and by the same rules. In the early forties he had said,

> The great difficulty is to get modern audiences to realize that you are preaching Christianity solely and simply because you . . . think it *true*. . . . [This] forces your audience to realize that you are tied to your data just as the scientist is tied by the results of the experiments. . . . What is being discussed is a question about objective fact—not gas about ideals and points of view. *(GiD,* 90-91)

In 1963 he was still saying it:

> [Alec Vidler] wants . . . to retain some Christian doctrines. But he is prepared to scrap a good deal. "Traditional doctrines" are to be tested. Many things will have to be "outgrown" or "survive chiefly as venerable archaisms or as fairy-stories." He feels quite happy about this undefined programme of jettison because he trusts in the continued guidance of the Holy Spirit. A noble faith; provided, of course, there is any such being as the Holy Spirit. But I suppose His existence is itself one of the "traditional doctrines" which, on Vidler's premises, we might any day find we had outgrown. *(LM,* 32)

This tendency to deny or soften the objective, factual character of Christian belief remained one of Lewis's chief targets until the very end.

There is a second way of seeing the unfairness of Farrer's criticism. Although he did not publicly respond to Flew's Challenge, Lewis was well aware of the issue of falsifiability and its implications for religious belief. No one seems to have noticed that in both *Miracles* (1947) and in a 1943 paper entitled "Dogma and the Universe" Lewis had set forth his own formulation of the Falsification Criterion. He had not only grasped the logical point at issue but employed it for his own polemical purposes almost ten years before Flew published the controversial paper that almost single-handedly launched the whole contemporary discussion.

As early as 1943 Lewis had anticipated Flew's diagnosis of the "endemic" disease of language that leads to the phenomenon of death by a thousand qualifications. Here is what he wrote:

> When the doctor at a post-mortem diagnoses poison, pointing
> to the state of the dead man's organs, his argument is rational
> because he has a clear idea of that opposite state in which the
> organs would have been found if no poison were present. In
> the same way, if we use the vastness of space and the smallness
> of earth to disprove the existence of God, we ought to have
> a clear idea of the sort of universe we should expect if God
> did exist. But have we? . . . If the universe is teeming with life,
> this, we are told, reduces to absurdity the Christian claim—or
> what is thought to be the Christian claim—that man is unique,
> and the Christian doctrine that to this one planet God came
> down and was incarnate for us men and our salvation. If, on
> the other hand, the earth is really unique, then that proves that
> life is only an accidental by-product in the universe, and so
> again disproves our religion. . . . We treat God as the police
> treat a man when he is arrested; whatever He does will be used
> in evidence against Him. (*GiD*, 39–40)

This kind of objection to the Christian faith is not really based
on the observed nature of the actual universe at all, Lewis argues.
You can make it without waiting to find out what the universe
is like, for it will fit any kind of universe one chooses to imagine.
Doctors can diagnose poison without even looking at the corpse
if they have a theory of poison that they will maintain *whatever*
the state of the organ turns out to be.

What is this if not the very logical objection Flew was to make
in 1950?—except that Lewis makes it against the skeptic! Just as
a diagnosis of poison would be falsified if the state of the organs
proved to be the opposite of what the doctor had expected, so
a "diagnosis" that God does not exist would be falsified if the
empirical evidence was the opposite of what the skeptic had expected. If you disbelieve in God on the ground that life exists on
the earth alone, then the empirical discovery that the universe is
"teeming with life" falsifies your belief. If you refuse to admit
this and continue to maintain your original assertion, you thereby
reveal that it is not an empirical assertion at all but one you are
determined to maintain whatever evidence turns up, and thus your
atheism must be as vacuous as those religious utterances for which
Flew was later to chide the empirically indifferent believer. All
those who deny that God exists must be prepared to specify what
kind of evidence would require them to withdraw their claim. In
providing us with this information, they would be telling us, in

Flew's language, what would have to happen in order for them to admit that they had been mistaken. The shoe is snugly on the other foot.

In insisting that skeptics must allow something to count against their beliefs, Lewis firmly commits himself to the falsifiability requirement. But then that same requirement applies to the believer, and Lewis must be prepared to say what would have to happen in order for him to withdraw his claim that God exists. And he does. You will recall that in his essay "On Obstinacy in Belief" he claims that although believers must be obstinate in the face of apparently contrary evidence, even a great deal of it, they may not continue to put forth their assertions *no matter what*. They may not continue to believe in the teeth of uniformly contrary evidence. According to Lewis, two facts render the believer's position "tolerable." First, the evidence continues to be "mixed": along with apparently contrary evidence there is also favorable evidence. Second, believers claim to have knowledge of God by acquaintance, which enables them to appeal not only to the "logic of speculative thought" but also to the "logic of personal relations."

Since these two facts render the believer's position tolerable, it follows that if they should change, that position would become intolerable—though not immediately, of course. But in the long run, no one whose experience seemed utterly devoid of favorable evidence and the sense of God's presence could any longer rationally continue to put forth a believer's assertions. The opposite state would then obtain: the person's beliefs would have been falsified.

Although it would be misleadingly anachronistic to say that Lewis accepted Flew's Falsification Criterion and the challenge it poses, it is nevertheless perfectly accurate to claim that he was fully aware of its underlying logic and that he set forth a clear account of the kind of evidence he would have regarded as counting strongly, perhaps even decisively, against his belief in a good and loving God. Say what you will—even that his was a minority opinion based on an outdated conception of philosophy that earned for him the scorn of many of his colleagues—the fact remains that Lewis perceived with uncommon clarity that the apologist who would remain true to historic Christianity is inescapably "tied to his data."[23] Faith as trust presupposes faith as belief. Belief-in presupposes belief-that.

The falsification issue is not a purely theoretical question remote from all human concerns, but one that touches the religious life at a bedrock level. That this is so is driven home by one of Lewis's last books, *A Grief Observed*. Written shortly after the death of his wife, it is a grim and altogether remarkable account of how Lewis himself came to doubt the goodness and love of God. In the depths of his sorrow, he found that he had to come to terms with the problem of contrary evidence all over again. His desperate struggle to find a solution in which he could rest reveals that we have not heard the last of fideism.

Chapter Nine

GRIEF

Before marrying Helen Joy Davidman on April 23, 1956, at the age of 58, Lewis had been a lifelong bachelor. From all reports, the marriage was idyllic. Lewis once told his friend Nevill Coghill that "I never excepted to have, in my sixties, the happiness that passed me by in my twenties."[1] His reason for marrying her, however, was most unusual. Although it was not until 1957 that she was diagnosed as suffering from cancer, it had been apparent a year earlier that she was seriously ill. To make matters worse, in early 1956 the British Home Office had refused to renew her permit to remain in England; this meant that a dying woman with two young sons would soon have to return to America. To prevent this hardship, Lewis married her.

That this is not simply part of the growing C. S. Lewis legend is borne out by a letter in which he reflects about his marriage: "It is nice to have arrived at all this by something which began in Agape, proceeded to Philia, then became pity, and only after that, Eros" (*L*, 277–78). Soon after, his wife took a turn for the worse, and Lewis brought her home to die. Before doing so, however, a Christian wedding took place at her hospital bedside on March 21, 1957. Lewis regarded the first ceremony, performed at the Oxford registry office, as nothing more than a civil contract; before taking her into his home, he wanted to be married "in the sight of God as well as in the sight of man."[2]

Then something completely unexpected occurred. Joy Davidman Lewis's cancer went into remission. She progressed from being bedridden to being able to get around in a wheelchair to walking with a cane. She not only redecorated their home and entertained guests but periodically drove off trespassers by firing at them with a pistol.

According to Lewis's brother, three years of "complete

fulfillment" followed: "To his friends who saw them together it was clear that they not only loved but were in love with each other. It was a delight to watch them, and all the waste of Jack's years which had gone before was more than recompensed" (*L*, 23).[3] Lewis himself described his wife's sudden improvement as the closest thing to a miracle he had ever experienced,[4] and in an essay entitled "The Efficacy of Prayer" he wrote,

> I have stood beside the bedside of a woman whose thighbone was eaten through with cancer. . . . A good man laid his hands on her and prayed. A year later the patient was walking (uphill, too, and through rough woodland) and the man who had taken the last X-ray photos was saying, "These bones are as solid as rock. It's miraculous." (*WLN*, 3–4)

A holiday to Greece followed (one of her lifelong dreams), a trip that provided Lewis with "the last of the great days of perfect happiness." His essay on the efficacy of prayer appeared in 1959. Less than a year later, Joy Davidman Lewis was dead, a victim of the cancer they thought had been miraculously cured. And Lewis's faith came crashing down like "a house of cards" (*AGO*, 31). As "a safety valve against total collapse," he wrote *A Grief Observed*.

There is no case for Christianity in this book. Gone are the persuasive arguments and the witty analogies. Gone, too, are the confidence and urbanity evident in *The Problem of Pain*. The Law of Undulation is not so much as mentioned. Nor does Lewis display the slightest tendency to tell his moods "where they get off." Here we encounter only a lonely and grief-stricken man jotting down his thoughts and second thoughts under the pseudonym of N. W. Clerk.

A Grief Observed is not so much a book as a widower's diary. A few passages border on self-pity, a fact that prompted some critics to question Lewis's judgment in making his personal suffering so visible in a public document. One reviewer even accused him of spiritual exhibitionism. But such criticism is wide of the mark. Lewis fully recognized his maudlin tendencies. Then, too, if a bereaved man were to produce a masterpiece of controlled and lucid prose, some might raise their eyebrows about that and harbor doubts about his sincerity. The fact is that the book is not a pathological exercise in self-indulgence but a rational attempt to grasp the implications of suffering. Even when Lewis is at his most emotional, one does not get the impression of a man out of control. It is as if he thought that by giving his emotions their head and allowing himself to experience their full impact, almost savoring them, he could better comprehend and come to terms with his loss. The result is an unflinching book, a book of many moods, the case history of a bereavement almost wholly free of artificial attempts to be "literary." The thoughts and emotions expressed are so utterly honest that the very privacy of Lewis's experience of the many faces of grief invests it with a kind of universality that a less personal journal could never have achieved.

First of all, there is undisguised grief in this book. Lewis had no patience with "pious jaw" about God's way being the best way or with glib dismissals of death. He recoiled from "all that stuff" about reunions on that other shore. His wife had died and he mourned for her. He spoke of the "sudden jab of red-hot memory" that could at any moment turn him into a whimpering child. Her absence was like the sky—spread out over everything. He knew that the things he wanted most were the things he could never have again: "the old life, the jokes, the drinks, the arguments, the love-making, the tiny, heartbreaking commonplaces" (*AGO*, 22). But it is a grief interspersed with moments of great reflective calm:

> Did you ever know, dear, how much you took away with you when you left? You have stripped me even of my past, even of the things we never shared. Today I have been revisiting old haunts, taking one of the long rambles that made me so happy in my bachelor days. . . . Every horizon . . . summoned me into a past kind of happiness, my pre-H happiness. . . . But . . . I find that I don't want to go back again and be happy in *that* way. . . . For this fate would seem to me the worst of all; to reach a state in which my years of love and marriage should appear in retrospect a charming episode— like a holiday—that had briefly interrupted my life and returned me to normal, unchanged. (*AGO*, 48)

Apparent also is the laziness of grief tinged with just a dash of self-pity: "What does it matter now whether my cheek is rough or smooth?" (*AGO*, 8). And a touch of that enviable complacency that a good marriage can bring: " 'It was too perfect to last.' . . . As if God had said, 'Good; you have mastered that exercise. . . .

Now you are ready to go on to the next' " (*AGO*, 40). There are even traces of a lover's jealousy. Just before she died, his wife said that she was at peace with God, and Lewis touchingly adds, "She smiled, but not at me" (*AGO*, 60).

But there are also doubt, rage, and protest in this book. Seldom has a religious writer assumed such freedom in refusing to pull punches. Although others have undergone similar experiences, few have been bold enough to contradict Psalm 91. Lewis bitterly demands to know why God is "so very absent in time of trouble." When you turn to him with gratitude and praise, you will be welcomed with open arms, he protests, but "go to Him when your need is desperate, when all other help is vain, and what do you find? A door slammed in your face, and a sound of bolting and double bolting on the inside. After that, silence. You may as well turn away" *(AGO,* 9). And again, "Talk to me about the truth of religion and I'll listen gladly. Talk to me about the duty of religion and I'll listen submissively. But don't come talking to me about the consolations of religion or I shall suspect that you don't understand" (*AGO*, 23). This little book is a remarkable document in which a morally outraged believer storms the heavens for an answer to the problem of suffering. Its first two sections are a paradigm of unconcealed doubt fearlessly expressed.

But there is something else in this book—the loss, if not of faith, then at least of a belief in faith's intelligibility. Lewis did not cease to believe in God, but he gave vent to equally erosive difficulties: "The real danger is of coming to believe such dreadful things about Him. The conclusion I dread is not 'So there's no God after all,' but 'So this is what God's really like. Deceive yourself no longer' " (*AGO*, 9–10). Readers familiar with *The Problem of Pain* may be puzzled by this. After all, had not Lewis squarely faced the problem of suffering in that book? Had he not also told us in *The Four Loves* that we are not to apply to heaven for earthly comfort, and that in the end there is no earthly comfort? Clearly something had happened in the meantime. But what? How is it that the same man who had so staunchly defended God's goodness should now declare that the behavior of God resembled that of "a spiteful imbecile practicing mean jokes," "a bad God," "a Cosmic Sadist," and an "Eternal Vivisector"? Why did God now seem to have all the characteristics we ordinarily regard as evil: "unreasonableness," "vanity," "vindictiveness," "injustice," and even "cruelty" (*AGO*, 27–28)? The answer is contained in the following remark: "Sooner or later I must face the question in plain language. What reason have we, except our own desperate wishes, to believe that God is, by any standard we can conceive, 'good'? Doesn't all the *prima facie* evidence suggest exactly the opposite?" (*AGO*, 26).

You will recall that in *The Problem of Pain, Reflections on the Psalms,* and elsewhere, Lewis insists that the goodness of God must be understood in terms of our ordinary moral standards. God, he argues, must be regarded as good *in our sense,* for only then will his goodness be of a kind that we can recognize. Although many religious believers may wonder whether such a demand is permissible, Lewis considered it not only permissible but necessary. Throughout his writings he emphatically rejects the view that things are good simply because God commands them. He assures his readers again and again that Christianity does not require them to reverse their moral standards. In *Reflections on the Psalms* he goes even further and asserts that the opposite view makes of morality a "toss-up" and of God a "tyrant." It would be better, he insists, to believe in no God at all and to have no ethics than to hold such a view. Yet when in his hour of need Lewis applies these same moral standards to God, he finds him wanting. Not only does God not seem good, but the *prima facie* evidence suggests that he is evil. Hence Lewis explores the hypothesis of the Cosmic Sadist.

We need to pay the closest attention to Lewis's doubts because their real character and momentous implications are easily missed. Austin Farrer provides us with a clear statement of the usual explanation—that when his wife died Lewis was confronted with the reality about which he had so "airily theorized" in *The Problem of Pain* and found that his theories were of no consolation in his "hour of trial," so that he had to discover the "existential" solution.[5] This explanation is not only superficial but inaccurate. It overlooks what was really troubling Lewis in *A Grief Observed*—not just his wife's death (although that was horrible enough), but the circumstances that had preceded it: the false hopes, the "miraculous" cure, the sense of having been toyed with.

> What chokes every prayer . . . is the memory of all the prayers H. and I offered and all the false hopes we had. Not hopes raised merely by our own wishful thinking; hopes encouraged, even forced upon us, by false diagnoses, by X-ray photographs, by strange remissions, by one temporary recovery that might have ranked as a miracle. Step by step we were "led up the garden path." Time after time, when He seemed most gracious He was really preparing the next torture. (*AGO*, 26–27)

The wistful allusion to the one temporary recovery that "might have ranked" as a miracle is a poignant afterthought to the thanksgiving expressed in "The Efficacy of Prayer." It is also revelatory of the hurt that further reflection had only aggravated.

If, with Farrer, we restrict ourselves to Lewis's need for an "existential" solution, we will miss what is unique about this book. We will fail to grasp that what it recounts is not a purely psychological crisis of faith but a logical crisis. Lewis did not simply find it difficult to accept his wife's death and to cope with the grief that engulfed him. Her death did provide the psychological occasion for his doubts, but it did not constitute their logical ground. Lewis himself had been put to the test, but so had God's goodness. The question was not "How can I continue to force myself to believe that God is good?" but "How can I continue to *mean* it? Does the term *good* mean anything at all when applied to God?"

It is not only Lewis's expositors who have failed to diagnose the true character of his doubts. Lewis himself missed their real import. After his initial protest had spent itself, he began to wonder whether his crisis of faith had been anything more than an emotional reaction. He asked himself whether, from a rational point of view, his wife's death had introduced anything new into the problem of suffering, and he concluded that it had not. After all, he already knew that people suffered, sometimes intensely. Although things were different when it was oneself who suffered, this was not a difference "in reality but only in imagination" (*AGO*, 31).

I think Lewis was wrong about this. In saying this I fully realize that I run the risk of appearing highly presumptuous. It would be the height not only of folly but of arrogance for me to claim that I know Lewis better than he knew himself. That is not what I am claiming. I am not suggesting that Lewis's *psychological* diagnosis of himself was faulty. In saying that he was wrong in tracing his crisis of faith to his emotions, I am putting forth a claim about what we find in Parts I and II of *A Grief Observed*.

In the language of *Mere Christianity,* did Lewis's wife's death give rise to genuine logical objections to Christianity? Or did it only plunge him into an emotional crisis that, while fully understandable, was basically irrational and the result of "a mere mood"? According to Lewis, believers are confronted with a genuine objection when they find that the arguments or reasons on which their faith depends no longer provide intellectually adequate answers, when they no longer enable them to deal adequately with contrary evidence. Believers are being overcome by a mere mood, on the other hand, when they feel that their religious beliefs are false while they fail to recognize that their arguments and reasons are as solid as ever. That Lewis was psychologically devastated by his wife's death is beyond question. But is his crisis of faith to be explained simply in terms of his emotional reaction to it?

One strong *prima facie* reason for thinking so is that Lewis himself offered this explanation: if he thought so, who am I to disagree? But this is only part of the story. As one proceeds through *A Grief Observed* it becomes quite evident that Lewis was far from satisfied with this diagnosis. Having traced his crisis of faith to an emotional reaction, he did not conclude without further ado that his doubts had been irrational and that God was good after all. His difficulties remained and he continued to grope for further logical reasons for believing in God's goodness. Throughout the book Lewis grieves like a husband, but he thinks like an apologist. In light of this, we would be greatly over-simplifying matters if we accepted a psychological diagnosis he himself regarded as inconclusive. It is true that he gradually came to terms with his personal grief—by the end of the book he no longer *feels* like making the protest—but this is not enough to justify the claim that he had adequately answered the *logical* objections he had raised earlier.

That the kind of evil present in *A Grief Observed* did introduce new difficulties that could not be handled by the arguments set forth in *The Problem of Pain* can be seen in a second way. In that earlier book, Lewis traces the existence of pain and suffering to two causes: a "fixed" and "inexorable" nature on the one hand, and the abuse of freedom on the other. But the evil gnawing away at him in *A Grief Observed* cannot be accounted for in either of these ways; it appears to be the result of divine agency. It is God himself who seems guilty of cruelty, trickery, and deception—of leading Lewis "up the garden path." He felt that he had been toyed with and duped into believing that his wife had been miraculously healed only to discover that still greater horrors awaited him. Unlike the evils considered in *The Problem of Pain,* those that brought his faith down like a house of cards were of a kind in which God was directly implicated. Just as *Surprised by Joy* is not purely autobiographical, neither is *A Grief Observed.* In it, the problem of suffering is confronted anew, and Lewis finds that he needs a new strategy for dealing with it, a strategy that will enable him to reclaim his wavering belief in God's goodness.

The new strategy is found in Parts III and IV. In Parts I and II, Lewis writes as a Platonist who judges God's goodness in terms of ordinary moral standards. Confronted with his wife's death and the cruel set of circumstances that had led up to it, he tries valiantly to catch glimpses of that goodness in order to confirm that God is good *in our sense.* But his efforts are futile. In his anguish, he calls upon God to justify his ways to man. Like Job, Lewis wants to retain his integrity. But unlike Job, for whom this meant retaining his belief in his own innocence, Lewis wants to retain his belief that God really is good, that what appears to be evil really is evil, that our "black" is not God's "white." God is not to be let off the hook. He must be held accountable for his actions. Otherwise he will be indistinguishable from a Cosmic Sadist.

But in Part III everything changes. The protest is dropped and the charges against God are withdrawn. A turning point is reached, and the tone of the book alters so abruptly that the reader is at a loss to explain Lewis's sudden change of heart. Here is the crucial passage:

> If my house has collapsed at one blow, that is because it was a house of cards. The faith which "took these things into ac-

count" was not faith but imagination. . . . [My faith] has been
an imaginary faith playing with innocuous counters labelled
"Illness," "Pain," "Death," and "Loneliness." I thought I
trusted the rope until it mattered to me whether it would bear
me. Now it matters, and I find I didn't. *(AGO,* 31)

The reader is startled to learn that it is no longer God but Lewis
who is at fault. God is not evil after all; rather, Lewis's previous
faith, he announces, had been imaginary. God had known all
along that his faith was a house of cards and could not allow him
to labor under the delusion that it was true faith. If Lewis was
to learn the truth about himself, God had to knock his house
down. "Nothing else will shake a man . . . out of his merely
verbal thinking and merely notional beliefs." A person has to be
"knocked silly" before he "comes to his senses." Only "torture"
can "bring out the truth." (*AGO*, 32).

As a result, the Cosmic Sadist becomes an unnecessary
hypothesis. Once Lewis has been reduced to self-abasement, he
no longer blames God. In fact, he praises him for dispelling his
illusion and thereby enabling him to set about rebuilding his
spiritual house. If it too is knocked down, that will only prove
that is was as faulty as the previous one. Yet a distinction must
be made: "In which sense may [my faith] be a house of cards?
Because the things I am believing are only a dream, or because
I only dream that I believe them?" (*AGO*, 33). Clearly the latter.
And so Lewis recants.

> All that stuff about the Cosmic Sadist was not so much the
> expression of thought as of hatred. I was getting from it the
> only pleasure a man in anguish can get; the pleasure of hitting
> back . . . "telling God what I thought of Him." And of
> course, as in all abusive language, "what I thought" didn't
> mean what I thought true. Only what I thought would offend
> Him . . . most. (*AGO*, 33)

The hypothesis of the Cosmic Sadist is therefore not Lewis's final
word on the subject of pain and suffering. It is one possible
interpretation of the facts that he temporarily entertains but
ultimately rejects in favor of the new hypothesis of God as the
Great Iconoclast who shatters our illusions for our own good.

That is why Lewis goes on to claim that a God who is good
in this sense is every bit as formidable as a Cosmic Sadist. The

GRIEF   149

more we believe that God's goodness is a goodness that shatters
our illusions, the less we can believe that there is any point to asking that our sufferings be removed or lessened. What we can be
sure of is this: if we suffer, our suffering is necessary. Like Job,
Lewis suffered. Like Job, he was morally outraged and stormed
the heavens for an answer. And like Job, he received no answer
and accepted this as proof that his questions had been illegitimate:
"Heaven will solve our problems, but not, I think, by showing
us subtle reconciliations between all our apparently contradictory
notions. The notions will all be knocked from under our feet. We
shall see that there never was any problem" (*AGO*, 56). Even the
closed door, bolted and double-bolted from the inside, begins to
appear in a different light. It was not God's indifference but
Lewis's frantic need that had slammed it shut in his face. Although
there is still no answer from God, it is "a rather special sort"
of no answer: not a locked door but "a silent, certainly not
uncompassionate, gaze," as if God is saying, "Peace, child; you
don't understand" (*AGO*, 54–55). As a result, Lewis no longer
tries to justify the ways of God to man; instead, he denies that
we need a justification.

The shift from the hypothesis of the Cosmic Sadist to that
of the Great Iconoclast is the new strategy by which Lewis
attempts to reclaim his belief in God's goodness. His change of
heart is prompted not by the discovery of new evidence but by
his coming to see his situation in a new way. What had seemed
so cruel is declared to be good because it has been instrumental
in forcing him to see that his faith had been imaginary. Through
his wife's death, he has finally achieved self-knowledge—another
proof that all things work together for good for those who love
God.

So where is the problem? Why not just say, with Farrer, that
by exchanging the hypothesis of the Cosmic Sadist for that of
the Great Iconoclast, Lewis "deepened" his faith, found the
"existential" solution, and emerged a "stronger" Christian? It
is a tempting solution, but it will not work. The problem is that
the shift from the hypothesis of the Cosmic Sadist to that of the
Great Iconoclast is a shift from Platonism to Ockhamism on the
question of the connection between God and morality. W. H.
Lewis states, and Chad Walsh repeats, that *A Grief Observed* is
Lewis's "most harrowing" book.[6] Yes, it is. But it is harrowing

in a far more unnerving sense than Walsh seems to realize as he directs our attention to the "tentative reassurances" toward which Lewis gradually moved. The Bantam Book edition triumphantly calls the work "a masterpiece of rediscovered faith" that will be "a source of comfort and inspiration" to anyone who has ever lost a loved one. This estimate seems to have become the received opinion, but it cannot bear scrutiny. True, by the conclusion of this riveting book a rediscovery of sorts has occurred, but few who grasp the nature of the rediscovered faith and note the process by which it is rediscovered will be likely to regard it as a source of "comfort and inspiration." The rediscovered faith is not a more "tentative" form of the old faith; it is rather a new faith with a philosophical foundation different from that of the earlier apologetic writings.

A Grief Observed is a harrowing book not just because it deals with suffering, death, and a tottering faith, but because it reveals that Lewis's faith was rediscovered at the enormous cost of leaving unanswered and unanswerable the very questions he had all along insisted must be answered, the very questions that had proven fatal to his earlier faith. Having insisted that God's goodness must be understood in terms of ordinary moral standards and having registered his protest on precisely these grounds in Parts I and II, in Parts III and IV he lays these standards aside and embraces the opposite view. The shift from the hypothesis of the Cosmic Sadist to that of the Great Iconoclast is at bottom a shift from the Platonic view that God says things are good because they are good to the Ockhamist view that things are good simply because God says they are.

The shift occurs the moment Lewis begins to suspect that the hypothesis of the Cosmic Sadist is too anthropomorphic. According to such a view, God is like the man who tortures his cats, and that is unbearable. Lewis recoils from this view and assures himself (and his readers) that when he called God a sadist and an imbecile, it was "more a yell than a thought" (*AGO*, 27). After that, we hear no more about the Cosmic Sadist—but in recoiling from that hypothesis, Lewis also recoils from his own Platonism, for it is that view that had prompted him to see God as a sadist in the first place. He saw that if you followed the logic of Platonism to its conclusion, God turns out to be much more evil than anyone would have supposed. In no longer taking the sadist idea seriously, Lewis can no longer take Platonism seriously either.

According to the Platonic view, you cannot say that a good God is every bit as formidable as a Cosmic Sadist. Notice, however, that although Lewis drops the label of the Cosmic Sadist, he continues to attribute to God the quality that prompts it. God is no longer called a sadist, but his behavior still requires an explanation. Lewis reclaims his belief in God's goodness by asserting that his earlier faith had been unreal—a house of cards. This "explanation" has just enough surface plausibility to convince Lewis's followers that he has not lost his rigor. But it will not do.

Notice what has happened. The very behavior on the part of God that the distraught mourner has denounced as cruel, spiteful, and sadistic has been dramatically reassessed. God is now called good because he has relentlessly driven home the point that Lewis's faith had been unreal. But how does Lewis know that he is right about his previous faith? How can he be certain that having been shattered he has achieved self-knowledge? His only "reason" for claiming that his faith had been a house of cards is that this alone enables him to see God's behavior as good. But that is no reason at all. Lewis does not show us that God is good in spite of appearances to the contrary, and then conclude that his faith had been a house of cards. He does exactly the opposite. He assumes that his faith had been unreal and then concludes that God is good. That is not a reason; it is a case of special pleading. It is not hard to understand why Lewis felt driven to this conclusion: any other assessment would have required him to say that his previous faith was unfounded, that God is in fact evil. The appeal to self-knowledge is therefore nothing more than a desperate *ad hoc* maneuver designed to insulate his shaken belief in God's goodness from the ravages of contrary evidence.[7]

The God who knocked down Lewis's house of cards is not a Platonically conceived deity who is good in our sense, but rather an Ockhamistically conceived being who is declared to be good no matter what he does. Lewis's "rediscovered" faith is a faith in a God whose goodness is so unlike our own that it can be called good only by laying aside our moral standards together with our ordinary criteria for determining who has true faith and who does not. It is in this alarming sense that Heaven is said to "solve" our problems. *Good* now means "whatever God wills or permits."

In *A Grief Observed* Lewis becomes an Ockhamist and embraces the view of the "terrible theologians" that he had previously deplored.

I do not think that Ockhamism, or the fideism to which it leads, is a tenable philosophical position. At the same time, there are solid reasons for thinking that the Ockhamist view of God's goodness partakes more deeply of and more authentically expresses the biblical view of divine goodness than does the Platonic alternative. According to the Ockhamist, the very attempt to solve the Problem of Evil along the lines pursued by Lewis in *The Problem of Pain* is mistaken in principle. Suffering is a problem (and hence an obstacle to belief in God) only for those who think that their own judgments, based on ordinary moral standards, are legitimate. This the Ockhamist denies. Instead of wondering whether suffering is compatible with a God who is good in Platonic terms, the Ockhamist insists that God is not subject to ordinary moral standards. To expect the God of Christianity to take our moral protests seriously is to mistake him for some other God, and to demand a justification for his conduct is an act of impiety.

Although there are in the Bible isolated examples of people, such as Job, who question God's goodness on the basis of ordinary moral standards, they are exceptions to the general rule that God is to be obeyed no matter how flagrantly his commands may violate the precepts of ordinary morality. Think, for example, of the command that Abraham sacrifice Isaac, that Elijah slay the prophets of Baal, that Joshua's army annihilate the inhabitants of Canaan right down to the last woman and child, that the she-bears tear into pieces and devour the boys who had called Elisha "baldhead," that Samuel lie to Saul about annointing David king of Israel, that the Israelites despoil the Egyptians as the exodus took place, and that Annanias and Sapphira be struck dead for lying to Simon Peter. Think of Uzzah being done away with for trying to prevent the Ark of the Covenant from falling, or of Moses being forbidden to enter the promised land simply because he had angrily beaten a rock with his staff. All these apparently immoral and capricious commands are ascribed to a God who is said to be good. But good in what sense? Surely not in the Platonic sense.

This Ockhamistic conception of God's goodness is the view

held by the vast majority of orthodox religious believers, most of whom have either never heard of the Platonic alternative, or have heard of it but reject it as foreign to the biblical view. Orthodox Christians unhesitatingly affirm that obedience to God is absolute and unconditional. He is to be obeyed because he is God, not because we have judged him good by some human standard.

Theologians have long insisted that the most fundamental property of the biblical God is not goodness but holiness. To say that God is holy is not an extravagant way of saying that he is good. *Holy* does not mean "*very very* good." The root meaning of the Hebrew term for holiness is "set apart" or "other." In the Old Testament, to say that God is holy is to say that he dwells in light unapproachable. There is none like him. He answers to no one. Creatures were called into being at his command and they are obliged to acknowledge his radical authority over them. To acknowledge that God is holy is to acknowledge that one is a person of unclean lips, that one has no claim on him. This root meaning is preserved in the New Testament, in which believers are called saints and said to be holy in a derivative sense: not because they are good but because they have been set apart as a peculiar people who are in the world but not of it. In the Bible God and man do not share a common moral world. There is a radical discontinuity between them. In response to his doings, we are not to "hotly criticize" his behavior and produce our moral standards; we are to be still and know that he is God and that his ways are not our ways. One cannot be a Christian without coming to terms with this doctrine. There is no way around it. One must bow the head and bend the knee. This recognition of the ultimacy and nonaccountability of God is precisely the rock of offense on which a consistently Platonic approach founders and is finally broken. Given this conception of God's goodness, evil is not a problem.

Consistently held, Ockhamism undercuts another belief that many Christians may be considerably less eager to abandon, one of the most firmly entrenched lingering vestiges of Platonism— the belief that one day all will be made plain. Ockhamism provides no basis for thinking that on the last day God will gather the saints around him and let them in on what he has been up to, reveal his "plan," after which they will see that all was for the best.

On the contrary, God will explain nothing for the very good reason that there is nothing to explain. If we are Ockhamists, we already know what he is up to: he is allowing suffering to exist. For God to take the Platonists' questions seriously and say, "Yes, I see your point," would be for him to acknowledge that the issues they raise are legitimate and that the burden is on him to come up with a face-saving answer. To acknowledge this, however, would be to surrender his status as the Creator of the world who possesses absolute prerogatives. St. Paul was very firm about this: "Hath not the potter power over the clay? May the clay say to the potter 'Why hast Thou made me thus?' God forbid" (Romans 9:21–22). For us to question God is an affront to his holiness. For God to meet men as equals, as if he and they were both reasonable parties engaged in some cooperative enterprise, would violate the Creator-creature relationship. Those who refuse to accept what God has done unless they find it plausible, convincing, and "justified" are refusing to acknowledge what that relationship defines them to be—creatures. It is to reenact the Fall. Imagine Adam asking, "But look here, that command about the tree was arbitrary. What's so bad about picking fruit *apart from your prohibition*?" But that is just the point. The prohibition made it wrong. For God to feel called upon to "justify" his prohibitions on independent moral grounds is unthinkable. This is often true even in human relationships. When the private asks the sergeant "But apart from your command, why do we have to stand here at attention in the blazing sun?" the sergeant is not reduced to groping for good reasons. Similarly, when the private obeys the sergeant, it is not because he agrees that it would indeed be nice for the entire platoon to be found standing straight and tall, but simply because he has been commanded to do so by someone with legitimate authority over him. Good soldiers do not raise searching questions about their orders; they obey them.

Just as the sergeant does not countenance the private's questions, neither, according to the Ockhamist, does God countenance ours. He is to be obeyed not because he is invariably right but because he is God. If you disagree with him, you are in the wrong by definition. Hence, all those who scrutinize God's commands on moral grounds have simply not come to terms with their creaturely status. God is not flattered by being called good only after being subjected to rigorous cross-examination and acquitted.

According to the Ockhamist view, then, we cannot ask separate questions about *what* God commands and *whether* he is good in commanding it. If there is any "lesson" in the book of Job, that is it. Job demands answers from God, fails to get them, and toward the end no longer seems to mind. Either the story is hopelessly confused or the point is that his questions are illegitimate. Heaven does not solve Job's problems (any more than it solves Lewis's) by showing him "subtle reconciliations" of his apparently contradictory notions. In the Bible the answer to the Problem of Evil is God's assertion of himself as God. His ways are not temporarily obscured by a regrettable lack of clarity that will one day be dispelled; they are shrouded in an unfathomable mystery that cannot be solved by the acquisition of further facts. Although it sounds decidedly odd, it is nevertheless entirely accurate to say that, according to the Ockhamist view, redeemed souls have forgotten about their moral scruples and are prepared to declare without reservation that "The Lord, He is God." The worship and adoration of the hosts of heaven is elicited by the fact that God is their Creator and Redeemer, not by the assurance that he has finally explained himself to their complete satisfaction (and presumably great relief).

Believers who hold this view do not see themselves as participating in what the Lewis of *The Problem of Pain* calls devil worship. It never occurs to the Ockhamist that God may be evil. If he has knocked down Lewis's house by causing him to suffer, so be it. Such suffering is good, and God will inflict it as often as proves necessary.

But Lewis's rediscovered faith rings false. Parts III and IV of *A Grief Observed* are unconvincing. Although Lewis does accept Ockhamism, his acceptance is half-hearted. He quickly realizes that in taking the Ockhamist route he has made it impossible for himself to see God as good in any sense conceivable to man, and he continues to long for this reassurance that only the Platonic view can provide.

To say that the rediscovered faith rings false is not, of course, to say that Lewis ceases to be a Christian, but rather that he never succeeds in making the Ockhamist conception of God his own. The rediscovered faith lacks not only the conviction of his earlier writings but even the conviction of Parts I and II of *A Grief Observed*. All the conviction is in the protest, in the "mad, midnight ravings.'' In Parts III and IV Lewis appears to be attitudinizing, trying to conjure up the requisite feelings, pretending to convey bedrock religious sentiments that he does not have. The will-to-believe is present, but it cannot seem to find adequate expression. Although Lewis assures us that Heaven will answer our problems by showing us that they are illegitimate, the doubts of Parts I and II have not been uprooted. He continues to cast wistful, backward glances at the Platonic view. His assent to Ockhamism is ''notional'' rather than real. He wears this view awkwardly and self-consciously like a new suit of clothes improperly tailored to his intellectual and emotional contours.

Although Lewis found a refuge of sorts in Ockhamism, he was still disquieted by the problem of suffering, and he continued to be disquieted even as he assured us that previously he had not understood. But *what* had he not understood? That the Platonist's question will not be answered until the hereafter? Or that Heaven will solve our problems by disallowing them? He could not make up his mind. So which view does he really hold at the conclusion of the book? The only possible answer is: neither. In *A Grief Observed* Lewis arrives at a halfway house that provides him with neither the consolation of Platonism nor the settled resignation of Ockhamism.

That Lewis could not make the Ockhamist view his own and continue to vacillate between it and the Platonic alternative is evident in a letter I received from him shortly before his death. I had asked whether he was still prepared to apply the Platonic view to God's behavior and to actions carried out in obedience to his commands as found in the Old and New Testaments. I had mentioned, among other examples, Joshua's slaughtering of the Canaanites and Simon Peter's striking Annanias and Sapphira dead as a punishment for lying. In his reply, Lewis confirmed my suspicions. I reproduce his letter in full.

Abs. from Magdalene College
Cambridge

3 July 1963

Dear Mr. Beversluis

Yes. On my view one must apply something of the same sort of explanation to, say, the atrocities (and treacheries) of

Joshua. I see the grave danger we run by doing so; but the dangers of believing in a God whom we cannot but regard as evil, and then, in mere terrified flattery calling Him "good" and worshipping Him, is a still greater danger. The ultimate question is whether the doctrine of the goodness of God or that of the inerrancy of Scripture is to prevail when they conflict. I think the doctrine of the goodness of God is the more certain of the two. Indeed, only that doctrine renders this worship of Him obligatory or even permissible.

To this some will reply "ah, but we are fallen and don't recognize good when we see it." But God Himself does not say that we are as fallen as all that. He constantly, in Scripture, appeals to our conscience: "Why do ye not *of yourselves* judge what is right?"—"What fault hath my people found in Me?" And so on. Socrates' answer to Euthyphro is used in Christian form by Hooker. Things are not good because God commands them; God commands certain things because He sees them to be good. (In other words, the Divine will is the obedient servant of the Divine Reason.) The opposite view (Ockham's, Paley's) leads to an absurdity. If "good" means "what God wills" then to say "God is good" can mean only "God wills what He wills." Which is equally true of you or me or Judas or Satan.

But [two illegible words] having said all this, we must apply it with fear and trembling. *Some* things which seem to us bad may be good. But we must not consult our consciences by trying to feel a thing good when it seems to us totally evil. We can only pray that *if* there is an invisible goodness hidden in such things, God, in His own good time will enable us to see it. If we need to. For perhaps sometimes God's answer might be "What is that to thee?" The passage may not be "addressed to our (your or my) condition" at all.

I think we are v. much in agreement, aren't we?

Yours sincerely,

[Signed]

C. S. Lewis

Coming from the author of *A Grief Observed,* this is a curious view. The Platonic notion of a hidden good is superfluous for the Ockhamist. Lewis's letter reveals that he never extricated himself from the Platonic view. Until the end of his life, he continued to believe in his heart of hearts that God must be good in our sense—even if his goodness is not immediately evident—and that it is for this reason alone that he is worthy of worship. But if Lewis continued to believe this, what becomes of the Ockhamist "solution" of *A Grief Observed,* which requires us to believe that the search for "invisible" or "hidden" goods is mistaken in principle and symptomatic of an imaginary faith?

Lewis was apparently not aware of the decisive reversal of his thought in the second half of this book. The upshot is that he became vulnerable to the same criticisms he had earlier leveled against Ockhamism. If the behavior of the Great Iconoclast is identical with that of the Cosmic Sadist, on the basis of what empirical evidence can we distinguish the one from the other? You cannot say that whereas the Sadist is evil, the Iconoclast is good, because all you mean by "good" is whatever the Iconoclast does, and, as Lewis points out, the same claim can be made of the Sadist. In laying aside ordinary moral standards, Lewis deprives himself of any logical ground for preferring one to the other. If the Great Iconoclast is really "every bit as formidable" as a Cosmic Sadist, then our "black" *is* God's "white."

In his poem, "The Apologist's Evening Prayer," Lewis implores God to take away his trumpery. Whether there is a God or not, his wife's death accomplished that purpose. Whatever trumpery may have been present before, in *A Grief Observed* it is present no longer. What remains is C. S. Lewis minus his apologetic—or better, C. S. Lewis with his new apologetic, which is already showing signs of having been burdened with a heavier load than it can bear. The Apostle to the Skeptics has himself become a skeptic—if not about the existence of God, at least about his nature. If an inspection of Parts I and II reveals an abandoned fortress with a crumbling foundation, a perusal of Parts III and IV discloses a makeshift shelter hastily pieced together in the hope that it would last the night.

I am touched by C. S. Lewis in his twilight years. Not just because of his sadness, nor even because of the wretched hypothesis of the Great Iconoclast to which the once "bonny fighter" was finally reduced, but because of the suspect but eagerly seized consolation it seems to have given him. Although I am glad that in the end he came to feel that his burden had been partly lifted, I deplore the self-debasing, *ad hoc* strategy by which this was accomplished.

I have already taken note of Austin Farrer's remarks about Lewis's need for an "existential" solution. Although this unhelpful term usually obscures much more than it illumines, we should not pretend that it is opaque in this instance. We all know perfectly well what he means. All of us will one day die, and before we do, many of us will have to endure the deaths of those we love. Whatever misgivings we may have about the term, we will then have to find something like the "existential" solution of which Farrer speaks. Like most men, Lewis had difficulty finding it. Chad Walsh reports that when he visited Lewis for the last time in 1961, he found him "subdued and at loose ends."[8] In light of this picture of human collapse, it would be worse than heartless for us to lie in wait for him, brandishing his inconsistencies in his face as he tries to pick himself up. Yet something must be said, for it appears that the apologist who had launched his career by saying that he was not asking us to accept Christianity if our best reasoning told us that the weight of the evidence is against it[9] finally arrived at precisely this impasse. And in order to move beyond it, he felt compelled to confess publicly that his faith had been unreal.

But wasn't Lewis too hard on himself? Surely the reported facts allow for a less self-deprecatory conclusion. His earlier Platonism provided him with two other alternatives. He could have concluded that suffering only *appears* to be incompatible with believing in a good God and proceeded to resolve the problem by producing new reasons for believing this. Or he could have concluded that suffering *is* incompatible with believing in a good God and abandoned Christianity forthwith. But he availed himself of neither strategy. Instead he redefined goodness.

The hypothesis of the Great Iconoclast followed. Its attractions were, of course, obvious. Armed with it, Lewis could say that what is evil by human standards is really good and thereby transform contrary evidence into favorable evidence by redefinition. The absence of God thus becomes one of the ways in which he is present. But that is no solution. The dictum "Whom the Lord loveth he chasteneth" seems comforting only until one realizes that it makes God's goodness compatible with whatever happens. If I am happy, that proves that God is good and is showering me with "blessings." If I suffer, that also proves that God is good and is shattering my illusions. And if I am religiously shaken by the shattering process, that only proves that my faith was not real in the first place.

But perhaps Lewis's faith *was* real all along. Perhaps his wife's death provided him with decisive counterevidence that showed that his belief in a good God was false. It certainly looks as if, having arrived at exactly the sort of situation he had defined as "intolerable" in "On Obstinacy in Belief," he simply refused to draw the conclusion that he had insisted must, after a certain point, be drawn. To avoid drawing it, he turned to the hypothesis of the Great Iconoclast. But surely to no avail. To embrace a hypothesis simply because it enables one to retain a belief one wants desperately to retain is a sure indication that rationality has been sidestepped. And for Lewis to continue reassuring himself that God is really good only made matters worse. I might just as well argue that the fact that my wife is constantly having affairs with other men does not falsify my claim that she is faithful to me, that it simply reveals that my concept of fidelity is too narrow, and that instead of doubting her faithfulness, I should defend her by invoking the principle that reality is iconoclastic. To the extent that I grow despondent about her apparent indifference toward me, I might claim that there is only a *prima facie* incompatibility between my claim and her behavior. But the one thing I ought never to do is this: I ought never to say that she is unfaithful. I should steadfastly endure her behavior and remain "obstinate" in my belief in her faithfulness until I am at last delivered from my absurdly restrictive categories and patently juvenile expectations. Then and only then would I realize that she had been faithful to me in a much "deeper" sense than that of "mere" sexual exclusiveness. Then and only then would I realize that asking for a faithful wife in the ordinary sense is like asking for a grandfather in heaven.

The Shattering Thesis of *A Grief Observed* is not, of course, a hitherto unheard-of idea in Lewis's writings. It can be found in *The Problem of Pain*. What is new is not the thesis but Lewis's recognition of its logical impact on the believer. It is trite to say, with Farrer, that one's own suffering is more difficult to endure than the suffering of others. Of course it is. The point is that in *A Grief Observed* Lewis wrestles not only with the psychological consequences of his wife's death but with the logical consequences of applying the term *good* to the Being who allowed it. The fundamental crisis of the book is a crisis of *meaning*, a crisis of such paralyzing magnitude that Lewis tries to distance himself from it in every possible way—including the perspective implied by his title. The grief is one that in the end he preferred to *observe* rather than to experience. It is almost as if he were recounting the bereavement of someone else.

This, of course, is not a criticism. It is an observation that reveals that Lewis finally perceived with numbing clarity the very difficulties that *The Problem of Pain* presents. In that book, he argues that God's goodness is most evident in just those situations in which he seems most cruel. He finally realized that this claim is a hollow, empty sham. In *A Grief Observed*, he experiences for himself the cold comfort of *The Problem of Pain* and recognizes that he had been a Job's comforter, someone who found it necessary to "palter" with ordinary moral standards. And he could no longer accept his own arguments. The good God of *The Problem of Pain* is identical with the Cosmic Sadist.

In the meantime, what has become of the Falsification Criterion and of the necessity of being able to specify what empirical evidence would require believers to acknowledge that their religious assertions must be withdrawn? It is but a short step from saying that God is good no matter what to saying that one must believe in him no matter what—but it appears to be a step that Lewis, however unwillingly, did in fact take.

We are emphatically assured by one expositor after another that the agonizing experience recounted in *A Grief Observed* does not constitute a falsification of the assertion that God is good. But then what would? Lewis's final answer appears to be: Nothing. But that is a fatal admission. It reveals that his belief in God's goodness has become wholly vacuous, that there is no way to deal with the problem of contrary evidence. Lewis claims that his faith somehow survived. I am sure that it did. But it no longer invites the assent of the rational man.

Chapter Ten

SPECIMEN

Ockhamism, pursued to its logical conclusion, leads to a form of fideism. As we have seen, the fideist is not disturbed by the problems Lewis raises in *A Grief Observed*. Doubts about God's goodness are to be dispelled not by providing a "justification" of God's behavior based on Platonic standards of goodness but by recalling that God's will is the standard and that he needs no justification. What God does is good by definition. If Lewis could have assimilated this view, his doubts would have been put to rest once and for all. In becoming a thoroughgoing Ockhamist, he could have joined the ranks of the Wittgensteinian fideists and quietly reinterpreted the language of religion in a way that no longer involved truth-claims. But he could not, and it was precisely this philosophical and temperamental inability to take the Ockhamist-fideist route that makes his apologetic writings unique and worthy of study.

The author of *A Grief Observed* is not an Ockhamist but a dispossessed Platonist worried about contrary evidence and its bearing on his belief in God's goodness. Worries about contrary evidence put in a brief appearance in *Mere Christianity* and *The Problem of Pain,* but they are handled briskly and with great confidence. They crop up again in "On Obstinacy in Belief," in which, despite the fact that his confidence has ebbed considerably, Lewis still manages to set forth an intelligible position. By the time he wrote *A Grief Observed,* however, his confidence was nonexistent, his worries all-consuming, and his argument incoherent.

How, then, did his faith survive? Apparently Lewis did exactly what he had advised his readers to do. He remained "obstinate" in his beliefs and fell back on the arguments on which his assent to Christianity had been initially based, and when the problem of contrary evidence became really acute, he substituted the Ockhamist view of God's goodness for the Platonic view and clung to it for as long as he could—at least until his crisis of faith had passed its psychological peak.

If my criticisms of Lewis's arguments for the existence of God are sound, however, the grounds of his initial assent are insufficient. If there are no reasons for believing in an infinite Object of desire, or a Power behind the Moral Law, or a cosmic Mind, then these arguments are invalid, and the problem of contrary evidence reemerges with a vengeance. Even if we waive my objections, Lewis's own strategy in *A Grief Observed* undercuts his earlier arguments. If God cannot be called good in any recognizable sense, then the Moral Argument can no longer be used to prove the existence of a Power urging us in the direction of moral goodness. The Argument from Reason also collapses, for it, too, depends on the belief that our moral judgments are grounded in some objectively good reality. Similarly, the claim that men desire some infinite Object that is both good and good for them loses its force if the term *good* can serve just as accurately to describe the activities of a Cosmic Sadist.

Deprived of the grounds of his initial assent, Lewis is left with a deity of dubious moral character. Although he continues to insist that worship is impermissible and immoral unless the being worshiped is recognizably good, Lewis appears to worship him anyhow—not only in the absence of evidence but in the teeth of contrary evidence. *A Grief Observed* reveals many things about Lewis, but none more important than the fact that he was undone by the problem of contrary evidence.

If this were simply a psychological claim, it would be nothing more than an *ad hominem* argument with no bearing on apologetics. The truth of Christianity is not called into question simply because one of its most famous apologists experienced a crisis of faith from which he never fully recovered. But I am not talking psychology. Throughout this study I have focused on the logical issues involved in Lewis's defense of Christianity. His is an arresting case history precisely because he neither confused psychology with logic nor abandoned his search for a rational religion based on rock-solid evidence. It is for this reason that his apologetic writings shed such a significant light on the contemporary religious debate among Anglo-American philosophers.

One of the crucial issues in that debate is whether Wittgenstein-ian fideism provides believers with an elucidation of religious language that satisfactorily preserves and adequately expresses the content of their beliefs. Those who follow this debate will soon come to a fork in the road: they will have to decide whether religious language in fact puts forth truth-claims that stand in some important and discoverable relation to empirical evidence, or whether religious language is not empirically meaningful but meaningful in some other way. The first position is that of Lewis and traditional apologists; the second, that of the fideists.

In turning from Platonism to Ockhamism, Lewis flirted for a time with fideism. Yet he soon realized that it enabled him neither to surmount the problem of contrary evidence nor to formulate a coherent view of God's goodness. As a form of fideism, Ockhamism depends on an apologetic method radically at odds with that upon which his entire career as an apologist had been based. And Lewis knew it. The inconsistencies and hesita-tions discernible in *A Grief Observed* demonstrate that beyond all doubt. At the same time, their very presence testifies to his firm grasp of the content and logical character of religious language. Inconsistency is never a virtue, but the kind of incon-sistency that leaps from the pages of this book reveals a degree of intellectual and moral integrity as remarkable as it is rare. Think of the less vulnerable alternatives that Lewis might have pursued. He could have clung to the view that after conversion religious belief is no longer a hypothesis and coaxed from it an empirically unfalsifiable safety. He could have explored much further the notion of the "logic" of personal relations and relied more heavily on the idea of faith as trust. He could have developed the strategy of obstinacy more fully. Yet, although he touched on all these possibilities, he staunchly refused to trivialize belief in God by making it compatible with whatever happened and thereby render it wholly discontinuous with all empirical considerations. He could not claim a greater assurance than he had himself attained. While offering a solution of sorts to the problem of suffering, he could not pretend that it was any less precarious than he saw it to be. His rediscovered faith was a halfway house, and again Lewis knew it. It is as if having seen the attractiveness of fideism, he had also perceived that its losses outweighed its gains. That way was not really open to him.

By an unexpected stroke of irony, therefore, the following conclusion emerges. If Lewis's employment of religious language is at all typical and representative of believers in general, then obedience to the Wittgensteinian dictum that we "look and see" how religious language is actually used reveals that the making of truth-claims *is* one of its irreducible functions. Hence Lewis's writings provide far more promising data for Wittgensteinian analysis than do the eccentric linguistic practices of the Wittgensteinian fideists themselves.

In his now-famous Cambridge Inaugural Address, Lewis describes himself as a dinosaur, one of the last survivors of a vanishing breed, and he expresses the hope that even where he fails as a literary critic, he might still be useful as a specimen.[1] Although he never makes a corresponding claim about his work as a Christian apologist, I find it undeniably moving that it is just because he failed in this role that he remains so useful as a religious "specimen." A specimen of what? Of a faith firmly based on the New Testament requirement of counting the cost, a faith not so far removed from philosophy that it could afford to ignore relevant questions of meaning and evidence, but at the same time not so far removed from that of his unlearned fellow believers that it could afford to make damaging concessions whenever philosophical sophistication seemed to require them. Despite his erudition as a Medieval and Renaissance literary historian, Lewis really was a "very ordinary layman" of the Church of England. And it is for just this reason that his more modest wish has been fulfilled. We can make good use of our specimen.

Although there have been Christian philosophers of far greater stature than Lewis, I know of no apologist in any age who has struggled with the intellectual difficulties involved in Christian belief in so grippingly visible a way and at such personal cost. Read Lewis's books desultorily and you will readily discover why his critics find them so infuriatingly facile and cavalier. But read them chronologically and attentively and you will also understand why they continue to attract so vast an audience. A mentality is at work in these books that is more than the sum of its often troublesome parts.

Yet toward the end it became a divided mentality, a mentality at odds with itself. Lewis was finally reduced to a fundamental, unresolved, and unresolvable set of inconsistencies.

These inconsistencies are symptomatic of his awareness of the choice he knew he had to make but could not bring himself to make. His final dilemma is all too clear: *Either* religious language consists of empirically meaningful assertions, we must retain the ordinary meanings of ethical terms, and we are left with the Cosmic Sadist, *or* we must believe in the Great Iconoclast, adopt an alternative ethical vocabulary, and live with the fact that religious language is empirically vacuous. What he wanted but could not have was the best of both worlds: the ordinary meanings of ethical terms, empirically meaningful religious assertions, and the Great Iconoclast. Although he could not abandon his faith, neither could he in all honesty take permanent refuge in what he knew were *ad hoc* diversionary maneuvers. Attracted and repelled by both Platonism and Ockhamism, in the end he could make neither his own.

The problem is not his alone. *A Grief Observed* dramatically illustrates the predicament of the orthodox believer caught between the indefensibility of traditional natural theology on the one hand, and the failure of contemporary fideism to preserve the content of the faith on the other. Here is the all-too-human Lewis who eagerly grasped at the straw provided by the hypothesis of the Great Iconoclast as well as the self-correcting Lewis who saw through this pathetic strategy and resolutely refused to settle for anything less than the truth-claims he defends in his earlier books. Even in the depths of his personal anguish, he remained the foe of all who advocate Christianity on grounds other than its truth.

Yet after *A Grief Observed* we can no longer read those earlier books as we once read them. For we now know that, whatever we may think of them, Lewis himself came to have grave doubts about the views he had so confidently and even joyously defended in them—doubts out of which he could not find his way. This fact casts an eerie retrospective light over his entire career as an apologist.

Taken as a whole, then, Lewis's apologetic writings do not embody a religion that satisfied his own definition of rationality. His arguments for the existence of God fail. His answer to the Problem of Evil is unacceptable. His characteristic way of misrepresenting the views of the opposition stands as a permanent warning to future apologists. He is even guilty of trying to harmonize incompatible philosophical traditions. And so the failures accumulate, the inconsistencies remain, and the case for Christianity has not been made. The old road is a dead-end, and the new one leads in the wrong direction. Yet if anyone wants to know what orthodox Christianity is, what it requires in terms of personal commitment, and what difficulties it must ultimately face, he need only read C. S. Lewis. Although the Lewis cult has made him out to be something he never was, and although Lewis the man must be distinguished from Lewis the myth and elemental force, his apologetic writings repay study—even if not for the reason he wrote them.

NOTES

INTRODUCTION

1. This was Lewis's term (borrowed from Richard Baxter) for the kind of Christianity he advocated. By "mere Christianity" he means the central core of doctrine that "all Christians believe." Convinced that there is such a thing, he deliberately avoided controversial doctrinal issues that divide Christians and focused on what is common to them. "You will not learn from me," he warns, "whether you ought to become an Anglican, a Methodist, a Presbyterian, or a Roman Catholic" (*MC*, 6).

2. The critic was Alistair Cooke (see "Mr. Anthony at Oxford," *New Republic*, 24 April 1944, pp. 578-80).

3. For examples of this sort of criticism, see E. L. Allen, "The Theology of C. S. Lewis," *Modern Churchman* 34 (January–March 1945): 317-24; R. C. Churchill, "Mr. C. S. Lewis as an Evangelist," *Modern Churchman* 35 (January–March 1946): 334-42; Robert Eisler, rev. of *Miracles,* by C. S. Lewis, *The Hibbert Journal* 45 (July 1947):373-776; W. Norman Pittenger, "Apologist Versus Apologist," *Christian Century*, 1 October 1958, pp. 1104-7; Mary Scrutton, "Confused Witness," *New Statesman and Nation*, 1 October 1955, p. 405; Victor S. Yarros, "An Invitation to Rough Debunking," *American Freeman*, December 1947, p. 449. Anyone who really wants to dip into the vast literature (pro and con) on Lewis should consult J. R. Christopher and Joan K. Ostling's *C. S. Lewis: An Annotated Checklist of Writings about Him and His Works* (Kent, Ohio: Kent State University Press, 1974). Others are at work on an updated edition.

4. These volumes are, respectively, *Light on C. S. Lewis*, ed. Jocelyn Gibb (New York; Harcourt, Brace and World, 1965); *Letters of C. S. Lewis,* ed W. H. Lewis (London: Geoffrey Bles, 1966); *C. S. Lewis: A Biography,* by Roger Lancelyn Green and Walter Hooper (New York: Harcourt Brace Jovanovich, 1974); *The Inklings*, by Humphrey Carpenter (Boston: Houghton Mifflin, 1979); *They Stand Together: The Letters of C. S. Lewis to Arthur Greeves, 1914-1963,* ed. Walter Hooper (New York: Macmillan, 1979); and *C. S. Lewis at the Breakfast Table*, ed. James T. Como (New York: Macmillan, 1979).

5. See Phillips, *The Ring of Truth* (New York: Macmillan, 1967), p. 118. It is an astounding remark, equaled only by that of Dr. Eric Routley, who "entirely believes" that Phillips was visited by Lewis and wishes that he "would from time to time haunt" him in the same way (see *C. S. Lewis at the Breakfast Table*, p. 37).

6. A recent ad for the Lewis calendar reverently declares that it "seems to

bless whatever room it hangs in with a quiet sense of peace." One wonders what unique benefits the aprons, sweatshirts, and tote bags provide.

7. See, for example, Corbin Scott Carnell, *Bright Shadows of Reality* (Grand Rapids: William B. Eerdmans, 1974); Richard C. Cunningham, *C. S. Lewis: Defender of the Faith* (Philadelphia: Westminster Press, 1967); Margaret Patterson Hannay, *C. S. Lewis* (New York: Frederick Ungar, 1981); Paul L. Holmer, *C. S. Lewis: The Shape of His Faith and Thought* (New York: Harper and Row, 1976); Carolyn Keefe, ed., *C. S. Lewis: Speaker and Teacher* (Grand Rapids: Zondervan, 1971); Clyde S. Kilby, *The Christian World of C. S. Lewis* (Grand Rapids: William B. Eerdmans, 1964); Peter Kreeft, *C. S. Lewis,* Contemporary Writers in Christian Perspective series (Grand Rapids: William B. Eerdmans, 1969); Kathryn Lindskoog, *C. S. Lewis: Mere Christian* (Downers Grove, Ill.: Inter Varsity Press, 1981); Gilbert Meilaender, *The Taste for the Other* (Grand Rapids: William B. Eerdmans, 1978); Brian Murphy, *C. S. Lewis* (Mercer Island, Wash.: Starmont House, 1983); Richard L. Purtill, *Lord of the Elves and Eldils: Fantasy and Philosophy in C. S. Lewis* (Grand Rapids: Zondervan, 1974), and *C. S. Lewis's Case for the Christian Faith* (New York: Harper and Row, 1981); Robert Houston Smith, *Patches of Godlight* (Athens, Ga.: University of Georgia Press, 1981); Gunnar Urang, *Shadows of Heaven* (Philadelphia: Pilgrim Press, 1971); Sheldon Vanauken, *A Severe Mercy* (New York: Harper and Row, 1977); Chad Walsh, *C. S. Lewis: Apostle to the Skeptics* (New York: Macmillan, 1949), and *The Literary Legacy of C. S. Lewis* (New York: Harcourt Brace Jovanovich, 1979); and William Luther White, *The Image of Man in C. S. Lewis* (Nashville: Abingdon Press, 1969).

In compiling this list, I am not consigning all these books to the same category. Some are much better than others, and several contain useful summaries of Lewis's ideas in addition to interesting biographical information. A few even venture to be critical. But on the whole these authors are so deeply under Lewis's spell that their criticism is perfunctory and its implications unclear. Cunningham, for example, acknowledges what appear to be serious shortcomings in Lewis's work—his tendency "to oversimplify difficult issues . . . to evade while giving the appearance of answering an objection, and to contrive an either-or which does not exhaust the genuine logical alternatives" (p. 201)—but he tells us neither which arguments are guilty of these flaws nor why he remains so impressed by them; instead, he retreats into autobiography: "Though not always persuaded by [Lewis's] logic, I am almost always moved by his spirit" (p. 12). Chad Walsh is also aware of Lewis's tendency to set up two options as if they were the sole alternatives (see *Literary Legacy,* p. 207); yet he, too, shrinks from his own insight and leaves the point dangling. Similarly, Margaret Patterson Hannay directs our attention to Lewis's tendency to make "controversial pronouncements," only to reassure us that when he occasionally overstates or misstates a point, he may be employing "a deliberate teaching method" (p. 175). Dabney Hart defends him along similarly maddening lines: Lewis "delights in hyperbole, in teasing, in setting up straw men; but these provocative techniques . . . are always intended to invite the reader to explore for himself" (*C. S. Lewis's Defense of Poesie,* Ph.D. diss., University of Wisconsin, 1959, p. 13); this foolproof strategy enables us to reduce Lewis's critics to silence simply by observing that whenever he appears to be mistaken, he is just making sure we are wearing our thinking caps.

My reason for calling attention to all this is not to make sport of serious writers. Examples such as these reveal that some of Lewis's most committed followers have spotted genuine problems in his work but recoil from the implications of their discovery. In finding excuses for him, they pull their punches and minimize recognized logical blunders by dwelling on the glories of his prose style, thereby running the dual risk of exaggerating the significance of his work and trivializing their own.

CHAPTER ONE

1. Regarding Kierkegaard's *Fear and Trembling*, Lewis asked, "What on earth is the man talking about?" He could not comprehend the writings of the existentialists and referred to the work of Kierkegaard and Sartre as "philosophical moonshine" (*C. S. Lewis at the Breakfast Table*, ed. James T. Como [New York: Macmillan, 1979], p. 160).

2. For the classic statement of this objection, see W. K. Clifford's "The Ethics of Belief," in *Lectures and Essays* (London: Macmillan, 1879), pp. 345-46.

3. That is, if there was ever a purely philosophical conversion to *theism*, it was Lewis's. He, of course, never claimed that his later conversion to Christianity was philosophical.

4. Lewis's use of the term *prove* is ambiguous. There are, of course, passages in which he concedes that proofs for the existence of God are not knockdown demonstrative proofs and that they are only intended to establish God's existence as "overwhelmingly probable": "I do not think there is a *demonstrative proof* (like Euclid) of Christianity. . . . The case for Christianity is well given by Chesterton; and I tried to do something in my *Broadcast Talks*. As to *why* God doesn't make it demonstratively clear: are we sure that He is even interested in the kind of Theism which wd. be a compelled logical assent to a conclusive argument?" (Lewis, quoted by Sheldon Vanauken, in *A Severe Mercy* [New York: Harper and Row, 1977], p. 89). And, "The Christian does not necessarily claim to have a demonstrative proof; but the formal possibility that God might not exist is not necessarily present in the form of the least actual doubt. . . . [Belief in God] seems to me to be assent to a proposition which we think so overwhelmingly probable that there is a psychological exclusion of doubt, though not a logical exclusion of dispute" (*WLN*, 15-16).

CHAPTER TWO

1. *Republic*, 506. Cf. *Symposium*, 192, 211.

2. Lewis used the term *inkling* in Plato's sense. Temporal goods provide a dim but nevertheless genuine glimpse of man's true end. "The Inklings" was also the name adopted by a group of writers whose nucleus included Lewis, J. R. R. Tolkien, Charles Williams, Lewis's brother, and others. According to Tolkien, the term was "a pleasantly ingenious pun . . . suggesting people with vague or half-formed intimations and ideas plus those who dabble in ink" (quoted by Luther White in *The Image of Man in C. S. Lewis* [Nashville: Abingdon Press, 1969], p. 222).

3. Some of Lewis's expositors disagree. Cunningham, for example, declares that Lewis was not setting forth an argument at all but simply telling a story. If he is right, *Surprised by Joy* is nothing more than a descriptive autobiographical account of Lewis's conversion. But is he right? If Lewis's account is purely descriptive, what is he describing? Cunningham's answer is that he is describing how he progressed from atheism to Christianity. There is, of course, a distinction between *stating* an argument and *defending* it, but Cunningham overlooks the fact that Lewis did indeed think that the Argument from Desire is sound and that Joy not only pointed him to God but will do the same for anyone who experiences it. Richard Purtill, on the other hand, thinks that there is an argument in *Surprised by Joy* and that it proves the existence of an infinite Object of desire. Like Lewis, he denies that the proof is logically "compulsive" but insists that it is "overwhelmingly probable: longings do not arise unless they can be satisfied" (Purtill, *C. S. Lewis's Case for the Christian Faith* [New York: Harper and Row, 1981], p. 21) If we ask Purtill how he knows this, his answer is that "If our 'infinite longings' do not mean that an infinite object exists to satisfy them, then they mean that we shall never be satisfied." But this is only to argue that I must be right because it would be intolerable if I were wrong. Perhaps there are some desires that will not be satisfied—ever. The possibility cannot be ruled out *a priori*. Nor can it be refuted by stamping one's foot.

4. Clyde S. Kilby is one of the rare exceptions. Although impressed by *The Pilgrim's Regress* and convinced that in it Lewis not only equals but surpasses Bunyan in several respects, he nevertheless candidly recognizes some of its shortcomings—for example, that "the story is weakened by excessive exposition" and that Lewis "sounds at times like an angry young man drawing a caricature . . ." (*The Christian World of C. S. Lewis* [Grand Rapids: William B. Eerdmans, 1964], p. 36). Richard Cunningham's assessment is representative of the more usual response: *The Pilgrim's Regress* is a "penetrating critique" of "various modern movements" in which Lewis "with rapier strokes" proceeds to "lay bare the major weaknesses of science, rationalism, humanism, Freudianism, aestheticism, subromanticism, and many others" (*C. S. Lewis: Defender of the Faith* [Philadelphia: Westminster Press, 1967], p. 158). I should have thought this a rather tall order for an allegorical novel.

5. In *C. S. Lewis: A Biography,* by Roger Lancelyn Green and Walter Hooper (New York: Harcourt Brace Jovanovich, 1974), p. 113.

6. *Of the Laws of Ecclesiastical Polity*, ed. A. S. McGrade and Brian Vickers (London: Sidgwick and Jackson, 1975), 1, 11, 4.

7. Tertullian declares "How shall I admire, how laugh, how exult when I behold so many proud monarchs groaning in the abyss of darkness, so many magistrates liquefying in fiercer flames than they ever kindled against the Christians, so many sage philosophers blushing in red-hot fires with their deluded pupils" (quoted by Chapman Cohen in *Essays in Free Thinking* [London: Pioneer Press, 1928], p. 25). Cf. St. Thomas Aquinas: "In order that nothing be wanting to the happiness of the restored in heaven, a perfect view is granted them of the tortures of the damned" (*Summa Theologica*, 3, Q. 94, art. 1). Or Jonathan Edwards who, in speaking of the damned, was transported to the heights of ecstasy: "Their eyes, their tongues, their hands, their feet, their loins, and their vitals shall forever be full of glowing, melting fire, fierce enough to melt the very rocks and elements;

and, also, they shall eternally be full of the most quick and lively sense to feel the torment . . . not for one minute, nor for one day, nor for one year, nor for one age, nor for two ages, not for an hundred ages, nor for ten thousand or million ages, one after another, but forever and ever, without any end at all, and never, never be delivered" *(Works* [Worcester: Isaiah Thomas, 1809], 8:167).

8. Plato, *Meno*, 77b–78b. On this Robert Houston Smith has good things to say: "Lewis came close to holding a two-tiered philosophy of religion: an orthodox Christianity that met the needs of his piety and upon occasion served as a refuge from insoluble intellectual problems, and a near-Platonic mystical religion that he shared with a handful of aesthetic and spiritual adepts" (*Patches of Godlight* [Athens, Ga.: University of Georgia Press, 1981], p. 226). This observation sheds light on a matter that has been altogether neglected for too long—namely, the dichotomy between Lewis the Christian and Lewis the Platonist. Although in matters of religion he claimed to be a very ordinary layman of the Church of England, he never claimed that either the path that led him to Christianity or the Platonically motivated quest for Joy and the satisfaction it seemed to hold forth were ordinary; in fact, he denied that his experience was typical and regarded himself as someone whose route to God had been very different from that of most people. For an appreciative but critical discussion of *Surprised by Joy*, see Margaret Masterman's "C. S. Lewis: The Author and the Hero," *Twentieth Century* 158 (December 1955): 539-48.

9. Barfield, in *Light on C. S. Lewis*, ed. Jocelyn Gibb (New York: Harcourt, Brace and World, 1965), p. xvi.

CHAPTER THREE

1. White, *The Image of Man in C. S. Lewis* (Nashville: Abingdon Press, 1969), p. 86. The same strategy is used by Chad Walsh, who defends Lewis by observing that "a series of ten-minute broadcast talks cannot deal with all the *if's*, *and's*, and *but's*" *(C. S. Lewis: Apostle to the Skeptics* [New York: Macmillan, 1949], p. 164). Cf. the remarks of Margaret Patterson Hannay: "These ten-minute broadcasts began in August, 1941, when London lay in ruins, most of Europe was under Hitler's control, and England stood virtually alone. On Wednesday evenings the English tuned in to hear C. S. Lewis. . . . It was no time for theological subtleties. . . . The listeners were air raid wardens, young RAF pilots about to leave on highly dangerous missions, wounded soldiers . . . and an entire population under the strain of rationed food, worry about the safety of those they loved, and the constant danger of air attack. So the tone is familiar, chatty, and the concepts are deliberately presented in their simplest form" (*C. S. Lewis* [New York: Frederick Ungar, 1981], p. 211). While it cannot be doubted that Lewis's radio audience listened under far from ideal conditions, I cannot help thinking that Hannay's remarks are intended not simply to provide us with a heightened sense of the occasion but to disarm criticism in advance—as if anyone crude enough to find fault with the talks thereby betrays an insensitivity to Nazi war crimes and a lack of compassion for those British listeners who tried to snatch a quiet moment of consolation from the theology Lewis offered them.

2. William's reaction is noted by Humphrey Carpenter in *The Inklings* (Boston: Houghton Mifflin, 1979), p. 184.

3. See Carpenter, p. 185.

4. Lewis deplored these vices in other writers—especially when they were directed at him: "I take it very hard that a total stranger whom I have never knowingly injured or offended, on the first discovery of a difference in theological opinion between us, should publicly accuse me of being a potential torturer, murderer and tyrant" (*GiD*, 329). And again, "I still think the abolitionists conduct their case very ill. They seem incapable of stating it without imputing vile motives to their opponents. If unbelievers often look at your correspondence column, I am afraid they may carry away a bad impression of our logic, manners and charity" (*GiD*, 340).

5. Hume, *An Enquiry Concerning the Principles of Morals,* L. A. Selby-Bigge, ed. (Oxford: Clarendon Press, 1951), pp. 272–73.

6. Westermarck, *The Origin and Development of Moral Ideas* (London: Macmillan, 1906), pp. 18–19.

7. Ayer, *Philosophical Essays* (London: Macmillan, 1963), pp. 245–49. As Lewis himself justly complained after W. Norman Pittenger imputed views to him that he had repeatedly repudiated, "How many times does a man need to say something before he is safe from the accusation of having said exactly the opposite?" (*GiD*, 178–79).

8. Vanauken, *A Severe Mercy* (New York: Harper and Row, 1977), p. 106. For a similar assessment, see *Patches of Godlight* (Athens, Ga.: University of Georgia Press, 1981), in which Robert Houston Smith contends that although Lewis's arguments are "not entirely flawless," he must nevertheless be "accorded high marks" for his use of reason (p. 232). Smith regards the Lord-or-lunatic dilemma as one of Lewis's "most memorable premises" (p. 265).

CHAPTER FOUR

1. Carpenter, *The Inklings* (Boston: Houghton Mifflin, 1979), pp. 216–17.

2. See *C. S. Lewis at the Breakfast Table*, ed. James T. Como (New York: Macmillan, 1967), p. 163.

3. Como, p. 21.

4. Carpenter, p. 217.

5. Ibid.

6. Como, pp. 161, 163. Richard Purtill begs to differ with the prevailing opinion. According to his account, Anscombe "in fact" merely pointed out that Lewis had "overstated his case slightly" and "in typical philosopher's fashion challenged him to define some of his key terms" (*C. S. Lewis's Case for the Christian Faith* [New York: Harper and Row, 1981], p. 24). This explanation, with its Olympian philosophers-will-be-philosophers attitude, not only fails to account for the deep psychological effects of Anscombe's criticism upon Lewis but also reveals that Purtill does not adequately recall her arguments.

Anscombe's own public assessment of the encounter came almost thirty-five years later. In the preface to *The Collected Philosophical Papers of G.E.M.*

Anscombe (Oxford: Basil Blackwell, 1981), Vol. II, which contains the paper she read to the Socratic Club, she recalls the meeting as well as its emotional aftermath: "The meeting . . . has been described by several of [Lewis's] friends as a horrible and shocking experience which upset him very much. Neither Dr. Harvard (who had Lewis and me to dinner a few weeks later) nor Professor Jack Bennett remembered any such feelings on Lewis' part. . . . My own recollection is that it was an occasion of sober discussion of certain quite definite criticisms, which Lewis' rethinking and rewriting showed he thought were accurate. I am inclined to construe the odd accounts by some of his friends—who seem not to have been interested in the actual arguments or subject matter—as an interesting example of the phenomenon called 'projection' " (p. x).

7. Anscombe, pp. 224–25.

8. Anscombe, p. 227.

9. Anscombe, p. 231.

10. Curiously Lewis does not mention Anscombe in the revised edition of *Miracles*, nor does he in any way acknowledge that he has reworked his argument against naturalism to take into account her criticism.

CHAPTER FIVE

1. *The Emperor's Clothes: An Attack on the Dogmatic Orthodoxy of T. S. Eliot, Graham Greene, C. S. Lewis and Others* (Bloomington: Indiana University Press, 1958), pp. 68, 257. Several of Lewis's disciples have responded to this charge, but they have contented themselves with recording emphatic denials that Lewis stressed sin rather than charity and with accusing Nott of varying degrees of intellectual irresponsibility ranging from having read Lewis's work superficially to having not read it at all. Their protests are not wholly unjustified, but one wishes that they had addressed themselves to her substantive criticism instead of just taking offense at the language in which she expresses it. Peter Kreeft, for example, deals with Nott obliquely by observing that "most readers who dislike Lewis dislike him violently" because he is "too rationalistic," "too romantic," "too fantastic," "too moralistic," or "too religious"—and he accounts for the unwonted vehemence of their dislike by noting that "those who have followed the Great Offender most closely have always been closest to His holy unpopularity" (*C. S. Lewis*, Contemporary Writers in Christian Perspective series [Grand Rapids: William B. Eerdmans, 1969], p. 43). Such a defense will not do; one cannot silence criticism by canonizing its object.

2. "Apologist Versus Apologist," *Christian Century*, October 1958, pp. 1105–6.

3. John Wain reports that Lewis "used to quote with approval General Booth's remark to Kipling: 'Young man, if I could win one soul for God by—by playing the tambourine with my toes, I'd do it' " *(C. S. Lewis at the Breakfast Table*, ed. James T. Como [New York: Macmillan, 1979], p. 69).

CHAPTER SIX

1. In Chapter One I call attention to Lewis's distinction between Faith-A (belief that) and Faith-B (belief in). Here and throughout this chapter I am discuss-

ing only Faith-B. Lewis thought that once people have been convinced that there is a God (Faith-A), they should hold fast to their beliefs and trust God (Faith-B) in the face of apparently contrary evidence. He likened this kind of trust to that of a child who is told by its parent that although it will hurt to remove the thorn from its finger, the pain is inflicted for benevolent purposes.

2. In advocating "obstinacy," Lewis was not, of course, suggesting that believers should have closed minds or be otherwise pigheaded about their beliefs. But neither are they open-minded in the ordinary sense.

3. He wants it to be understood, that is, as the *logical* conclusion and not some spurious retreat into psychological "assurance." Lewis thought that the distinction between the "logic of speculative thought" and "the logic of personal relations" could be explained with sufficient clarity to deprive the skeptic of the charge that the appeal to a personal relationship introduces a purely private and therefore dubious form of evidence into the discussion. Although he was prepared to grant, and even to insist, that the believer has a kind of direct, personal knowledge of God that the unbeliever necessarily lacks, he was not inclined to view it as an alternative to the publicly available evidence he thought exists and can be appealed to as the basis for the case for Christianity.

4. If, however, there are no good reasons for believing that God exists in the first place, then the grounds of the initial assent can no longer serve as the rational justification for "obstinacy" in the face of apparently contrary evidence. In that case, the believer's only recourse is to try to meet the problem of contrary evidence on its own terms. Lewis remained convinced that the believer's situation is not that desperate and that Christians can therefore "fall back" on the grounds of their initial assent—a claim which, of course, presupposes that those grounds are acceptable. But if, as I have argued, they are not, then the distinction between the initial and later assent (as well as the distinction between the logic of speculative thought and the logic of personal relations) collapses.

CHAPTER SEVEN

1. See, for example, J. L. Mackie, "Evil and Omnipotence," *Mind* 64 (April 1955), pp. 200–212; H. J. McCloskey, "God and Evil," *The Philosophical Quarterly* 39 (April 1960), pp. 97–114; Antony Flew, "Divine Omnipotence and Human Freedom," in *New Essays in Philosophical Theology*, ed. Antony Flew and Alasdair MacIntyre (New York: Macmillan, 1955), pp. 144-69; and John Stuart Mill, *Three Essays on Religion* (London: Longmans, Green and Co., 1874), pp. 52–53, 113–14, 176–77. See also J. E. Barnhart, *Religion and the Challenge of Philosophy* (Totowa, N.J.: Littlefield, Adams and Co., 1975), pp. 111-33.

2. Perhaps the most casual remarks on the subject to be found in the entire history of Western philosophy occur in George Berkeley's *A Treatise Concerning the Principles of Human Knowledge* (1710; New York: Liberal Arts Press, Inc., 1957). Although "monsters, untimely births, fruits blasted in the blossom, rains falling in desert places, miseries incident to human life, and the like, are so many arguments that the whole frame of nature is not immediately actuated and superintended by a spirit of infinite wisdom and goodness," we are assured that "the very blemishes and defects of nature are not without their use, in that they make an agreeable sort of variety and augment the beauty of the rest of creation,

as shades in a picture serve to set off the brighter and more enlightened parts."
Again, "as for the mixture of pain or uneasiness which is in the world . . . this
is indispensably necessary to our well-being"; hence, "it is merely for want of
attention and comprehensiveness of mind that there are favorers of atheism"
(pp.101-2). Berkeley concludes that "Although God conceals Himself from the
eyes of the sensual and lazy . . . yet to an unbiased and attentive mind nothing
can be more plainly legible than the intimate presence of an All-wise Spirit" (p. 101).

3. *Institutes of the Christian Religion,* trans. John Allen (Philadelphia:
Presbyterian Board of Christian Education, 1928), iii. 23.

4. Clark, *Religion, Reason and Revelation* (Philadelphia: Presbyterian and
Reformed Publishing Co., 1961), p. 241.

5. See Flew, "Divine Omnipotence and Human Freedom."

6. McCloskey, "God and Evil."

7. Ibid.

8. McCloskey, 203-5. See also Michael Scriven, *Primary Philosophy* (New
York: McGraw-Hill, 1966).

9. *PP*, 134. It is hard to know how seriously to take Lewis's appeal to demons.
For a Christian to believe that there are devils is one thing; to employ them as
an explanatory hypothesis is something else. After all, you cannot very well shore
up an already questionable belief in a good and omnipotent God by invoking the
even more questionable belief in devils, since the validity of the latter is surely
dependent on the validity of the former. Clearly, if belief in a good God must
be abandoned, belief in demons will go with it.

10. There is not *a* problem of pain—there are *many*, and the suffering of children is one of the grimmest. Compare Lewis's response to that of Peter De Vries
in his gripping novel *The Blood of the Lamb* (Boston: Little Brown, 1961), in
which the father of a dying child says, "What baffles me is the comfort people
find in the idea that somebody dealt this mess. Blind and meaningless chance seems
to me so much more congenial—or at least less horrible. Prove to me that there
is a God and I will really begin to despair" (pp. 207-8). Or again, another of
De Vries's characters, who has stood by helplessly as his daughter dies of leukemia,
finally renounces his faith:

> I could not decline the burden of resumption. The Western Gate is closed.
> The exit is barred. One angel guards it, whose sword is a golden head smiling
> into the sun in a hundred snapshots. The child on the brink of whose grave
> I tried to recover the faith lost on the edge of my brother's is the goalkeeper
> past whom I can now never get. In the smile are sealed my orders for the
> day. One has heard of people being punished for their sins, hardly for their
> piety. But so it is. As to that other One, whose voice I thought I heard, I
> seem to be barred from everything it speaks in comfort, only the remonstrance
> remaining: "Verily I say unto thee, Thou shalt by no means come out thence,
> until thou hast paid the uttermost farthing." (Pp. 243-44)

11. Mill, *An Examination of Sir William Hamilton's Philosophy* (1875; London: Routledge and Kegan Paul, 1979), pp. 102-3.

CHAPTER EIGHT

1. Ayer, *Language, Truth and Logic* (New York: Dover, 1936), p. 35.
2. Ayer, p. 45.

3. Ayer, pp. 116, 120.

4. Flew, "Theology and Falsification," in *New Essays in Philosophical Theology,* ed. Antony Flew and Alasdair MacIntyre (New York: Macmillan, 1955), pp. 97–99.

5. See H. E. Allison, "Faith and Falsifiability," *The Review of Metaphysics* 22 (1969): 515; and M. J. Charlesworth, *Philosophy of Religion: The Historic Approaches* (London: Macmillan, 1972), p. 154.

6. See Dallas M. High, *Language, Persons and Belief* (New York: Oxford University Press, 1968), p. 151n; and James A. Richmond, *Theology and Metaphysics* (London: SCM Press, 1966). Wisdom originally set forth the Parable of the Gardener in his essay "Gods," in *Logic and Language: First Series,* ed. Antony Flew (Oxford: Basil Blackwell, 1955), pp. 187–206.

7. See especially "Performative-Constative," in *Philosophy and Ordinary Language*, ed. Charles E. Cahn (Urbana, Ill.: University of Illinois Press, 1963), pp. 22–54; *Philosophical Papers* (Oxford: Clarendon Press, 1961); and *How to Do Things with Words* (Oxford: Clarendon Press, 1962).

8. See Braithwaite's essay "An Empiricist's View of the Nature of Religious Belief," in *Christian Ethics and Contemporary Philosophy* (London: SCM Press, 1966), pp. 53–73.

9. Braithwaite, pp. 58, 67–68. Braithwaite is, of course, well aware that many religious adherents *do* believe these "stories" and thus *do* intend to be making assertions. But, he says, "One can recognize [a person's] intention without sharing his presuppositions." He contends that in making assertions on the basis of their beliefs, believers are "either not philosophizing or [are] philosophizing in a manner which is now impossible for us . . . to practice with sincerity" (p. 89). But this is problematical. Suppose I were to propose that we give a gift to the mail carrier this Christmas as a token of appreciation for delivering our mail faithfully all year long through all kinds of weather, and that my neighbor were then to point out that in fact we never received any mail or, worse still, that the postal service had been abolished years ago. Would it not be rather feeble for me to reply, "Oh, I know all that, but thanking the mail carrier doesn't require me to believe that there really is someone who delivers letters; in saying 'Let us thank the mail carrier' I was simply announcing my intention to be an appreciative person"?

10. See Flew and MacIntyre, p. 100.

11. For this discussion, see "Religion and Morals," in *Faith and Logic*, ed. Basil Mitchell (London: Allen and Unwin, 1957), pp. 183–84.

12. See, respectively, Zuurdeeg, "The Nature of Theological Language," *The Journal of Religion* 40 (1960): 1–8; Evans, *The Logic of Self-Involvement* (New York: Herder and Herder, 1969); and Miles, *Religion and The Scientific Outlook* (London: Allen and Unwin, 1959).

13. Wittgenstein, quoted by Anscombe in "What Wittgenstein Really Said," *The Tablet*, 17 April 1954, p. 373. Anscombe unhelpfully adds, "I do not know whether he was right about this."

14. Malcolm, *Ludwig Wittgenstein: A Memoir* (London: Oxford University Press, 1958), p. 72.

15. See Nielsen, "Wittgensteinian Fideism," *Philosophy* 42 (1967): 191–209.

16. Passmore, *A Hundred Years of Philosophy* (London: Gerald Duckworth, 1957), p. 459; and High, p. 135.

17. Flew and MacIntyre, p. 108.

18. See Cavell, "Kierkegaard's *On Authority and Revelation,"* in *Must We Mean What We Say*? (New York: Scribner's, 1969), p. 175.

19. See, for example, Phillip's *The Concept of Prayer* (London: Routledge and Kegan Paul, 1965) and *Faith and Philosophical Enquiry* (London: Routledge and Kegan Paul, 1970).

Of all the Wittgensteinian fideists, Phillips is the most emphatic in stressing that "if the philosopher wants to give an account of religion, he must pay attention to what religious believers do and say" (*The Concept of Prayer*, p. 1). Yet his very attentiveness often produces startling results. Among the conclusions he draws from the general claim that religious language does not consist of empirical assertions are the following:

a. The Christian who believes in the Last Judgment does not thereby believe in a future event. Moreover, the unbeliever who denies that there will be a Last Judgment does not thereby contradict the believer who claims that there will be (*Faith and Philosophical Enquiry*, pp. 111–14).

b. Believing that God exists does not involve believing that "an additional being exists" (*Death and Immortality* [London: Macmillan, 1970], pp. 1–2, 12).

c. In order to pray it is not necessary that we believe that we are talking to someone who actually exists. Indeed, according to Phillips, God does not exist; rather, he is "real" (*The Concept of Prayer*, pp. 23–25; cf. p. 57). Although he does maintain that prayer changes things, he holds that petitionary prayer is not a literal form of request, "a way of getting things done" (*The Concept of Prayer*, pp. 112–13, 121). Such a view reduces prayer to superstition.

Phillips does not mean to deny that Christianity is true, but he is at pains to insist that such truth as it possesses has nothing whatever to do with the facts. "To ask [the Christian] whether religious beliefs are true," he says, "is not to ask him for evidence for them, but rather to ask him whether he can live by them, whether he can digest them, whether they constitute food for him" (*Death and Immortality*, p. 71). Like Braithwaite, Phillips realizes that many believers *do* mean to say that the truth of Christianity is factual, but he suggests that such believers "make mistakes," that their religion is "shallow" and flawed by "distortion" (*The Concept of Prayer*, pp. 10–11). Such believers, among whose ranks stand Lewis, have been mislead along with such unbelievers as Flew by the "surface grammar" of religious language, says Phillips; only the Wittgensteinian fideists have penetrated to the "depth grammar."

20. The essay can be found in *Faith and the Philosophers* (New York: St. Martin's Press, 1964), pp. 103–9. A lot has been written in the field of the philosophy of religion since the time this essay appeared, but to pursue more recent developments would be irrelevant to the thought of Lewis, who died in 1963.

21. Ayer, 118.

22. Farrer, quoted by Jocelyn Gibb in *Light on C. S. Lewis* (New York: Harcourt, Brace and World, 1965), pp. 25, 31.

23. See *GiD*, 90–91. Ayer himself describes Lewis as one of those who fought "a rearguard action" against analytic philosophy and recalls "a flashy debate" with him at the Oxford Socratic Club "which entertained the audience but did neither of us much credit" (*Part of My Life* [London: Collins, 1977], pp. 296–97).

CHAPTER NINE

1. Lewis, quoted by Roger Lancelyn Green and Walter Hooper in *C. S. Lewis: A Biography* (New York: Harcourt Brace Jovanovich, 1974), p. 270.

2. Green and Hooper, 268.

3. At the age of four, Lewis officially rejected the name "Clive" and not only announced that he was "Jacksie" but would answer to no other name. Later "Jacksie" became "Jack."

4. Green and Hooper, 268.

5. See *Light on C. S. Lewis*, ed. Jocelyn Gibb (New York: Harcourt, Brace and World, 1965), pp. 31–32.

6. See *Letters of C. S. Lewis* (London: Geoffrey Bles, 1966), p.55; and Walsh, Afterword to *A Grief Observed* (New York: Bantam, 1976), p. 151.

7. For Lewis to say that God caused his wife to suffer and die in order to convince him that his faith had been a house of cards is a rather self-centered "solution" which overlooks the fact that it was primarily she who suffered. Had her faith been imaginary too? And what about the faith of her two sons? I do not mean to raise idle or indelicate questions about a grimly serious subject, but in view of Lewis's explanation I think we are entitled to know just where we are to draw the line in "accounting" for suffering by appealing to those whose characters are to be "improved" by it.

8. Walsh, Afterword to *A Grief Observed* (New York: Bantam Books, 1976), p. 157.

9. One cannot weigh evidence as one weighs grapefruits. When can we say that the weight of the evidence has turned against believing in a good God? What scale can we use? Insofar as he accepts the Falsification Criterion, Lewis is committed to the view that as long as the evidence enables the meaning of the term *good* to remain intact, it is intelligible to speak of the evidence as supporting or favoring belief in a good God, but when the contrary evidence becomes so overwhelming that the term *good* loses its meaning and believing in a good God becomes compatible with whatever happens, then the evidence is no longer favorable and the "weight" of the evidence is against it. The scale is a logical one involving *meaning*. Beyond a certain point, the term *good* becomes empty.

CHAPTER TEN

1. *"De Descriptione Temporum,"* in *They Asked for a Paper* (London: Geoffrey Bles, 1962), p. 25.

INDEX